Embracing Autonomy

The Americas in the World

JÜRGEN BUCHENAU AND STEVEN HYLAND JR., SERIES EDITORS

The Americas in the World series publishes cutting-edge scholarship about the Americas in global and transnational history, politics, society, and culture as well as about the impact of global and transnational actors and processes on the hemisphere. The series includes both works on specialized topics as well as broad syntheses. All titles aim at a wide audience.

Also available in the Americas in the World series:

The Dollar: How the US Dollar Became a Popular Currency in Argentina by Ariel Wilkis and Mariana Luzzi

North American Regionalism: Stagnation, Decline, or Renewal? edited by Eric Hershberg and Tom Long

EMBRACING AUTONOMY

Latin American–US Relations
in the Twenty-First Century

Gregory Weeks

UNIVERSITY OF NEW MEXICO PRESS | ALBUQUERQUE

© 2024 by the University of New Mexico Press
All rights reserved. Published 2024
Printed in the United States of America

Names: Weeks, Gregory Bart, author.
Title: Embracing autonomy: Latin American-US relations in the twenty-first century / Gregory Weeks.
Other titles: Latin American-US relations in the twenty-first century | Americas in the world.
Description: Albuquerque : University of New Mexico Press, 2024. | Series: The Americas in the world | Includes bibliographical references and index.
Identifiers: LCCN 2023051881 (print) | LCCN 2023051882 (ebook) | ISBN 9780826365804 (cloth) | ISBN 9780826365811 (paperback) | ISBN 9780826365828 (epub) | ISBN 9780826366429 (pdf)
Subjects: LCSH: Latin America—Relations—United States—21st century. | United States—Relations—Latin America—21st century. | Autonomy. | BISAC: HISTORY / Modern / 21st Century | POLITICAL SCIENCE / International Relations / General | History / Latin America / Central America
Classification: LCC F1418 .W278 2024 (print) | LCC F1418 (ebook) | DDC 327.7308—dc23/eng/20231201
LC record available at https://lccn.loc.gov/2023051881
LC ebook record available at https://lccn.loc.gov/2023051882

Founded in 1889, the University of New Mexico sits on the traditional homelands of the Pueblo of Sandia. The original peoples of New Mexico—Pueblo, Navajo, and Apache—since time immemorial have deep connections to the land and have made significant contributions to the broader community statewide. We honor the land itself and those who remain stewards of this land throughout the generations and also acknowledge our committed relationship to Indigenous peoples. We gratefully recognize our history.

Cover illustration: courtesy of DesignCuts
Designed by Felicia Cedillos
Composed in Alegreya

CONTENTS

Acknowledgments   vii

1. A Conceptual Framework   1
2. Electoral Revolution in Latin America (1998–2002)   15
3. Political Pragmatism and Autonomy (2003–2005)   43
4. New International Institutions (2006–2008)   68
5. Maturation of Autonomy (2009–2015)   92
6. Latin America Plays the Field (2016–2020)   119
7. The Embrace of Autonomy Continues (2021–2023)   144

Notes   161
Bibliography   169
Index   199

ACKNOWLEDGMENTS

The analysis in this book developed over years, and I've presented pieces of it at a number of different conferences. Alan McPherson, Jürgen Büchenau, and Steven Hyland all read the entire manuscript and provided numerous suggestions that improved it. Vince Gawronski, Jonathan Hiskey, Mary Rose Kubal, Frank Mora, Steve Morris, and Lars Schoultz provided feedback at different times as I wrote. Thanks to Guy Mentel for publishing my opinion piece on this topic at the *Global Americans* website.

This book took longer to write than anticipated, as I took on a new administrative role at UNC Charlotte. I appreciate the support of the College of Liberal Arts & Sciences, and specifically Dean Nancy Gutierrez and Interim Dean John Smail. Thanks to Michael Millman, senior editor at the University of New Mexico Press, for his patience as he periodically—but very nicely—checked in on my progress.

Finally, my thanks go out as always to my family. My wife, Amy, and my children Ben, Grey, and Elizabeth remind me on a constant basis that there are more important things than academia and not to take myself too seriously.

1. A CONCEPTUAL FRAMEWORK

INTRODUCTION

The first two decades of the twenty-first century have been remarkably disruptive of traditional Latin American–US relations. Relationships that were once close became distant, even hostile, while once prickly partnerships have smoothed over, at least partially. Leftist governments won major elections, which changed the pitch of rhetoric toward the United States, although a number of these also later lost power, even by means of shaky constitutionality. Meanwhile, new actors from outside the hemisphere have appeared on the scene for the first time. All the while, Latin American governments have worked to chart a course that could provide them with new opportunities to grow and prosper. Those courses often have entailed steering around the United States.

This book emphasizes the growing relevance of Latin American policy choices for understanding Latin American–US relations. So often—indeed too often—in studies of Latin American–US relations, scholars view the Latin American side of the relationships as largely reactive or even passive, as Latin American policy makers in those countries are reduced to peripheral actors or, at the extreme, even puppets. This analysis departs from other general treatments of Latin American–US relations not by putting US policy aside but by bringing in the Latin American and global contexts more closely. The goal is to avoid the incomplete picture provided by a narrow focus on the policies of the United States.

But this is not a study of rebellion against the United States, or even a critique of US policy. Instead, it is an examination of the major shifts that have taken place in the region in recent decades and how they have shaped Latin American–US relations. These shifts were sparked by events in the 1980s and 1990s but did not solidify until the end of the twentieth century. In 2000, Latin America was a far different place than it was in, say, 1980. Economic policy had radically transformed, as had the global political environment.

UNDERSTANDING AUTONOMY

The predominant Latin American approach to understanding Latin American–US relations centers on autonomy. If you do some searching, you will find that this literature is almost exclusively in Spanish and Portuguese.[1] Professors at Latin American universities have written most of what little there is in English, while the literature produced in the United States stays mostly centered on US theoretical developments and rarely bothers to examine what else might be out there.

The etymology of *autonomy* is Greek from the words for "self," "rule," and "law." At root it is about not being subservient to another and having the latitude to deal with your own affairs without external coercion. In the history of Latin American–US relations, autonomy became important because of the US proclivity to interfere in the affairs of countries, many times to the point of invasion and occupation, which by definition involves the loss of autonomy.[2] Because of this history, autonomy in Latin America carries with it a normative component. Seeking autonomy is not just possible but desirable.

While the concept of autonomy is difficult to find in non–Latin American works on international relations (IR), in Latin America it has been a topic of considerable debate for several decades and still going strong.[3] Juan Carlos Puig, an Argentine academic, lawyer, and eventually minister of foreign relations, was (and long after his death still remains) the major scholarly voice on the topic.[4] For Puig, autonomy is about the ability to make policy decisions without outside interference. Puig accepted the notion of international anarchy, meaning lack of a world government, which is core to realist theory, and the dominance of certain great powers (most notably the United States) from dependency theory. But he considered autonomy to fall outside those theoretical perspectives in that there is still space for weaker states to make their own autonomous decisions to defend their interests. For Puig, autonomy was about the rational calculation of what independent policies were possible before the United States threw up obstacles. The concept of autonomy continues to take realist and dependency theories seriously but reshapes the debate.

The essence of dependency theory is that less developed countries are locked into an economic relationship with the developed world that leaves them in a permanent position of weakness. The hierarchical structure of the global economic system allows countries like the United States to import raw materials at low prices from Latin America, produce finished goods, and then export those industrial goods back to Latin America at higher prices. Because of this relationship, the region was unable to generate enough capital on its own to promote economic development (and ideally industrialization). There is no single "dependency theory," as they range from a uniform argument that all Latin American countries have similar relationships to the developed world, to more attention to different ways in which countries have become inserted into the global economy, which in some cases can leave room for successful dependent development.[5]

Broadly speaking, the Latin American political responses to the dependent relationship took two forms. Even before dependency theory was fleshed out in academia, the United Nations' Economic Commission for Latin America and the Caribbean (ECLAC in English, CEPAL in Spanish) had proposed new models of economic development that would shield local economies from the more powerful "developed" economies. States could carve out economic autonomy by raising tariffs and subsidizing domestic industries, thus protecting them from imports and nurturing them to compete with imports (Franko 2007, 63). Raúl Prebisch (1962, 2), an Argentine economist who became executive director of ECLAC in 1950, was ambivalent about protectionism, writing that the "solution does not lie in growth at the expense of foreign trade." Prebisch hoped that growth would make it unnecessary to restrict imports, but growth was essential for the model to function. Marxists, meanwhile, argued that only revolution would break the economic bonds to the United States. Both of these responses were efforts to spark autonomous economic policy, which by definition meant reducing US influence, to differing degrees.[6]

Realism is also a structural theory founded on the assertion that global politics are defined by anarchy. There is no world police or military force, so individual states are left to seek their own security.[7] In this situation, states with weaker military and economic capabilities are the most vulnerable. State behavior should therefore be understood in terms of relative capabilities. Those who have more power than others act accordingly with their own self-interest driving them. In the Latin American context, one important takeaway was that states in the region faced retribution if they pursued policies (either domestic or foreign) that the United States deemed as threatening. States that attempted to break entirely from US influence, most notably Cuba, found themselves under unrelenting attacks.[8]

From the perspective of autonomy, realist theory is quite pessimistic, as the relatively weaker Latin American countries have little leeway. One of the few ways is to *balance*, whereby countries group together to serve as a counterbalance to the largest power. Latin American leaders had been trying to do this with minimal success since independence. The other main option is *bandwagoning*, which means aligning your own state interests more closely to the United States and drastically decreasing autonomous actions. Puig accepted realist assumptions about international anarchy and power, but also dependency assumptions about economic structures.

For Puig, autonomy focused on resistance to the great power, which for Argentina (and the rest of Latin America) meant the United States. That entailed solidarity among those states. He considered autonomy to be a zero-sum game, where gains by lesser powers came at the expense of the more powerful.

Latin American debates about autonomy also tend to pay close attention to national economic policy and to regional integration. Puig himself saw regional integration as a critical step toward autonomy.[9] He differentiated between "heterodox autonomy," which accepted (or at least was resigned to) the position of the great power and sought to work within its limitations, and "secessionist autonomy," which involves, in his words, "cutting the umbilical cord."[10] Either way, the objective of becoming more autonomous is to move as far away from a position of dependence as possible.

The concept was challenged and shaped over time. Puig had an essentially realist conception that resembled balancing, whereby weaker countries form alliances to balance the power of the strongest power. During the Cold War some Latin American leaders believed that autonomy must include a measure of separation from the United States. For example, many Latin American countries were members of the Non-Aligned Movement, which sought to provide an informal alliance of countries that excluded the North Atlantic Treaty Organization (dominated by the United States) and the Warsaw Pact (dominated by the Soviet Union). It often criticized US policy toward less developed countries, beginning with Vietnam.

Once the Cold War ended and Latin American countries opened up economically to the world, that emphasis on separation shifted. For example, Roberto Russell and Juan Gabriel Tokatlian developed the concept of "relational autonomy," which is distinct because it rejects the notion of self-sufficiency and instead emphasizes that "both the defense and the expansion of autonomy enjoyed by Latin American countries today can no longer depend on national or subregional policies of isolation, self-sufficiency, or opposition" (Russell and Tokatlian 2003, 13). National interests are therefore embedded within complex relationships with other governments and international institutions. In general, even though the conceptual development of autonomy took place during the Cold War, the numerous projects in the first decade of the twenty-first century ensured that it remained relevant and widely mentioned in the Latin American literature (Zapata 2017).

Carlos Escudé was instrumental in developing the notion of "peripheral realism," which questioned the goal of autonomy.[11] He argued that autonomy was too often considered an end to itself in the developing world, as it connoted success in pursuing national goals. Instead, all countries, but especially middle-sized ones, have considerable freedom of choice and do not always need to seek complete autonomy. Further, less powerful countries should avoid openly confronting the greater powers because they know they will lose and this will hurt the general population. He frames this as "total foreign policy autonomy = absolute domestic tyranny" (Schenoni and Escudé 2016, 4). For strategy, Escudé focused in particular on attracting investment and otherwise boosting the economy, which would best serve the citizens of less developed countries.[12] The Brazilian theorist Helio Jaguaribe echoed the relevance of size, pointing out the need to have adequate natural and human resources to exercise international autonomy in the face of imperial (meaning US) influence.[13] From that perspective, smaller countries had little chance to increase their autonomy because they could not withstand the effect of being the target of US antagonism.

According to Escudé, autonomy should consider the costs associated with using that freedom. Escudé argues that the pursuit of autonomy can be damaging because the costs are so high. What peripheral realism argues is a careful balance between autonomy and "playing along" with the great power in order to achieve specific national goals. The caveat is that this holds "as long as this does not entail sacrificing its own material interests, which are paramount" (Jaguaribe 1979, 55). In this view, states should not embrace autonomy just for the sake of autonomy. They must tie those efforts to specific interests they are trying to achieve. Otherwise, the punishment meted out by the stronger power is simply not worth the gain.

Clearly, an important part of this debate is the question of whether a country is entirely free of US constraints or not. Vigevani and Cepaluni (2009, 3) take the position that autonomy falls along a continuum between the ideal types of total dependence and total autonomy. This book will consider autonomy in the same way, with total separation from the United States at one end and military occupation on the other. Of course, neither currently exists and in fact the former has never existed while the latter has not existed for many years. In the twenty-first century, Latin America has become more autonomous than ever before, but constraints still exist. And although much of the pursuit of autonomy in Latin America has been explicitly aimed at breaking away from US control, increasingly it is intended more broadly to maximize economic and diplomatic gains. The United States therefore becomes one actor—albeit a powerful one—among several, or many.

A group of mostly Latin American scholars and former policy makers published a collection of essays in 2021 advancing the concept of "active non-alignment" (Fortin, Heine, and Ominami 2021). It mirrors autonomy in many ways, and some of the authors previously published works on autonomy. A difference is its call for a regional commitment to autonomy not just from the United States but from any other major power as well. With its emphasis on national interests, active non-alignment also hews closely to realism.

This book bases its analysis on three assertions. First, Latin Americans take autonomy seriously and therefore so should we all. Second, centering on autonomy means shifting our focus away from US policy and toward policy decisions made in Latin America. Third, power imbalance is part of the analysis, but it varies widely, as Latin American policy makers all face different opportunities and constraints, and those need more exploration.

This book will not advance a normative argument about the optimal positions for Latin American governments to take. Rather, it argues that Latin America has gradually expanded its scope of autonomous action in the twenty-first century, but outright rejection of the United States is not necessarily a primary goal at any given time.

The literature on Latin American–US relations in the United States tends not to consider autonomy in any systematic manner. To be sure, there are plenty of works criticizing US policy and calling for greater independence from the negative aspects of US power. Nonetheless, these generally downplay Latin American actions and assume US dominance. To avoid throwing stones from my own glass house, I should note that in the first edition of my own textbook on the topic, I argued that "Latin Americans have often struggled against US dominance and at times have been successful in that effort" (Weeks 2008, 4). It's not that this is incorrect, but that it is incomplete and one-sided. Latin American autonomy can at times be directed specifically at struggle against the United States, but more often than not it has other aims.

PURSUING AUTONOMY IN LATIN AMERICA

As Russell Crandall pointed out more than a decade ago, "Mononational research tends to produce mononational explanations and to ignore the role of players from countries other than those whose words are examined" (Crandall 2006, 4). Since then, a number of authors have pushed back on the power imbalance emphasis and showed how Latin American governments mattered more than generally appreciated, not passive but rather instrumental in shaping outcomes (Long 2015; Mora and Hey 2003; McPherson 2014). The same was true of individuals. Even efforts during the Cold War both by the United

States and the Soviet Union to co-opt and control Latin American intellectuals was frustrated by their ability to define their own version of nationalism that was beholden to neither (Iber 2015).

Of course, seeking autonomy is not exclusive to the twenty-first century, or even to the twentieth. The Liberator himself, Simón Bolívar, wrote repeatedly about the need to keep the United States at arm's length. In 1825, by which time much of the region had won independence wars, he worked (in vain) to bring unity to the region, arguing that allowing the United States either to ally itself closely with his Colombia or to join any regional confederation would possibly antagonize England, whose favor Bolívar hoped to maintain.[14] But we need to go beyond this "arm's length" argument as well. Latin America is often creating autonomous spaces without the explicit goal of reducing engagement with the United States.

The core of autonomy for Latin America from the United States is seen in new, deeper, and more numerous relationships that do not include the United States. Broadly speaking, they can be political or economic. Political relationships include the creation and strengthening of international institutions, diplomatic initiatives, military agreements, and diplomatic summits. Economic ties include trade agreements, foreign investment, and loans. These are all things Latin American governments currently focus on, even more so than in the past.

Scholars and pundits alike often draw a causal link between Latin American states becoming more autonomous and a decrease of US influence.[15] What I will argue is that although autonomy does entail a decreased dependence on the United States, and in fact even a challenge to US hegemony in some cases, US influence remains high.

Part of the problem with the debate is that terms tend not to be clearly defined. Hegemony has been usefully defined as "one state is powerful enough to maintain the essential rules governing interstate relations, and willing to do so" (Keohane 1984, 34–35). Almost always it refers to a preponderance of economic and military power. Hegemony, however, does not necessarily mean the exercise of power without constraint. The United States cannot dictate the nature of its bilateral and multilateral relationships.

While strong for most of the twentieth century, US hegemony in the Western

Hemisphere eroded since the end of the Cold War, but we are not necessarily in a "posthegemonic" era, at least not yet. Many of the rules governing interstate relations in the Western Hemisphere are still defined in large part by the United States. Nonetheless, independent Latin American policies have consistently and sometimes successfully challenged these rules. This book takes the position that Latin American autonomy and US hegemony coexist.

That brings us to "influence." In international relations, the essence of influence is for a state to get other states to behave in a way that matches its preferences and desired policy outcomes. Given the United States's wealth, ability to provide benefits, and shared history, US influence remains high in Latin America. Just as hegemony does not necessarily mean control, influence does not mean always achieving all policy goals. Even hegemons cannot always get what they want. Another theme in the book will be to determine how much Latin American autonomy and US influence are mutually exclusive. This is more complicated than hegemony, but clearly US influence is high by virtually any standard.

In the Latin American–US context, the United States holds a hegemonic position by virtue of its large power imbalance in the region. By any measure, the United States is far more powerful than any other country and it has more influence. Its ability to convince another state to do something in the US interest is higher than any other state. But that influence always has limits, even for a hegemonic power. In the twenty-first century, US influence is high but, more than in the last century, there are multiple other influential actors.

EMBRACING AUTONOMY

We must also take global historical and political contexts in mind. Three almost simultaneous processes facilitated Latin American autonomy as the twentieth century came to a close.

First, in the 1980s virtually all of Latin America undertook a broad array of structural adjustments, including a shift of their economies away from protectionism and toward exporting as the engine of economic growth. This entailed privatization of state industry, the end of government subsidies, deregulation, and the lowering of trade barriers. The United States certainly pressured Latin American policy makers to enact such policies, though they found plenty of elite interest in the region. Like-minded presidents and economic ministers believed such reforms were necessary to bring their countries out of debt.

In some countries the sometimes disastrous results of these reforms led to simmering discontent that eventually manifested itself in support for leftist candidates and movements. These movements were defined in large part by their efforts to seek autonomy from US economic hegemony. Fueled by the ideals of dependency theory, many leftist leaders called for solidarity against the imperial designs of the United States and for a more global approach to economic development that marginalized US influence to the extent possible.

But in other cases, such as Chile, Colombia, and Mexico, there was no electoral swing from right to left; instead they stayed somewhere in an ideological middle. At the same time, Latin Americans—both political and economic actors—began actively seeking new global partners. For radicals and moderates alike, this new economic model challenged prevailing assumptions about the traditional role of the United States.

Second, this new focus on export-led development also prompted *all* governments—regardless of ideology—to start looking beyond the Western Hemisphere for those trading partners, sources of investment, and possible loans. For those countries that continued to favor market-oriented policies into the 2000s, such as Mexico and Colombia, more partners meant more markets for exports and opportunities for imports. While not the primary aim, this expansion resulted in more autonomy from the United States.

For countries trying to break away from the free market model, such as Bolivia and Venezuela, more partners meant sources of income that did not entail dependence on the United States. Aid and loans from China, for example, did not have the same strings that came with US funding and they decreased Washington's ability to use the withholding of aid and loans as punishment. Still other countries, such as Brazil, straddled the two orientations by sticking with the market model while also pushing back on the United States. All those governments were embracing autonomy, albeit for different reasons.

In 1995 the United States constituted 45.9 percent of Latin America's export trade. Despite ups and downs over time, by 2019 it was nearly the same at 44.5

percent.[16] Extra-hemispheric countries, however, had become newly relevant. China is the most prominent example. In 1995, China's share of Latin American trade was 1.1 percent. That rose to 3.4 percent in 2005 and 12.4 percent in 2016. For foreign direct investment (FDI), new partners abounded.

Latin America increasingly exported to and imported from China, and clearly this impacted the US share.

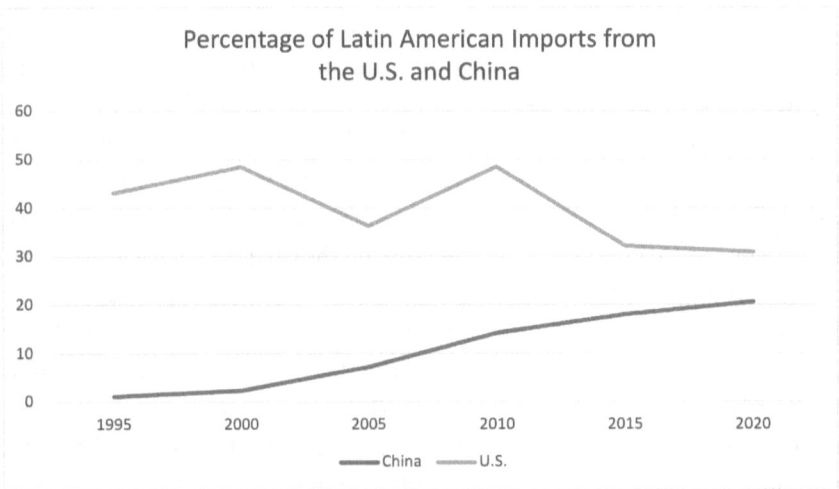

Figure 1. Source: World Bank Trade Data. https://wits.worldbank.org/countrystats.aspx?lang=en.

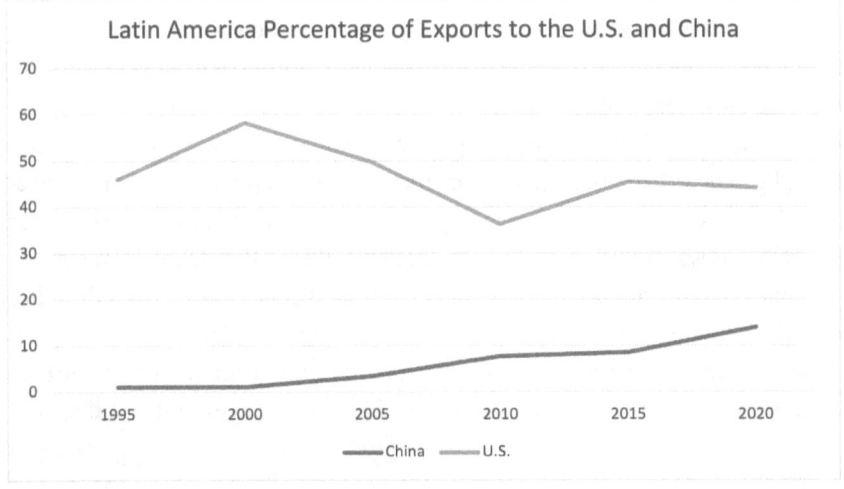

Figure 2. Source: World Bank Trade Data. https://wits.worldbank.org/countrystats.aspx?lang=en.

What we see, then, is that US dominance is gone, but its influence—and even its hegemonic position—is not. Autonomy should not be viewed in a zero-sum context. Greater autonomy and US hegemony are not mutually exclusive. Subsequent chapters will explore this in greater depth.

Further, the type of export does not tell us much either about autonomy. For example, countries with the highest dependence on the export of primary products, such as El Salvador and Venezuela, have taken very different stances while both also remain heavily reliant on US consumers. In general, there are incentives for all countries to look beyond the United States while not jettisoning it, more so than in the past.

Third was the end of the Cold War, which had its last gasp in 1991 with the dissolution of the Soviet Union. That was a pivotal moment in Latin American–US relations because the automatic antagonism toward leftist political movements in Latin America, virulent during the Cold War, gave way to flexibility and pragmatism. During the Cold War, when leftist presidents took power the United States worked quickly to invade or to encourage military coups (Guatemala in 1954, Brazil in 1964, the Dominican Republic in 1965, and Chile in 1973 are prominent examples). Governments that came to power through revolution (Cuba in 1959 and Nicaragua in 1979) soon faced hostility: unremitting violence, covert action, and harassment.

In 1998, only seven years after the fall of the Soviet Union, Hugo Chávez's resounding victory in the Venezuelan presidential election presaged a slew of similar elections across the region. These governments always had some measure of anti-US foreign policy message in their rhetoric, and they threw wrenches in the works of US trade agreements, military base negotiations, regional alliances, and even votes in international institutions, including the United Nations. In the past, US policy makers would have given serious thought to overthrowing such governments, either covertly or through invasion. In the absence of a global ideological threat, coexistence proved more palatable, as was autonomous foreign policy making. This does not mean that US policy makers did not respond negatively at all, because at times they did, including support for coups, but that response was far milder than in the past.

The result was more space for Latin American governments to pursue autonomy in whatever form. In terms of Escudé's argument, the costs of antagonizing the great power decreased markedly. In strictly realist terms, the most powerful state perceived fewer threats to national security interests and therefore did not respond as in the past. In concrete terms, Latin American leaders went about creating new institutions, forging new agreements, pursuing new trade and investment partners, and criticizing US policy in ways that would have risked retaliation before.

It is a cliché to make the claim that a book is "rethinking" or providing more "nuance," but that is indeed an important part of the pages that follow."[17] The goal of this book is to provide a clearer understanding of where Latin America stands vis-à-vis the United States here in the twenty-first century, which is different from any other era and which requires reconsideration of how relations developed and where they appear to be heading. By doing so, we can get a better grip on the trajectory of Latin American–US relations and how they develop in turbulent times.

Finally, a brief note on what this book is not designed to do. It is not a comprehensive review of Latin American–US relations, which can be found elsewhere (yes, even in my own textbook, but plenty of other places as well). Since the focus is largely on Latin America, there is less on the intricacies of US policy making. And since its focus is conceptual, there are fewer details about specific policy areas. It's not that these aren't important or interesting, of course, but I feel (or at least hope) that conciseness helps with reconsideration.

THE BOOK'S STRUCTURE

The book is organized chronologically, with each chapter tracing the evolution of autonomy. The original intent was to have each chapter cover the same number of years, but as the project advanced, it became clear that such uniformity did not match important events and changes in Latin American perspective on the United States. Hopefully the finished product flows well thematically even if the coverage of years varies.

Chapter 2 will address the electoral revolution in Latin America from 1998 to 2002. Hugo Chávez was elected in 1998 and represents the first critical example of the ideological shift in Latin America. Chapter 3 will examine a pivot toward political pragmatism from 2003 to 2005. It is bookmarked by Lula's inauguration in Brazil and by Michelle Bachelet's election in Chile, whose government entailed a combination of autonomy and a deep economic relationship with the United States. Chapter 4 centers on the development of new international institutions in Latin America that did not include the United States, from 2006 to 2008. It will examine the Union of South American Nations (UNASUR) in particular, which was founded in 2008. Chapter 5 analyzes what we might call the "maturation" of autonomy from 2009 to 2015. In the wake of the global financial crash, the election of Barack Obama saw improved relations with the United States, but new actors like China simultaneously deepened their involvement in the region. Chapter 6 brings us to the election of Donald Trump in the United States and how his administration disrupted existing relationships. Chapter 7 examines the first part of the Joe Biden administration and the trajectory of Latin American–US relations.

2. ELECTORAL REVOLUTION IN LATIN AMERICA (1998–2002)

THE COLD WAR, WHICH colored every aspect of Latin American–US relations for two generations, ended in 1991. President George H. W. Bush proved more pragmatic than his predecessor Ronald Reagan, which launched shifts in U.S policy priorities (LeoGrande 1990). Without global ideological struggle hanging over US policy, Bush was more willing to accept compromises even in hotspots like Central America, where long-standing civil wars were ending. That set a new tone. Given his decision to invade Panama in 1989, President Bush did not ignore Central America, but part of the new tone also involved moving US foreign policy attention elsewhere, especially the Middle East.

Elected president in 1992, Bill Clinton had no interest in the Cold War underpinnings of Latin American–US relations. His focus on Latin America was even more pragmatic than Bush and rarely a priority. He was, like all other post–Cold War presidents, accused of "ignoring" Latin America (Crandall 2008, 20). He had been elected on a platform centered on improving the US economy, so in Latin America he emphasized free trade and market reforms along with democratization. Unlike the Cold War period, his view of democratization was not limited strictly to candidates that US policy makers considered acceptable. US interests mattered—they always do—but protecting them became a more flexible exercise.

Flexibility opened a political door previously slammed shut. In the absence of a global ideological war, the United States was much less focused on undermining the political advancement of the Latin American left. That opening meant greater latitude for the left to seek new partnerships and to have the option—even if not necessarily taken—of expanding autonomy from the United States. The United States was no less hegemonic than before, but it was less concerned about imposing control. That context falls under Juan Carlos Puig's category of "heterodox autonomy," though he views it in terms of weaker countries taking advantage of "weaknesses and errors" of the hegemonic center (Puig 1980, 152). In the immediate post–Cold War era, however, indifference was likely more relevant than weakness or error. Simply put, the United States government did not feel so paranoid anymore and had other issues on its plate.

Back in that more paranoid past, the United States government overtly or covertly attacked leftist governments or movements that seemed capable of upending the conservative status quo. That was especially prevalent in Central America and the Caribbean, but it spread to South America as well, where leftist governments found themselves the victims of sanctions, pressures, or covert operations. The biggest target was always Cuba, which had greatly resembled a US colony in the first third of the twentieth century, and was thereafter controlled by the dictator Fulgencio Batista, who enjoyed US support until almost the very end of his time in power.

Fidel Castro represents the most extreme historical case of Latin American autonomy from the United States. Counter to peripheral realism, he remained committed to promoting radical autonomy even when it started to generate highly negative effects on Cubans. For Castro, the revolution was everything no matter how harshly the United States responded. Only Venezuela in more recent years resembles the Cuban experience.

The 1959 revolution quickly deepened and the imposition of the US embargo cut off trade between the two countries. As a result, Castro shifted trade elsewhere, primarily the Soviet Union. Until the end of the Cold War, at any given time roughly 80 percent of Cuban exports went there. Later, Cuba shifted to China and European countries. Fidel Castro was a driving force in the Non-Aligned Movement, on organization founded in 1961 that situated itself outside Cold War confines, aligned in neither ideological camp. In a famous 1979 speech to the United Nations, he declared:

We are 95 countries from all the continents representing the vast majority of humanity. We are united by determination to defend cooperation among our countries, free national and social development, sovereignty, security, equality and self-determination.[1]

Setting aside the question of Cuba's clear alignment with the Soviet Union against the United States, Castro's message was one of autonomy. When the Soviet Union fell apart, Cuba maintained a strong connection to Russia based on those decades, but the economic dependence never returned.

The Cuban revolution and Fidel Castro's leadership personally inspired many among the Latin American left. At the turn of the twenty-first century, no government followed his particular model of revolution or sought to employ the same high level of repression and control (though over time some would copy it more). But many admired the very idea of a small country successfully thumbing its nose at the United States and so hoped—or at least claimed to hope—they could do the same in modified form. Cuba had diversified its trading partners such that by 2018 its four main export partners were Venezuela, Spain, Russia, and Bolivia, while it imported from China, Spain, Germany, and the United States.[2] Even after the Cold War ended, Cuba played an active role on the world stage, not by sponsoring revolution but by helping to create and nurture international institutions that excluded the United States, such as the Community of Latin American and Caribbean States (CELAC), created in 2011. The very purpose of CELAC was to keep the United States at bay while fostering regional integration.

CELAC is an example of how Cuba's Cold War autonomy served as an inspiration for the leftist leaders elected in the final years of the twentieth century and early in the twenty-first. Cuba was a key member of CELAC after years of exclusion from the Organization of American States, which expelled it in 1962. It was just the most recent example of the many ways in which Fidel Castro and Cuba served as models for the Latin American left. The most important president that Fidel Castro mentored was Venezuelan Hugo Chávez.

Chávez, a former army lieutenant colonel, coup plotter, and self-professed champion of the poor, won handily in 1998 with 56 percent of the vote. When he took the oath of office, he broke with protocol and said, "I swear in front of my people that over this moribund constitution I will push forward the democratic transformations that are necessary so that the new republic will have an adequate magna carta for the times" (quoted in Jones 2007, 226). Chávez took office the following year, on the cusp of the twenty-first century. His stated project was radical and leftist but initially its scope was not entirely clear.

At that time the administration of President Bill Clinton, which previously had denied Chávez a visa because of his participation in the coup attempts, responded hesitantly but favorably toward him, taking care to make clear that it did not like the rumors circulating that the army would stage a coup to prevent him from taking office (Bachelet 2017). The US government then agreed to give him a visa. Chávez did push back against US policies, for example refusing to allow use of Venezuelan airspace for US planes involved in the drug war, and diplomatic niceties remained the norm for the time being (Duarte Villa 2004).

The Latin American response to Chávez's election was decidedly mixed. In the 1990s the region leaned conservative. There were center-left presidents in Brazil and Chile, but in Bolivia, Colombia, Mexico, Peru, and all of Central America, the right was largely in control. Everywhere, free market models were the norm. Colombia's foreign trade minister tepidly said that bilateral commercial relations should not be affected by the election result (IPS Correspondents 1998). Panamanian president Ernesto Pérez Balladares said that the election represented "the reaffirmation of the democratic system" (Spanish Newswire Services 1998a). Former Honduran president and then president of the Central American Parliament, Carlos Roberto Reina, called Chávez's victory "a tragedy for America" (Spanish Newswire Services 1998b). Argentine president Carlos Menem made no public announcement but Chávez said that Menem had called him (Xinhua News Agency 1998). Naturally, Fidel Castro was ecstatic, saying that Cubans "share with the Venezuelans your jubilation" (Agence France Presse 1998).

There was a darker side to the putative regional free market consensus. Under the surface, the free market boat was running aground. Chávez and his drive for autonomy from the United States stemmed from the economic reforms the government of President Carlos Andrés Pérez pushed through in the late 1980s. These included cutting spending, slashing government subsidies, and privatizing state industries. The message was that by sweeping out old models and enduring pain in the short term, you could refresh those struggling economies. Latin American governments across the region had been doing the same in the 1980s, and protests—even riots—erupted in response. Similar scenes played out elsewhere in Latin America, almost everywhere. Governments that implemented those structural changes generally found themselves losing elections or forced out of power.

That had been Venezuela in the late 1980s. After the government implemented its package of policies, the economic and political consequences came quickly. The proximate cause in Venezuela was a 100 percent increase in the price of gasoline, which in turn increased public transportation fees (López Maya 2003). Protests that began at Caracas's main transportation points soon exploded and the president used security forces to put them down. Then all hell broke loose.

THE VENEZUELAN COMANDANTE

Chávez's view of autonomy was radical and emancipatory, based in no small part on the core tenets of dependency theory. At home he promised to write a new constitution. His broader vision of regional autonomy had not coalesced yet, but the kernel was there. It involved political and economic union, using the independence hero Simón Bolívar as a rhetorical (and even theatrical) vehicle. The use of the word "Bolivarian" denoted not just an emphasis on Venezuela's political history, but on the belief in a Latin American community, free of US manipulation and entirely skeptical of US motives.

Chávez's message was anticapitalist, though he denied he was aiming to copy the models of Cuba or the Soviet Union. Instead, he proclaimed his economic project was "twenty-first-century socialism," a catchy but ill-defined term that fell uneasily between state capitalism and socialism. It rejected both capitalism and communism and in practice meant a greatly enhanced role for the state without taking over the entire economy. His message, soon to be emulated by Rafael Correa, Evo Morales, Néstor Kirchner, Cristina Fernández de Kirchner, and other presidents on the way, was that Latin America needed new partners, new opportunities, and new ways of thinking. They did not necessarily share his economic vision but that was not a requirement for changing the way Latin America viewed the world.

He employed what Rafael Sánchez (2016) has nicely summed up as a populist style based on "monumental governmentality." Like his hero Bolívar, Chávez consciously assumed a bigger-than-life persona. Like Bolívar, he loved dancing and—even along with singing—that became part of this image that purported to represent the will of the nation.[3] Embodying that will allowed a heterogeneous country to unite by seeing themselves in their leader (Sánchez 2016, 4). For many Venezuelans, Chávez was much more than just president. He was *Venezuela*. In the way he made those direct personal connections, he was a populist.

The term "populism" is a contested term, used to apply loosely to a broad swath of leaders. It can refer to economic policy or political style. This book will follow Levitsky and Roberts (2011, 6) in emphasizing the latter: "the top-down political mobilization of mass constituencies by personalistic leaders who challenge established political or economic beliefs on behalf of an ill-defined *pueblo*, or 'the people.'" It often manifests as leftist, though there are also Latin American examples to the contrary, such as Alberto Fujimori in Peru. Populists on the left inspired millions who felt the economic status quo had left them out. "Personalism" was all about forging a bond between the president and the common person, united against entrenched elites. Leftist populists took the strongest stance, accompanied by a barrage of anticapitalist, anticonservative, and anti-US language, in promoting new partnerships both within and outside the region, excluding the United States. In terms of autonomy, this last point is central.

His election was a first breaker of what became commonly known as the "pink tide," which denotes a surge of leftists coming to office through free elections. The "pink" referred to the notion that although these new presidents were leftist, they had no "red" inclinations toward communism but wanted something lighter. It is imperfect imagery, since the right did continue winning in some countries, most notably Colombia and Mexico, and there was considerable ideological diversity within the broad category of "left." But the thrust of the term was that something new was happening, and that newness was connected to increasing autonomy. Some of these new leaders openly criticized the United States, but many were more circumspect. What they did all share was a commitment to looking more globally for trade and investment. It was diversifying, playing the field so to speak, not breaking away. This is relational autonomy, as opposed to antagonistic autonomy (Russell and Tokatlian 2003).

One problem with the pink tide imagery is that Hugo Chávez tends to be viewed as its embodiment, but he was the exception, not the rule. When he took office, Chávez asserted his message of autonomy toward the United States in part through Colombia. He was critical of President Rafael Caldera (in office 1994–1998) because of his support for Plan Colombia, the large-scale military aid project the United States and Colombia established in 2000 to combat narcotics. Chávez bristled at Caldera's approval of US Drug Enforcement Agency flights that went into Venezuelan air space. This initial period of US-Venezuelan relations has been usefully called "tension without rupture" (Duarte Villa 2004, 28). Chávez viewed Plan Colombia as an imperialist policy aimed at embedding the US military more deeply into South America. Further, Chávez believed the United States would use the Organization of American States against him to intervene and label his government as illegitimate, just as it has with Cuba. Yet these points of contention did not constitute a breaking point. The US ambassador to Venezuela, John Maisto, took the position of "Watch what Chávez does, not what he says" (quoted in Foer 2006). For a short time, US-Venezuelan relations bent did not break.

Chávez's rise to power coincided almost perfectly with Vladimir Putin's in Russia. President Boris Yeltsin named him prime minister in late 1999 and he became acting president when Yeltsin resigned at the end of the year. The two presidents were not ideological soulmates or even temperamentally alike, so they never developed a close personal relationship. Theirs was instead a marriage of convenience. Both felt threatened by the United States and committed to upsetting the US sense of Latin America being its backyard. Chávez first went to Moscow in 2001 and the two leaders discussed possible Russian investment in Venezuelan oil and gas fields (United Press International 2001). The relationship grew gradually. By the time of Chávez's next visit in 2004, he had oil money and an appetite for weapons.

Finally, Chávez prioritized the Organization of the Petroleum Exporting Countries (OPEC) as a way to counter US influence. He traveled to member nations, including Iraq in 2000, and called an OPEC meeting that same year, its first since 1975 and only the second in its history (Bellos 2000). For Chávez, OPEC was the ideal global vehicle for creating leverage over the United States while increasing Venezuela's (and by extension his) stature. Chávez advocated for production cuts in the cartel as a way to boost prices.

THE RISE OF CHINA

Understanding the uneven push for Latin American autonomy requires looking beyond the region. As a dynamic economic area no longer a center of global struggle, the region offered great opportunity. As the 1990s began, China's primary concern in Latin America was about denying diplomatic recognition to Taiwan. China's global goal was to switch recognition because Latin America (especially Central America) had close ties to Taiwan. Chinese president Yang Shangkun made the first trip by a high-level official to the region in 1990, visiting five countries to counteract Taiwanese capitalizing on the negative image of China following the Tiananmen Square repression (Zhu 2010, 93). Subsequent trips gradually expanded that relationship to include economic agreements.

During this period, China experienced high levels of growth, and its demand for raw materials rose. Beginning in 1978, for a variety of reasons it shifted away from a centrally planned economic model.[4] The government introduced profit incentives into agriculture that dramatically increased production, gave state enterprises more leeway to make decisions and to keep profits, and moved from a closed economy to an export model. These reforms were clearly bearing fruit by the 1990s precisely as Latin America was opening itself economically as well.

Resource constraints, including a trade deficit in key commodities, prompted the Chinese government to look abroad for new sources (Jenkins, Peters, and Moreira 2008). China also joined the World Trade Organization in 2001, which was a gateway to greater global access to commodities and export markets. At the same time, the Cold War was over, which meant China could engage with Latin America without automatically sparking a crisis with either the United States or the Soviet Union. Simultaneously, Latin American countries had shed their protectionist past and were opening their economies.

In early 2001, Chinese president Jiang Zemin made his third visit to Latin America, bringing a delegation to six countries, noting explicitly along the way that a key goal was to establish agreements about commodities, specifically copper, wool, and oil (China Daily 2001). That marked the beginning of a concerted Chinese government effort to expand ties to the region (in addition to Africa) especially by increasing trade and investment. It is notable that ideology did not drive the choice of countries. Cuba and Venezuela were on the left, while Argentina, Brazil, and Chile were arrayed more to the center, and Colombia (though to a lesser extent) was on the right. China went to all of them.

In short, China's new focus on Latin America was driven by economic, not ideological, considerations. In general, the Chinese government has been careful, and still is up to the present day, not to make any claims to ideological affinity in an effort to allay US concerns. The 1990s were especially sensitive in this regard because the United States government was preparing to relinquish control over the Panama Canal. A number of congressional Republicans vociferously opposed shifting ownership of the canal to Panama, arguing that China would swoop in and seize it. As Rep. Dana Rohrabacher (R-CA) put it in 1999, "I can guarantee you that within a decade, a communist China regime that hates democracy and sees America as its primary enemy will dominate the tiny country of Panama" (quoted in Mufson 1999). The Chinese leadership understood that the United States viewed Latin America as its proverbial backyard and so were careful not to give the impression that they wanted to buy the house next door.

That point is important for our understanding of autonomy because Latin American policy makers across the ideological spectrum viewed China as a potential source of trade and wealth creation in conjunction with continued connection to the United States. This development was not about spurning the United States and choosing a new partner. It was not, in fact, about the United States at all. Instead, reaching out to China represented an organic extension of the economic models that all Latin American countries were trying to follow. "Globalization" can be a tired term, but Latin America's market reforms naturally led it to find as many new opportunities as it could. They were simply playing the field.

Hugo Chávez visited China in 1999, not long after taking office. When Jiang Zemin arrived in Venezuela in 2001, Chávez greeted him warmly, and soon the two countries established commissions for cooperation in energy, industry, science, and technology. Over the next fifteen years, China and Venezuela signed more than three hundred agreements, which the Venezuelan state media approvingly noted was all due to "the socialist leader and the beginning of the Bolivarian Revolution" (Correo del Orinoco 2016). Chávez would consistently frame the relationship in ideological terms. China would not.

Indeed, at the same time that Chávez and Jiang were signing agreements, China was pursuing similar ties with Argentina, which in the late 1990s was following an aggressively market-oriented economic policy that included pegging the Argentine peso to the dollar. President Carlos Menem traveled to China in 1990 and 1995, always taking a delegation of business leaders (Oliva 2010). By 2001, Argentine exports to China—largely consisting of soy—were over $1 billion (Oliva 2010). Neither country even bothered to mention ideology.

This narrative repeated and expanded across Latin America in the twenty-first century. An initially tentative relationship with China would strengthen, heads of state would visit each other, business leaders would do so more often, and they would sign agreements focused largely on the raw materials that China saw as essential for economic growth. By 2000, these relationships were consolidating. Later, economic cooperation would more explicitly include loans, at times for considerable sums. Whether or not it was an explicit goal, these agreements increased Latin American autonomy from its traditional heavy dependence on US markets. The specific timing of changes in the international system and in national-level attitudes toward economic development made it possible. Just ten years earlier, it would have been problematic.

Guatemala provides an instructive case for the nonideological dynamic of moving closer to China. Historically, Guatemala was heavily dependent economically on the United States and close ideologically. In 2000, the United States was by far its largest trading partner, constituting 39.72 percent of its imports and serving as a market for 36.11 percent of its exports.[5] At that point, China was barely a speck of Guatemala's trade, at 0.91 percent of imports and 0.13 percent of exports. Fifteen years later, trade with the United States had not changed much, with 37.13 percent of imports and 34.98 percent of exports. But China's share had increased to 10.59 percent of imports and 1.94 percent of exports. These numbers are still small when compared to some other Latin American countries, in large part because China's demand for fruit is nowhere near that of oil, metals, and soy. Plus Guatemala still recognizes Taiwan, which hampers the deepening of economic ties.

But China's growth, especially with its exports to Guatemala, did not occur at the expense of the United States. Instead, there were small decreases scattered among many different countries. If anything, US economic presence had increased. US foreign aid of all types totaled $78 million in 2001 and, with ups and downs along the way, reached $258 million in 2021. Thus while China's role in the Guatemalan economy grew noticeably, US influence was still high. Guatemala looked to the United States for economic assistance, for example, and for help combating narcotics. Guatemala's strong connection to the United States had not changed much despite this carving out of some autonomous space.

The essential point here is that the entire region was interested in working more with China, which involved autonomy from the United States. Trade with China lessened dependence on the United States and provided more options than before. But the immediate goal was about national prosperity, and only more rarely what it meant for bilateral relations with the United States. Hugo Chávez did actively want to move away from the United States, but other countries far less so.

THE EFFECTS OF SEPTEMBER 11, 2001

George W. Bush took office in January 2001. He was a known conservative from a prominent Republican family, but his views on Latin America appeared largely pragmatic, as had been his father's once the Cold War was over. As governor of Texas, he had worked with the Mexican government and had traveled to Mexico numerous times. Free trade suited him ideologically. Hugo Chávez was the kind of leader toward whom Bush would naturally be antagonistic because Chávez's rhetoric was anti-imperialist and volcanic. But prior to the attacks, the new president could let that slide. As one presidential advisor put it, "As long as Houston and Big Oil are happy, we're not going to say anything to fuck things up" (quoted in Anderson 2001).

In the background, however, hard-liners worked to undermine the Chávez government. One of the most vociferous was Otto Reich, a Cuban American diplomat who in the 1980s was the first director of the State Department's Office of Public Diplomacy for Latin America and the Caribbean and had done his best to put a positive spin on the Contra rebels in Nicaragua. He was investigated for illegal activities in this regard, and in 1988 the state comptroller issued a report about his office and one of its contractors, International Business Communications (IBC).

> Due to the difficulty the Committee staff encountered in its efforts to obtain relevant information from the State Department and to the that IBC had been involved in funneling money to secret Swiss Bank account, many answers to questions raised in the report were not immediately forthcoming (House of Representatives 1988).

Chávez was close not only with Fidel Castro but also with Daniel Ortega, the former Sandinista Reich had hoped to overthrow violently. Thus even if President Bush appeared satisfied not to rock the oil boat too much, his choice of appointees sent obvious signals of a hard-line position.

Chávez, who launched his political career on the promise of breaking away from imperialist bonds, did not need much prompting to make autonomy his stated goal. His speeches bristled with the language of dependency theory. He got some of his inspiration from reading Noam Chomsky, an American foreign policy critic. He even recommended Chomsky's *Hegemony or Survival* in a speech to the United Nations in 2006 (thus assuring that it went from obscure leftist critique to bestseller).

Nonetheless, Chávez's extravagant goals could hardly be realized without resources. In December 2001 the *New York Times* saw a potentially dire situation as Venezuela increased spending but faced uncertainty about how to continue paying for it: "The value of the country's oil has fallen 40 percent since last year, and the worldwide economic slowdown could ensure that prices remain low" (Forero 2001). Autonomy cost money, and Venezuela was short on it.

This forecast might have been true if Al Qaeda operatives following orders from Osama bin Laden had not hijacked four planes, destroyed the World Trade Center, attacked the Pentagon, and murdered almost three thousand people on September 11, 2001. That set off a chain of events that eventually reached Latin America. The Bush administration quickly responded by invading Afghanistan, whose Taliban government harbored bin Laden. That invasion did not have economic ramifications for Latin America because there was little trade or interaction with Afghanistan. Over time, however, the administration began building a case in the United Nations for an invasion of Iraq, making two critical and erroneous arguments that Iraqi dictator Saddam Hussein was aiding Al Qaeda and also had weapons of mass destruction that threatened US national security. When the administration found itself unable to find many takers in Latin America for invasion, it resorted to bullying.

Mexican president Vicente Fox recounts in his memoir that Bush barraged him with phone calls. Given Mexico's history of being invaded, Fox could never even contemplate voting in favor of the war unless he was convinced both that all diplomatic avenues had been exhausted and that Hussein represented a threat to the entire world beyond any doubt (Fox 2007, 287). The Bush administration pushed forward and the conversations between the two presidents became icier and more formal, to the point of Bush telling Fox that either Mexico was with the United States or against it. At the time, Heraldo Muñoz was Chile's ambassador to the United Nations, and President Ricardo Lagos's position on Hussein was the same as Mexico's. After Chile and Mexico chose not to support the invasion, Bush advisor John Maisto told Muñoz that the president "was truly disappointed with Lagos, but he is furious with Fox" (Muñoz 2008, 170). He went on to say that Chile would now lose influence, and free trade negotiations would slow. Because of this resistance, the United

States and Great Britain decided not to attempt a UN vote and invaded the next week instead.

Both then and now, Iraq has some of the largest oil reserves in the world. It remained one of the world's top oil exporters despite three major wars. In its 2002 Annual Report, OPEC acknowledged jitters because of the 2001 terrorist attack and fear of a US invasion of Iraq, but reported a yearly average of $24.36 per barrel, within the expected band (OPEC 2004). In October 2003 the United States invaded, which prompted both production decreases and widespread uncertainty about supply. By 2005 that annual average was up to $61.08 (OPEC 2008). In July 2008, just before the global economic crash, the price hit $140 per barrel (OPEC 2010). The upward trend of oil prices was manna from heaven for Hugo Chávez, who otherwise likely would have found his promises impossible to keep. Oil revenue also made it possible for him to create and maintain major international agreements and new institutions. This has been called "oil diplomacy" or "petro-diplomacy" (Clem and Maingot 2015).

US foreign policy thus breathed fresh air into Bolivarian lungs. Yet Venezuela remained tightly tethered to the United States. US consumers eagerly filled their gas tanks with gasoline refined from Venezuelan crude, perhaps even at their local Citgo, the wholly owned subsidiary of the Venezuelan state. By 2001, just over half of that was exported to the United States. Chávez threatened countless times to turn off the spigot, normally to deter US interference of some kind. But Venezuelan crude is hard to refine and there are few options outside the United States, so few took those threats seriously. Part of Venezuela's problem was that production declined after Chávez took power. In 1999, Venezuela produced 3.1 million barrels per day (bbl/d) of petroleum products, which increased for two years until the 2002–2003 oil strike, which was intended to force Chávez out.[6] After 2002, total production never again reached three million bbl/d and in 2019 it totaled only 830,000 bbl/d. That steady reduction meant that Venezuela's leverage over the United States, which was already tenuous, eroded.

Venezuela was not the only country to benefit from the oil boom. Colombia and Ecuador (and Brazil to lesser extent) exported crude while Bolivia did the same with gas. Further, oil was not the only commodity that rose in price. The early 2000s saw the beginning of a "super-cycle" of international commodity prices (Gruss 2014, 3). Between 2000 and the global crash in 2008, prices for food roughly doubled, metals quadrupled, and fuel quintupled, while non-food agricultural goods remained stable (Gruss 2014, 20). China's demand for soy (Argentina and Paraguay) and copper (Chile and Peru) brought in significant revenue, but general global demand for iron ore, coffee, beef, zinc, and bananas did the same across the region. There were resources to encourage autonomy.

But 9/11 had effects other than just on oil. As mentioned, the Bush administration had antagonized otherwise friendly governments in Chile and Mexico with its insistence on invading Iraq, a decision that was deeply unpopular in Latin America across the ideological spectrum. Beyond that narrow policy area, the bigger question of fighting a global war on terrorism (or just "terror," as the president sometimes put it) was also unpopular. The Pew Research Center compared the image of the United States in 1999/2000 to 2002, and it had decreased in every country but Guatemala (Pew Research Center 2002). Conservative Honduras and Bolivarian Venezuela each saw a seven-point drop. By the end of Bush's second term in 2008, confidence in the president was abysmally low, where a large majority had either no confidence or not too much.[7]

In the days following the terrorist attacks, Latin America united in condemnation. On the same day, the OAS General Assembly issued a statement that "condemns in the strongest terms the terrorist acts visited upon the cities of New York and Washington, DC and reiterates the need to strengthen hemispheric cooperation to combat this scourge" (Organization of American States 2001). That was followed by resolutions on September 21 to prevent, combat, and eliminate terrorism but also to consider the attack on the United States to be an attack on all. The twist, though, was that these were condemnations of Al Qaeda and did not signal approval of US policy.

The US war on terrorism involved making assumptions that a majority of Latin Americans did not share. Latin America did not consider itself to be a target of Al Qaeda or other Middle Eastern terrorist organizations, whereas the United States framed the struggle as global.[8] Latin America actually has a large population of Middle Eastern descent—especially Palestinian—that typically was not radicalized. The September 11 attacks did not appear to change that fact. From the Latin American perspective, the attacks on the

United States, while deplorable, were more a backlash against US policy in the Middle East than a broader attack on the world. That the US government believed a military-centric response was most appropriate to what it considered a global threat worsened the divide. Neither civilian nor military leaders were anxious to take part.

But the Bush administration would not allow a middle ground. As the president said in a September 20, 2001, address to Congress, "Every nation, in every region, now has a decision to make. Either you are with us, or you are with the terrorists" (*Public Papers* 2001, 1142). That assertion was discomfiting to a region unconvinced there was a global war at all. Bush was unwittingly pushing Latin America away precisely at a time when it had decided to look elsewhere on its own.

There were exceptions for mostly practical reasons. The Dominican Republic, El Salvador, Honduras, and Nicaragua did send more than a thousand troops to Iraq in 2003 as part of a coalition with Spain known as the Brigada Hispanoamericana, yet all but El Salvador pulled them out the following year, citing domestic opposition (Carney 2011). These were smaller, economically dependent countries with sympathetic governments eager to stay in the good graces of the administration. Yet even they faced the overwhelming weight of skepticism at home, with upwards of 70 percent of Salvadorans disapproving (San Martin 2007).

Under the guidance of Otto Reich and fellow far right advisor Roger Noriega, the "war on terror" paradigm replaced the Cold War (Emerson 2010). Military aid increased and the United States Southern Command took a more central role in forging foreign policy. From 2000 to 2017, the United States spent just over $20.8 billion in security assistance to Latin America (Isacson and Kinosian 2017), the lion's share of which went to Colombia and Mexico as part of the ever-present "War on Drugs."

Mexican president Vicente Fox defeated the candidate of the long-ruling Institutional Revolution Party (PRI) and thereby started an uncertain and uneasy process of democratization. He was center-right and no antagonist of the United States. He and President George W. Bush got along well until the terrorist attacks of September 11, 2001, upended the relationship. The two presidents agreed to deepen law enforcement cooperation, and President

Bush lauded Fox's efforts. After leaving office, Fox would proclaim the "War on Drugs" to be a waste, with legalization as the logical solution, but that was only later.

That war also included Plan Colombia, an initiative conceived by Colombian president Andrés Pastrana and initially funded by the Clinton administration. Although Pastrana had an ambitious plan that included funding for social programs, the United States elected to fund its militarized side. Between 2000 and 2008, the United States averaged $540 million per year, with Colombia also spending approximately 1.1 percent of its GDP each of those years (Mejía 2016). The money bought weapons of all sorts:[9] Blackhawk helicopters, US military advisors and mobile units, private US contractors, intelligence assistance, coca eradication efforts, and much more. The results in terms of reducing the cultivation and trafficking of cocaine to the United States was mixed (Mejía 2016).

Relations between the United States and Colombia had been decidedly rocky in the 1990s, as the Clinton administration cut off aid to the government of Ernesto Samper, who was accused of receiving millions of dollars from the Cali drug cartel. Relations improved under Pastrana and then even more keenly under his successor Alvaro Uribe, a staunch ally of the Bush administration who saw Plan Colombia as essential to his country's survival. There were many ardent critics of Plan Colombia in both countries, but unlike many other policies in the post–Cold War era, it was entirely bilateral. Colombia had no interest in policy autonomy. Rather, it needed resources. During initial debates in the US Senate, Sen. Joe Biden lauded the plan and noted that "Europe and Japan are being asked to contribute as well" (United States Senate 2002). Any multilateral aspect of the plan was coordinated with the United States. Colombia had no interest in antagonizing the United States.

The attack on 9/11 also had important and long-lasting consequences for immigration. Just before the attacks occurred, President Bush and President Vicente Fox of Mexico were scheduled to discuss immigration, which had not been reformed since the 1986 Immigration Reform and Control Act. Whatever window might have been opened after Bush's election slammed firmly shut. The president created a new Department of Homeland Security, which took over immigration and many other functions. By 2003, the former Immigration and Naturalization Service (INS) was folded into the new Immigration and Custom Enforcement (ICE). The shift from "service" to "enforcement" in the name was apt, because the government's approach to immigration was enmeshed more than ever in national security.

At the turn of the twenty-first century, there were approximately 8.5 million undocumented immigrants, referring to immigrants lacking legal status (Pew Research Center 2018). That number would peak in 2007, and then decline again. These immigrants, always a source of controversy, became even more entangled in the domestic US debate over security. Policy makers left no room for negotiation with affected Latin American countries or even much consideration of immigration policy's impact on them. The Clinton administration had enacted a number of hard-line measures, and 9/11 solidified that trend.[10] At various moments over the next two decades, bills emerged and occasionally passed either the House of Representatives or the Senate, but they consistently ran into the brick wall of domestic politics. Immigration legislation remained limited and did not take Latin American realities (or opinions) into account.

We will periodically return to immigration over the course of the book, but Latin American autonomy in that area was slower to develop than in many others, and in most cases remained minimal. By virtue of geography and history, the places from where the lion's share of migrants came were more geographically close and historically more economically dependent on the United States. Therefore, they were more apt to accept US demands, since refusing them could carry penalties in other important areas. Further, unlike other areas of Latin American–US relations, Latin American governments could not enact any policy that would keep a migrant at home or encourage them to choose a different destination. Decreasing trade with the United States did not mean decreasing emigration there.

Latin American governments therefore argued their cases in the court of public opinion and in the halls of the United States Congress, where their lobbyists sought sympathetic ears. Since countries like Mexico, El Salvador, Guatemala, and Honduras could not offer sufficient economic and personal security to their own citizens, they sought humanitarian treatment for them. That required US legislation, which in the twenty-first century has typically been focused much more on security than on humanitarian impulses.

THE VENEZUELAN COUP

On April 11, 2002, a faction of the Venezuelan army forced Hugo Chávez out of office. Two days later, his supporters put him back. As noted in chapter 1, the end of the Cold War expanded the space within which Latin American governments made decisions autonomously. Before then, Chávez would have likely been treated by the United States the same way as Fidel Castro or Daniel Ortega, the targets of covert action and armed insurrection. In the twenty-first century, when Chávez made provocative and insulting remarks while discussing socialism and threatening nationalization, the United States government did not fund either. This is not to say US policy makers did not welcome regime change, but the intensity of the Cold War no longer infused bilateral relations.

In the weeks leading up to the coup, US officials met both military officers and members of the opposition, and one official admitted that when the topic of a possible coup came up, "We were not discouraging people" (Borger and Bellos 2002). This was a green light the opposition wanted. The 2002 oil strike had emboldened Chávez's political enemies and increased the antagonism between them and Chávez. In April, the opposition organized a march, which they steered toward the presidential palace Miraflores, where a progovernment rally was underway. The two came together violently. As the chaos and violence spiraled, dissident army officers demanded Chávez's resignation. He did not resign but agreed to surrender. Chávez supporters poured into the streets, protesting not just the coup but the antidemocratic opposition figures who tried to form a government. Within two days, loyalist officers prevailed and he returned to the presidency.

Three weeks after the coup, the US ambassador to the Organization of American States (OAS), Roger Noriega, repeated the Bush administration's position that Chávez was at fault. He argued that the coup occurred "after the Venezuelan military refused to fire upon unarmed, peaceful demonstrators"

(United States Department of State 2002). This version did not resonate with most of the region, especially as news trickled out that opposition leaders, both military and civilian, had met with Bush administration officials. This discordant note, which showed how the United States was out of step with the rest of Latin America, weakened US influence further. George W. Bush was consistently unpopular in Latin America, where his policies on Cuba, Venezuela, and terrorism in particular were met with skepticism or even hostility.

After his return to power, Chávez accelerated his push for autonomy through "soft balancing," which involves "frustrating the foreign policy objective of other presumably more powerful nations" (Corrales 2009, 98). To this end, Chávez rejected cooperation with the United States, built alliances with like-minded states, created counterproposals to thwart US objectives, and used investments (especially after the price of oil skyrocketed) to attract allies long-term. This last point is especially relevant. As the following chapters show, many of Chávez's initiatives did not outlast the future drop in oil prices. The balancing was predicated solely on the continued flow of free or cheap money or oil from the Venezuelan government.

Chávez's strategy resembles Juan Carlos Puig's idea of "heterodox autonomy." For all his rhetoric, Chávez accepted the hegemonic position of the United States and understood there were limits to what he could achieve. He could not counter US military force and did not try to do so. He could block US efforts to establish a hemispheric free trade area (the Free Trade Area of the Americas) but he did not make any serious moves in the direction of reducing economic dependence on the United States. In fact, Corrales (2009) makes the point that Chávez's most favored tactic was talking, which he did in prodigious amounts. But what was perhaps most important about soft balancing was that it coincided with other global forces. Just as Chávez laid the groundwork for his various projects, China was looking to the region. Other countries from outside the hemisphere similarly sent diplomats and trade representatives in larger numbers and at greater frequency than in the past. These two developments dovetailed.

Chávez's election was the harbinger of a slew of elections across Latin America that brought left or center-left presidents to power. Such terms are imprecise, as are *moderate, radical, centrist, conservative, far right*, or other similar permutations. They are used loosely, but there is no good way to do otherwise. Left and right are opposites, but there is a long continuum between them, and placing anyone precisely on some point in the middle is not simple. Nonetheless, viewing how leaders govern at least provides a sense of what their preferred policies are and what tactics they will likely choose to achieve them.

Jorge Castañeda, Mexican academic and former foreign minister, writes that the left is hard to pinpoint, but in economic and social terms it emphasizes social justice over economic growth, government intervention over market mechanisms, social spending over orthodox economics, and reduction of inequalities over efficiency (Castañeda 1993, 18). Such orientation may be more (even a *lot* more) or less radical, and he poses four different groups: traditional communist parties, nationalist or populist left, political-military organizations, and reformists. In the twenty-first century we see mostly populists and reformists.

This ideological diversity is worth examining. Scholars and pundits tend to divide the left into two categories. There is the moderate left and the radical left (Weyland 2009). Or, if you prefer, one is "open-minded" while the other is "close-minded" (Castañeda 2006). The point was that some leftists were populist, less democratic, and anticapitalist while others were more social democratic. In practice, those distinctions are difficult to make because few leaders fall neatly into one category or the other. The binary look is easy to digest but not a great reflection of reality. The key point is that being leftist per se had little bearing on whether a given leader necessarily framed autonomy in anti-US terms. This new crop of leftist governments questioned assumptions about economic development that had become conventional wisdom in the 1990s, but questioning mostly did not mean wholesale rejection either.

The "right" is the other side of the same coin. Luna and Kaltwasser (2014, 4) define it as "a political position characterized by the idea that the main inequalities between people are natural and outside the purview of the state." Economically, the market is the driving factor and at least in theory the state plays a minimal role, there mostly just to make sure basic rules are followed. Socially, there are often strong religious overtones, usually from the example of the Catholic Church but also increasingly from evangelical Christian denominations. The term is generally synonymous with "conservative."[11] The far right simply refers to those political actors who believe the most fervently in these positions and are less apt to compromise on them. Meanwhile, the most conservative leftist and the most left-leaning conservative come quite close to overlapping. This is where we find moderates and centrists, terms that typically are used interchangeably.

Aside from clarifying exactly what we mean by different terms, these different ideological positions serve as a reminder that leaders across the political spectrum have embraced autonomy, though for different reasons. The populist left and the reformist left tend to get lumped together but their autonomy goals differ, especially in terms of how they hope to position themselves vis-à-vis the United States.

Presidents like Ricardo Lagos of Chile and Fernando Henrique Cardoso of Brazil were both reformist presidents. Lagos, a social democrat (in the Party for Democracy party, or PPD), was elected in a second round in 2000. He is often lumped into the "leftist" category but is nowhere near Chávez ideologically. Chilean foreign policy in the twenty-first century is marked by a focus on autonomy, but that does not include any rejection of the United States. On the contrary, Lagos continued the process of negotiating a free trade agreement with the United States. As José Morandé (2003, 258) notes, with the end of the Cold War, Chile has greatly expanded its international reach so that "the Chilean economy expanded in commercial exchange to different regions of the world." Under Lagos, according to Claudio Fuentes, the Chilean government continued a policy resembling "soft power," where it negotiated free trade deals but explored many other areas of cooperation, conflict resolution, democratization, and humanitarian concerns (Fuentes 2006, 106).

In the 1960s, Cardoso was a major academic voice (in sociology) in defining and developing dependency theory, but by the time he was elected in 1995 he had moved decisively to the center. Like Lagos, he inherited a market-oriented economic model (of which he was an architect as minister of finance) and continued to nurture it, which in his case also meant privatizing state industries. This was no dismissal of neoliberal economics.

But after the global economic crisis of the late 1990s, sparked by currency devaluation in Asia that had global ripple effects and hit other developing countries, Cardoso followed "asymmetric globalization" (Pecequilo and do Carmo 2013). That perspective did not involve challenging the so-called "Washington Consensus," but rather pointing out how its positive effects were not distributed evenly across the globe. In response, Brazil took renewed interest in South American economic development, where it was a key player. Although Brazil did reject the US-proposed Free Trade Area of the Americas, that stemmed from what Brazil saw as uneven benefits and not because of any ideological commitment to keeping the United States at arm's length. Instead, Brazil looked to the South American Common Market, or Mercosur, a regional customs union with free trade among its members and a common external tariff. It was created in 1991 and is composed of Argentina, Brazil, Paraguay, and Uruguay, with a scattering of associate members. Brazilian leaders also focused on projects like the Initiative for the Integration of Regional Infrastructure in South America, which was intended to make South American countries more interdependent. Launched in 2000, it eventually was folded into the Union of South American Nations (UNASUR) even after Cardoso left office.

Then there was Luiz Inácio Lula da Silva (known as Lula). He was a decidedly leftist candidate, a longtime member of the Worker's Party (PT from the Portuguese acronym), and a vocal opponent of the military government. The PT transformed Brazilian politics, which had been characterized by weak and fragmented parties. By the 1990s it had become one of the strongest parties in Latin America, and in 1989 Lula almost won the presidency (Avritzer 2009, 45). The PT situated itself as worker-based and leftist, with the basic message of popular government. Its core message was domestic, about participatory budgeting, grassroots organizing, and strengthening of unions. Foreign policy was a relatively minor part of its identity, but Lula himself had a vision of forging a global policy that would raise Brazil's profile.

Lula represented the pragmatic side of the mostly leftist PT. He pledged to work within the 1988 constitution and even to work with the International Monetary Fund even as he tackled Brazil's chronic poverty (Hunter 2003). The election itself was not characterized by crisis or deep uncertainty. He ran on domestic issues and not on foreign policy. George W. Bush invited him to the White House not long after he took office, where both leaders wanted to emphasize their desire for close ties. Ideologically, this was highly unlikely, but the message itself was important symbolically.[12] Neither chose to target the other. Indeed, as historian John French points out in his biography of Lula, "Bush had been forced again and again—as late as 2007—to return to Lula for help in the region" (French 2020, 330).

Vigevani and Cepaluni (2012) situate Lula's foreign policy in part with the traditional positions of the PT, of which Lula was a key pillar, characterized by "autonomy by diversification." That position held that Brazil should be a global player, reaching out well beyond the Western Hemisphere while also maintaining a leadership role within the region without the United States. In fact, acting as a regional leader could serve as a springboard for a greater global influence. Cardoso had expanded Brazil's presence in the region, but less so globally.

Further, the Brazilian push for autonomy after the dictatorship predated not just Hugo Chávez but also the end of the Cold War. It began, albeit slowly, in the mid-1980s as Brazil democratized after two decades of a military dictatorship. Democratization brought new actors into the political process, which coincided with economic crisis. Debt, poverty, and inflation were all inheritances from the military government. In 1986, President José Sarney published an article in *Foreign Affairs* saying that "Brazil today is a medium-sized power, with a growing international presence as a result of its dimensions and interest" (116). That growing presence stemmed in no small part from its desire, even need, to find new export markets globally. The postauthoritarian era was leaving import substitution and state capitalism behind. By the time Lula took office, this new orientation had become consensus. Sarney, however, had also pointed out the difficult relationship Brazil had with the United States. With all presidents going forward, Brazil sought autonomy not to reject the United States per se, but rather to keep a comfortable amount of distance.

Lula moved to establish new commercial ties to South Africa, India, and China as well as Russia. He pushed for Brazil to have a permanent seat on the United Nations National Security Council (a long-standing goal) and for Brazilians to lead the World Trade Organization and Inter-American Development Bank. Unlike previous presidents, Lula included social policy in foreign policy, using his antipoverty programs at home promote the global struggle against inequality. This activism represented a break from Cardoso, with more emphasis on sovereignty and national interests (Almeida 2004, 165). We will return to Lula in the following chapter.

The key point here is that Brazil and Chile represented two of the most dynamic economies in Latin America and neither was interested in reducing its commercial and diplomatic ties with the United States. Certainly, neither had any interest in returning to a state-led development model. Instead, Brazil was diversifying its trading partners, which Chile had done years before. In 2001, 3 percent of Brazil's exports went to China and 2 percent of its imports came from there (CEPAL 2015). Just four years later exports rose to 6 percent and imports to 7 percent, and they kept going up (CEPAL 2015).

Brazil was invited to participate in the G20 in the wake of the financial crisis of the late 1990s (Doctor 2015).[13] Brazil's participation in this and other fora shows the balance between autonomy and engagement. While Lula in particular challenged the status quo, for example by advocating for a greater voice for emerging countries and reform of international institutions like the International Monetary Fund, he also made sure that Brazil was compliant or close to it in as many areas as possible, ranging from macroeconomic stability to reducing trade barriers and increasing transparency.

Like Ricardo Lagos and Fernando Henrique Cardoso, Lula did not make the United States a target. Put another way, he did not see rejecting the United States as part of his message to his constituency. Instead, his vision of autonomy was one where Brazil was a leader within a multilateral context. US-Brazilian relations showed a "limited divergence," where numerous disagreements caused frustration but not open confrontation (Soares de Lima and Hirst 2006, 33). Lula's goal was not countering the power of the United States per se, but finding optimal ways to achieve foreign policy goals while recognizing the reality of that power and what issues the United States prioritized.

DOLLARIZATION AS EXCEPTION

Not all Latin American leaders viewed economic autonomy as the ultimate goal, or even a central one. One important economic example is dollarization.

As the name suggests, dollarization means replacing a national currency with the US dollar. The idea is that given the stability of the dollar, supporters see inflation control and currency predictability as important benefits. Both domestic and foreign audiences will therefore have much greater confidence in policy makers and will therefore more likely invest and spend.

Dollarization is, as you might guess, the opposite of fiscal autonomy. Control over money supply and interest rates—key aspects of monetary policy—is gone. Those decisions are made entirely in the United States, and so the US Federal Reserve takes on a newly important role for the dollarizing country. Governments in those countries lose the ability to respond in traditional ways to financial crises, such as devaluing. They also lose seigniorage, which refers to the government earnings from the printing and selling of money. Panama, which was essentially a US colony at the time, dollarized in 1904.

Just as Hugo Chávez was elected with promises of resolving an economic crisis, so was Jamil Mahuad in Ecuador, who assumed the presidency in 1998. Like so many other countries, Ecuador had undergone a painful shift from state-led development in the 1960s and 1970s to an export-oriented economy in the 1980s and 1990s. By the end of the 1990s, the banking sector was hemorrhaging money, poverty was increasing, and the currency lost value at alarming rates. Mahuad bailed out the banking sector, but the cost of doing so entailed drastic cuts to social services. Unemployment and income inequality increased, and his approval ratings plummeted. By 2000 rumors circulated that the two likely outcomes were either resignation or coup (Rohter 2000).

To bolster his position and to assuage investors along with the International Monetary Fund, Mahuad chose the radical solution of dollarization in January 2000. It was an act of desperation, hammered through in haste. The dollar would replace the Ecuadorian sucre for all transactions. A week of protests forced him from office before January was out. He was soon offered a fellowship at Harvard (though in 2014 was convicted of embezzlement in Ecuador). Vice President Gustavo Noboa assumed office and continued the process. Indigenous groups in particular feared that dollarization would keep labor informal and flexible and lock in dependence on primary products, so they renewed their protests (Lucero 2001). Noboa's government responded with repression, and dollarization was completed in September 2000, but several months later Noboa signed a negotiated agreement that provided for cost-of-living adjustments and sustainable development. Ecuador was thus bound tightly to the United States.

As will be discussed in subsequent chapters, Rafael Correa, a leftist with a PhD in economics, would come to power in 2006 with fiery denunciations of the United States and of its imperial reach. But he never reversed dollarization. In 2016, just months before leaving after a decade in the presidency, he said dollarization was "monetary suicide" because it meant "adopting a foreign currency that behaves exactly in the opposite way we want it to" (TeleSur 2016). Nonetheless, dedollarizing would "cause an economic, social, and political chaos" (TeleSur 2016). Dedollarizing would immediately inject uncertainty back into the economy and potentially recreate the conditions that gave rise to dollarization in the first place. Ecuador would pursue autonomy in other ways, but remained—and for the foreseeable future will remain—tethered to the United States through the dollar.

El Salvador had a different route to dollarization, though it occurred at roughly the same time. Unlike Ecuador, there was no financial crisis or hyperinflation. Strongly tied to the United States for both imports and exports, El Salvador had earlier tried to harness that dependence as a way to reduce currency fluctuations. From 1993 to 2000 the Salvadoran colón was pegged to the dollar, though dollarization has long been a goal of the conservative ARENA party, whose candidate Francisco Flores won the 1999 presidential election. President Flores announced the policy in November 2000, the legislature passed it within a week, and it was implemented on January 1, 2001, a total of thirty-nine days from announcement to reality, without any real debate (Towers and Borzutzky 2004). In the absence of a financial crisis, Flores stated that dollarization would reduce interest rates and increase foreign investment, though it was not necessarily clear that those would not occur anyway. Later he would say that "without dollarization the country would be facing extremely grave fiscal problems" (Flores 2013). Not surprisingly, assessing the impact of dollarization in the country is an ongoing and, it is fair to say, neverending debate. Economist Luis René Cáceres (2017) notes the complexity of such assessment, and how important the role of the state is to nurture human capital and facilitate economic activity through judicious spending. Being tied to the United States per se in this view is less important than the strategies governments use to keep the system stable.

But of course, one inevitable consequence for El Salvador was to have an even closer trade relationship with the United States. From 2000 to 2015, the percentage of imports coming from the United States rose from 26.75 percent to 39.39 percent and exports to the United States went from 10.71 percent to 47.05 percent.[14] In 2000, El Salvador imported only 0.68 percent of its total from China and it exported nothing, whereas in 2015 imports were 8.11 percent and exports 0.8 percent. If anything, US influence was greater than ever before.

The twenty-first century commenced with Hugo Chávez taking up the banner of a new leftist surge that promoted autonomy from US hegemony. This deservedly gets the lion's share of attention, but was accompanied by other moves toward autonomy that did not base themselves in ideology. The pursuit of autonomy is often not specifically intended to free a country from the United States, but more so to expand its range of options. Those spaces were even more open because the ideological battles of the Cold War were over precisely at a time when China was showing interest in developing new relationships or deepening existing ones.

Other countries, notably Ecuador and El Salvador, actually dollarized, which tied them to the United States economically in specific ways no matter the ideology of whatever government in power. Further, even as Chávez loudly denounced the United States and found new insults for President George W. Bush, Lula was taking an entirely different tack, quieter but no less important. We will now turn to his foreign policy, which remained friendly both with the United States and Venezuela while asserting Brazil's place in the world even in the face of US resistance.

3. POLITICAL PRAGMATISM AND AUTONOMY (2003–2005)

IN THE PREVIOUS CHAPTER we saw that autonomy comes in different shapes and sizes. It might involve a radical turn away from the United States, like the oft-used example of Venezuela after 1998. Hugo Chávez certainly liked to frame his own views as universal, as Simón Bolívar coming back to life and unifying all of Latin America. But pragmatism tended to be a more common response. Open hostility toward the United States carried risks that many governments were unwilling to take, feeling they would not serve their own national strategic interests.

Take Brazil. It is the behemoth of the region, by far the most populous (by tens of millions) and the largest (by millions of square kilometers). Brazilian leaders have thus typically viewed the country as a natural global player rather than a Latin American one. A quest for autonomy does accompany those ambitions, but it comes with a solid dose of pragmatism, which in practice means working with the United States to some degree.

As Rossone do Paula (2018) has written, there are numerous messy discourses about what Brazil has been, what it is now, what it can be, and what it should be. Emerging as a global player that is becoming more autonomous in the international arena is one of them, particularly for the "should." Lula tapped deeply into the notion that Brazil had the requisite economic capabilities and diplomatic credentials to lead a way that was more South-South rather than fixed to the United States or any other developed country. His own background fighting against the Brazilian dictatorship and organizing workers further added to his street cred.

Lula was a counterpoint to Hugo Chávez, simultaneously a comrade and an independent voice, impossible to nail down in a "good" and "bad" spectrum. He had clear leftist credentials but often governed from the center. Even as he worked with the International Monetary Fund to keep strict monetary policies in place, conservatives in the United States Congress like Henry Hyde claimed he would form a Latin American axis of evil and possibly even facilitate a nuclear attack on the United States (Maxwell 2002). As it turned out, Lula did not annihilate any US cities.

As Soares de Lima and Hirst (2006, 32) note, under Lula Brazil had "recently acquired [a] vocation as a regional firefighter and crisis manager." Brazilian presidents were often interested in hemispheric affairs, but the intensity and desire for a leadership position varied. Some were highly active. Although not universally pro–United States, Juscelino Kubitschek (in office from 1956 to 1961) spearheaded a regional effort to promote Pan Americanism and closer ties to the United States, with the goal of increasing US aid to combat underdevelopment and by extension communism. Pushing hard despite frustration with a lack of US interest, Kubitschek's message finally got through to Presidents Dwight Eisenhower and John F. Kennedy, contributing to the Alliance for Progress (Long 2015). By contrast, the first postauthoritarian president, José Sarney (1985–1990), came to office facing immediate economic crisis, so he focused more squarely on South America, especially Argentina, to weather the storm.

José Saraiva (2014, 13) argues that although the quest for autonomy existed long before Lula, he gave it new life, a new national sense of self-confidence in the twenty-first century. Before him, Fernando Henrique Cardoso was more accepting of US power. As Cardoso wrote in his memoirs: "During my presidency, the United States considered itself as the world's only superpower. So, it was quite logical that much of our foreign policy would focus on our US relations" (Cardoso 2006, 256). He got along well personally with Bill Clinton and refrained from much criticism.

US relations centered on trade. President George H. W. Bush first proposed the Enterprise for the Americas initiative in 1990, which was intended to develop a free trade zone covering the entire hemisphere. The following year, Argentina, Brazil, Paraguay, and Uruguay signed an agreement to examine the possibility of a large free trade area. Bill Clinton was unable to move the idea much past rhetoric, but George W. Bush once again made it a priority. In 2003 and 2004, he and Lula worked together to determine what such an agreement might entail (Crandall 2011, 160). This collaboration demonstrates some of Lula's deftness at maintaining a more measured position with the United States. He wanted hemispheric agreements like Mercosur to deepen before launching a region-wide trade agreement, so remained friendly but cool.

His strong interest in Mercosur in a global context differentiated Lula from his predecessors, as did his even stronger nationalist orientation (Mariano 2015). Soon after taking office, he created a subsecretary of South American affairs to deepen Mercosur. Lula viewed regional South American integration, especially with the participation of Argentina, as critical for fostering a united front when negotiating economic agreements with the United States or the European Union (Mariano 2015, 185). His choice of foreign minister, Celso Amorim, favored an assertive policy and a strong global role for Brazil. They deemed the Free Trade Area of the Americas (FTAA) process rushed and overly beneficial to the United States. The FTAA was a US initiative intended to create a regional free trade across the region. So, while Lula worked with Bush, he was in no hurry and had little interest (and little incentive) in compromising.

Amorim (2010, 215) later noted with some satisfaction that the failure of the FTAA process worked out pretty well for Brazil, "especially for her efforts to promote South American integration." At the same time, commercial relations with the United States in general were positive, so Brazil's push for autonomy did not prompt backlash. Vivegani and Cepaluni (2012) consider Lula and Amorim's stance to be similar to President Ernesto Geisel's "Responsible Pragmatism" in the mid-1970s, which was meant to move closer to the Global South without aligning too closely with it. Autonomy did not mean antagonism, but rather careful participation. Brazilian scholars put this in various ways, including "moderate and propositional contestation" (Visentini and da Silva 2010, 63). More colorfully, at the 2008 Bahia Summit, Lula's presidential chief of staff Gilberto Calvalho told US ambassador Clifford Sobel that Brazil always wanted to diversify its trading partners but that a person "would have to have something wrong with his head" to think that Brazil could "leave the United States behind" (Wikileaks 2008). Fittingly, at that same moment Lula was in the office next door speaking with Cuban president Raúl Castro. That's how Brazil rolled.

In this sense, Lula did not mark any fundamental shift in Brazilian foreign policy. All previous Brazilian presidents emphasized autonomy in some fashion. Lula's own twist was more diversification, reaching out to a broader range of countries and using South America as a launching pad for more global aims. An example of diversification was Lula's courting of South Africa and India, which culminated in 2003 with the Declaration of Brasilia to create the India-Brazil-South Africa Dialogue Forum (IBSA, sometimes referred to as the G-3) (Alden and Vieira 2005, 1088). A Trilateral Commission served as the institutional arm of the agreement, facilitating talks, information exchange, cooperation, and joint initiatives, run through the respective foreign ministries. Starting in 2006, this led to annual or biannual summits.

As Lula put it in 2003 after feeling marginalized at the G-8 summit in France, "What is the use of being invited for dessert at the banquet of the powerful? We do not want to participate only to eat the dessert; we want to eat the main course, dessert, and then coffee" (quoted in Kurtz-Phelan 2013). This expanded culinary ambition took form in shared G-3 opposition positions at the World Trade Organization, coordination at the United Nations, and at times even common foreign policy positions. The last generally reflected commitment to dialogue over intervention, without open confrontation with the United States. Visentini and da Silva (2010, 56) describe Lula's process of seeking autonomy from the United States as occurring "very discreetly." That might be up to interpretation. US trade representative Robert Zoellick said in 2003 that Brazil's hard opposition to the Free Trade Area of the Americas would leave it resigned to negotiating trade deals with penguins in the Antarctic, a crack that the Brazilian press did not forget.[1] US officials were periodically critical of Lula's foreign policy, but he managed the relationship effectively, never letting it become truly antagonistic.

Lula's global focus also became evident with Iran. In 2005 the United States pursued sanctions to punish Iran for developing its nuclear program. Lula irked US officials when he argued that Iran had the right to develop peaceful nuclear power, which Brazil had already done to a limited extent with the Angra Nuclear Power Plant in Rio de Janeiro. According to Celso Amorim,

Lula's interest in Iran had two causes.[2] First, Lula wanted a global foreign policy "not limited by no-go areas of any kind" (Amorim 2017, 2). Second, he believed that Iran was important politically and economically, so Brazil would benefit from greater engagement. During his term he hosted Iranian president Mahmoud Ahmadinejad, went to Iran himself, and spent hours talking to other foreign leaders, including US presidents, about the US-Iran conflict. In fact, according to Amorim, in this regard relations with the Bush administration were equally positive as those with Obama. Lula wanted to be an intermediary and to an extent did play that role, along with Turkey. They helped broker a deal in 2010 for Iran to send enriched uranium abroad for processing (something Iran had rejected before), thereby at least postponing sanctions from Western countries. Lula's goal was to show the world that Brazil was a good negotiator, especially between middle powers and great powers, and to enhance the country's position in international institutions (Santos Vieira de Jesus 2010). Tied to all this was the image of a rising power standing firm against the United States, which tended to be more hostile and more skeptical of consensual solutions to Iran's development of nuclear power.

As with the rest of the Latin America, the bilateral trade relationship between Brazil and China took off in the early 1990s. In 1990, Brazil exported $381 million worth of goods to China.[3] President Cardoso declared (correctly) that Chinese demand for Brazilian products "will be a central fact of life for both countries for decades to come" (Cardoso 2006, 266). By the time Lula took office in 2003, exports to China had increased to $4.5 billion and continued to explode from there, rising to $44 billion when Lula left office in 2011, then plateauing soon thereafter as the Brazilian economy contracted. This move toward China was unrelated to Brazil-US relations. It began under Cardoso and continued after conservative Michel Temer became president in 2016. In fact, Jiang Zemin visited Brazil in 2001 as part of a six-country tour of Latin America and met with Cardoso.[4] China needed raw materials, which constituted about 61.5 percent of Brazil's exports in 2003 and 81.1 percent in 2016. By contrast, the bulk of Brazilian imports were machinery, electronics, and intermediate goods.

Lula visited China in 2004 with a large contingent of politicians and business leaders to discuss increasing trade, framing it as feeding China

(Chetwynd 2004). By 2009 Chinese trade with Brazil was greater than trade with the United States. Interestingly, in terms of dependence Brazil was more at an advantage with the United States because it exported far more finished goods there than to China. In 2003, the largest Brazilian export to the United States was machinery and electronics, which remained true in 2016, whereas with China it retained the traditional dependency balance of trade by exporting raw materials and importing Chinese industrial goods. Ironically, then, under Lula's leadership Brazil successfully pursued diversification but in a manner that was not always as advantageous as it might appear.

Lastly, Lula expanded Brazil's role in international peacekeeping, which dated back to 1957. By far the most important example in the twenty-first century was the United Nations Stabilizing Mission in Haiti, known by its acronym MINUSTAH. It came in the wake of the 2004 coup that overthrew Jean-Bertrand Aristide in the midst of violent insurrection, and the coup government requested UN intervention. The United Nations Security Council created MINUSTAH shortly thereafter. Brazil immediately took the lead and contributed the most soldiers, marking the first time it had commanded a peacekeeping operation. Faria and Paradis (2010) noted that Amorim called this type of foreign policy "non-indifference," meaning that intervention could be justified in limited cases in the name of social justice. They go on to write that Brazil's foreign policy took a "humanist" turn under Lula, which generated energy at the national level as well. At times Brazilian military leaders in Haiti talked about pushing back against US demands to use more force, which they opposed.

By and large MINUSTAH was popular in Brazil. Interestingly, there are those in Brazil who believe that far from promoting autonomy, it simply reinforced Brazil's subordinate role:

> [T]he Global North has the power of not only defining what peace is, and what it means, but also how it should be pursued and its construction operationalized throughout the globe. On the other hand, the Global South is responsible for building the kind of peace that reflects the characterization defined by the former. The Global South is the wo/manpower of such international division of labor of peacebuilding (Blanco 2017, 9).

Further, a major reason Brazil took the lead in the first place was that the United States, like other developed countries, was uninterested in doing so (Valença and Carvalho 2014). Under those circumstances, it is more difficult to see the operation as necessarily contributing to a more autonomous position, particularly when it was going along more or less exactly with US interests. Nonetheless, for Lula it was all part of a broader plan to project Brazil more globally.

Yet MINUSTAH also served US policy goals in that it constituted a wedge between Brazil and Venezuela. Hugo Chávez was derisive about the mission, which he considered an imperialist project to keep Haiti permanently subjugated. Defense Minister Nelson Jobim told US ambassador Thomas Shannon in 2010 that Chávez's accusation of a "US invasion" had no merit and that if anything the United Nations should improve and extend the mandate (Wikileaks 2010).

For different reasons, Chile was also painstakingly constructing its own international agreements literally all over the world. Unlike Brazil, its orientation was actually more global than it was regional. To a degree, autonomy included being unconstrained by the weaker economies of its neighbors. Chile's own trajectory in this regard was different from surrounding countries because it embarked on structural adjustment on its own during the dictatorship of Augusto Pinochet (1973–1990). Influenced by his University of Chicago–educated economic advisors (the so-called "Chicago Boys"), in the mid-1970s Pinochet oversaw the dismantling of Chile's long-standing state-led economic model. Since other South American countries remained economically unstable, Chile looked outside the region for free trade agreements. For Chile, the more the better because too few would mean becoming overly dependent on a small number of trading partners while also benefiting the politically influential export sector (Wehner 2011). Although the dictatorship built the export model, democratic governments after 1990 deepened it. Chile signed its first free trade agreement with Mercosur in 1996, and in 1997 the FTA with Canada was the first to be implemented (Wehner 2011).

As a result, Chile eagerly signed an FTA with the United States, which went into effect in 2004, gradually phasing out tariffs until full implementation in 2015. By that time, Chile already had several dozen FTAs and preferential trade agreements of various kinds, so closer ties with the United States did not entail any loss of autonomy in the traditional sense of subsuming Chilean interests to the United States. Instead, it shielded Chile from a sudden economic downturn with any given trading partner. This was particularly true with other South American countries, which were prone to going through cycles of economic stagnation (sometimes accompanied by high inflation) and currency devaluation, which of course disrupted trade. It did dilute US economic influence by making it just one of many, though that was not the primary goal.

TABARÉ VÁZQUEZ IN URUGUAY

Uruguay tends not to garner much attention in the United States, being small, peaceful, and distant. Yet it also joined the ranks of countries that elected center-left leaders. In 2004, Tabaré Vázquez won just over 50 percent of the vote, thus avoiding a second round and winning the presidential election. He was part of a center-left coalition, the first time the left gained power in the country. The two establishment parties, the Partido Colorado and the Partido Nacional, were pushed aside by Vázquez's Frente Amplio coalition in a historic election. As Uruguayan political scientists Daniel Buquet and Daniel Chasquetti (2005) point out, the left had been gradually increasing its share of votes, attracting younger voters in particular, and it wanted change.

Vázquez did not drastically shift foreign policy, but he did reorient it away from a generally pro-US stance toward a nonaligned stance, which provided more freedom to engage with both conservative and leftist governments. That was a conscious shift toward greater autonomy (Ferro Clérico 2006) and meant re-establishing diplomatic ties with Cuba, which were traditionally rocky. They were cut in 2002 after President Jorge Batlle sponsored a United Nations resolution condemning human rights abuses in Cuba, and Fidel Castro responded by calling him a "lackey" (Associated Press 2002). Vázquez also advocated for Venezuela's entrance into Mercosur.

But this did not mean rejecting the United States. Vázquez did not often mention the United States, and relations were not part of his campaign or platform. At the Summit of the Americas, a time when Hugo Chávez was leading the attack on George W. Bush's Free Trade Area of the Americas proposal, Vázquez and Bush quietly signed an agreement on investment (Ferro Clérico 2006, 128). President Bush visited Uruguay in 2007, eating barbecue at a presidential retreat the same month that Vázquez said he was an "anti-imperialist" president (Rutenberg 2007). This was similar to the nonaligned stance of many countries during the Cold War, which was founded largely on pragmatism. Despite some grumbling within his coalition, Vázquez maintained an entirely positive relationship with Bush and did not join in the antagonism.[5]

He prioritized Mercosur and its associate members in particular, along with the Andean Community, seeing them as conducive to regional economic growth. Outside Latin America, he continued the process of developing trade and investment agreements with the European Union. In 2007, he traveled to Brussels and signed a memorandum of agreement on EU-Uruguayan cooperation, which included economic, human rights, gender equality, and the environment (European Commission 2007).

International peregrinations started immediately with China, with Chinese officials arriving soon after he was sworn in to sign agreements and publicly affirm the importance of the bilateral relationship. Vázquez had previously visited China as leader of his Frente Amplio coalition, but went for the first presidential visit in 2009. Like with other countries, the main thrust of the trade agreements was to get Uruguayan primary products into the expanding Chinese economy.

In 2000, 3.2 percent of Uruguay's imports came from China and 3.97 percent of its exports went there.[6] When Vázquez took office in 2005, the imports had grown to 6.25 percent while exports had actually decreased slightly to 3.56 percent. When he left office, imports had risen to 13 percent and exports to 5.4 percent. Like virtually everywhere else, these trade relationships had yet to reach their ceiling. In 2000, the United States accounted for 9.8 percent of imports and 8.4 percent of exports. When Vázquez took office, those were 6.72 percent of imports and 23.1 percent of exports. When he left office, imports were at 10 percent and exports at 2.7 percent. When he was later again elected in 2015, China remained an important priority.

From that point forward, Uruguay took on a low-key but decidedly independent foreign policy stance over the course of several different presidential administrations. Domestic policies like legalizing marijuana and giving same-sex couples the right to marry had important international impacts, while later its insistence on promoting dialogue to resolve the Venezuelan crisis in 2019 (at which time Vázquez was once again president) set it apart from the United States and even much of the region.

NÉSTOR KIRCHNER AND ARGENTINA

In 1991, Argentina adopted a policy of currency "convertibility," whereby the peso was pegged one-to-one by law to the US dollar. As noted in chapter 1, the purpose of both convertibility and its more drastic cousin dollarization is to stabilize the currency, reduce inflation, and calm both investors and consumers. That system was threatened in 1999, when Argentina's major trading partner Brazil devalued against the dollar. Since Argentina could not respond in kind, its exports to Brazil were hit badly and the economy went into a tailspin. Gross domestic product shrunk and unemployment soared. Argentina turned in particular to the International Monetary Fund for emergency loans and a stamp of approval for international investors. Those loans came with strings, which entailed austerity measures that included significant cuts in government spending, including salaries and pensions. In 2001, capital flight increased and the government put a limit on bank withdrawals. Seeing this as an attack on convertibility itself (since the core of the notion was that the government would always convert), the IMF decided to stop providing loans. The Argentine economy collapsed and the government defaulted on debt.[7]

Given its conscious and deliberate attachment to the US dollar, convertibility was of course the antithesis of autonomy. In 2002, President Eduardo Duhalde ended the policy and the peso depreciated sharply.[8] In the midst of economic depression, Argentine voters looked for someone to resolve the problem and were receptive to a message that rejected the United States and blamed the ills of US-driven international capitalism for the country's suffering. Despite being a member of the establishment Peronist Party (formally known as the Partido Justicialista) and serving as governor, Néstor Kirchner stepped in that role after winning the May 2003 presidential election. Along with his basic message of economic stimulus, he specifically emphasized greater autonomy from the United States, which for him constituted "carnal relations" (Sanchez 2005). Following that particular metaphor, fellow Peronist Carlos Menem shared a bed with Washington, and Argentina suffered the consequences. At that point the Peronist Party and the Radical Party, previously bedrocks of the party system, were fractured by infighting, so that in the first round none of the main five candidates even reached 25 percent of the vote. In the second round between the two Peronists Kirchner and Menem, the latter withdrew after it became clear he was doomed to an electoral beating.

Kirchner's immediate challenge was economic and oriented toward pushing back at the United States and the International Monetary Fund. The shift he initiated shows the extreme flexibility of Peronismo, since Carlos Menem was from the same party and had governed as a pro-US, promarket president. But it also shows how Argentine politics are highly personalized and the state bureaucracy is not strongly professionalized (Malamud 2011). He went on the offense against bondholders, playing hardball and insisting they receive only a fraction of the face value of the bonds.

Morasso (2016, 3) labels Kirchner's foreign policy as "autonomist orientation." Referring to the United States as a hegemonic power, Kirchner ended the practice of aligning automatically with the United States and instead focused far more on regional unity (unlike Lula, Kirchner did not have broader global goals). That included developing close relationships with Hugo Chávez and Fidel Castro. Castro noted approvingly in an interview that Kirchner represented "the destruction of the symbol of neoliberal globalization" in Argentina (quoted in Ramonet 2010, 310). As time went on, Kirchner became increasingly open about his antagonism toward the United States.

What began as a rejection of economic policy that depended on the United States evolved into something more expansive. Kirchner came to office just as China started paying more attention to Latin America. In 2003, China accounted for 5.2 percent of Argentina's imports and 8.28 percent of its exports.[9] When he left office just four years later, those shares had jumped to 11.39 percent of imports and 9.26 percent of exports. Almost two-thirds of the exports (63.05 percent) were raw materials, whereas the imports were largely machinery, electronics, and consumer goods. Thus, Argentina was increasing its autonomy from the United States in economic terms. In the same 2003–2007 period, the share of Argentine exports to the United States dropped from 16.35 percent to 11.95 percent, and imports from 10.47 percent to 7.79 percent. In 2004 Kirchner went to China. Later the same year, Chinese president Hu Jintao traveled to Argentina and announced China would invest some $20 billion over the next decade (BBC 2004). The investments would include railways, education, tourism, and trade. In reality, the Chinese were more lukewarm than Kirchner claimed, as little of that came to fruition. Chinese loans would eventually come, but not immediately. Nonetheless, Chinese demand for Argentine goods served to reduce Argentina's debt. In 2005, Kirchner famously cancelled the country's debt to the International Monetary Fund, a move that the Bush administration opposed but which eased Argentina's debt burden. The growth of Chinese trade had the same effect and Argentina's debt shrunk by one-third (Davis 2010).

It is worth noting that the shift away from the United States did not change the fundamentally dependent relationship Argentina had with wealthier countries. Argentina continued to export primary products to China and receive finished goods in return, just as dependency theorists had been lamenting for years with regard to the United States. Argentina remained the weaker partner. In other words, greater autonomy from the United States did not entail any fundamental shift in Argentina's position in the global system. It remained relatively less industrial and needed to import manufactured goods.

Unlike Lula, Kirchner was more vocal about his dislike for George W. Bush's policies. In late 2005, the US president traveled to Mar del Plata, Argentina, to participate in the Summit of the Americas, aimed at promoting the Free Trade Area of the Americas (FTAA). A few blocks away, Hugo Chávez gave a speech to about twenty-five thousand people in a soccer stadium, all of whom were there to protest Bush (Rohter and Bumiller 2005). This is where Chávez declared the FTAA dead. Then, with Bush sitting stony-faced and Chávez applauding as hard as his hands would allow, Kirchner gave a welcoming speech that rejected free market principles, saying their theoretical underpinnings were empirically false and that any country that pushed them should accept some responsibility for their failure (*La Nación* 2005). They never saw each again after that, though unlike Chávez (and later Morales and Correa), Kirchner did not go out of his way to insult Bush.

For Argentine political scientist Alejandro Simonoff (2009), Kirchner's foreign policy was essentially Puigian, meaning a calculated expansion of autonomy without inspiring backlash from the United States. Kirchner rejected the Washington Consensus while seeking to strengthen Argentina's presence in the region. His policy choices reflected prioritizing autonomy and reducing dependency on one country, while not fully breaking ties with the United States. At least initially, that meant support for Venezuela, but not too much, and amicable ties with Brazil, but not too much. He was to the right of Chávez and the left of Lula.

This was the period when George W. Bush had a full contingent of Latin America policy hard-liners in his government. Assistant Secretary of State Roger Noriega criticized Kirchner, especially for his opening to Cuba (Relea 2004). Overall the administration made periodic remarks about its concern over the shift to the left in Latin America, but Noriega was especially vocal. That was also the immediate post-9/11 era, when US foreign policy was closely tied to finding and combating Islamic terrorism.[10] The United States saw threats all across Latin America, a view that was not widely shared in the region. Argentina (like many other Latin American countries) historically had a large population of Middle Eastern descent, and also shared the "Triborder Area" with Brazil and Paraguay, which was a haven for smuggling. The State Department issued annual reports on terrorist activity in Latin America and its assessment of how well each country was responding. Year after year, the administration left a contradictory message about Argentina. The report detailing 2004 is typical:

> The United States remains concerned that Hizballah and HAMAS raise funds among the sizable Muslim communities in the region, and that the high incidence of illicit activity could tempt terrorist groups to seek to establish safe havens in this largely uncontrolled area. Persons suspected of ties to terrorist groups have been spotted in the TBA, but no operational activities of terrorism have been detected (United States Department of State 2005).

Given Argentina's own experience with terrorism, specifically the 1992 attack on the Israeli embassy, which killed twenty-nine people, and the 1994 bombing of the Argentine-Israeli Mutual Association, which killed eighty-five people, Kirchner was adamant about his commitment to fighting terrorism, including in the Triborder Area.

The problem was that the Bush administration viewed terrorism through a militarized lens. It was a "war on terror" and armies fight wars: "the US emphasis is on intelligence sharing, border control, law enforcement, and freezing of assets. In Latin America, the first three have, with some variation, traditionally involved a significant military presence" (Weeks 2006, 62). Kirchner opposed that stance and was not receptive to the US request for Argentine troops to deploy to Iraq (Gentile 2003). For Kirchner, then, autonomy meant framing Argentina's participation in antiterrorism operations solely in his own way, resisting US pressures toward militarization. Few countries in the region jumped on board with the US vision.

BOLIVARIAN ALLIANCE FOR THE PEOPLES OF OUR AMERICA: ALBA

Regionally, the Summit of the Americas helped propel new autonomy initiatives. While the moderate left grew, so did its more radical counterpart. Hugo Chávez vociferously rejected the idea of the FTAA and proposed an alternative, the Bolivarian Alliance for the Peoples of our America (with the acronym ALBA from the Spanish Alianza Bolivariana para los Pueblos de Nuestra América). For Chávez, the FTAA was an imperialist project that would permanently stunt Latin American development. In an interview with Che Guevara's daughter Aleida, Chávez said he conceived of ALBA in December 2001 at the Caribbean Summit when he was talking to Fidel Castro. He called it "mischief" because FTAA in Spanish is ALCA (Área de Libre Comercio de las Américas) so he played around with the letters to create ALBA, a Spanish word meaning "dawn" (Guevara 2005, 102–3). At the time he had nothing but a cute word and the general notion that Latin America should have an alternative model, and when Fidel asked him a week later for a proposal, he had nothing. From there it gradually made its way from rhetoric to existence.

The first written agreement came in December 2004 and included only Cuba and Venezuela. It advocated solidarity among all Latin American nations, centered on a mutually beneficial exchange of goods and services, maximization of social benefits, reciprocal credit, and even educational and social exchanges (Backer and Molina 2009). Other countries, usually with smaller and dependent economies, eventually joined (e.g., Bolivia, Nicaragua, Honduras, Dominica, and St. Vincent and the Grenadines). As one sympathetic analysis noted, "ALBA is built on the idea of the inherent potential for Latin America's development independent of the United States and Europe, a development that has thus far failed to materialize" (Backer and Molina 2009, 701). The agreement was intended to be noble, keeping the poor always in mind. Indeed, the project rejects capitalist models entirely and instead has a firm base of solidarity.

An important part of ALBA was funding through different mechanisms for social and economic programs in member countries. ALBA's objective was both to "preserve Latin American autonomy and identity" and to "promote the fight against poverty and social exclusion" (Moreno 2007). Neither of these is cheap. Since Chávez and Castro created ALBA precisely as the price of oil shot up after the US invasion of Iraq, Venezuela had ample finances for that purpose. Indeed, it had no other sustainable source of funding.

Clearly, this was based on the normative goal of rejecting the United States. It was what brought the entire idea to Chávez in the first place. Citing Juan Carlos Puig, Oddone and Granato (2007) consider ALBA to be an example of "secessionist autonomy." The idea was that ALBA could serve to cut the umbilical cord to the metropolis, and together Latin American countries could find their own comparative advantage while still privileging domestic social progress and reduction of inequality. Critically, it did not endeavor to change any of the countries' economic dependence either on commodities or on the US market for trade. ALBA countries did not have the capacity to replace the United States and did not try to do so. Instead, they worked at the economic margins and carved out space for diplomatic relationships. The creation of ALBA has also been framed in realist terms as "soft balancing," an active nonmilitary strategy of blocking and frustrating US plans (Toro 2011). From that perspective, ALBA would pre-empt any US effort to forge a regional FTA. In that sense, ALBA was explicitly aimed at thwarting US policy.

Part of that project involved engaging more with extra-hemispheric actors who were adversaries of the United States. Watson (2017) argues that ALBA was a vehicle for Iran to expand its relations with Latin America, which it viewed as a way to increase its political support for a nuclear program. The same can be said of Russia, which under Vladimir Putin had developed a closer relationship with Venezuela and also wished to enhance its global position, especially in counterpoint to the United States. Chávez also reached out to Middle Eastern countries. Later, in 2010, in addition to Russia, he flew to Syria, Libya, and Iran, a trip he explicitly described as anti-imperialist. The enemy of his enemy was his natural ally. Chávez brought Eva Golinger—a US admirer of his—on the trip as well. As she wrote, "There were a lot of big egos involved and Chávez seemed to be the man of the moment whom they all wanted to captivate and woo (Golinger 2018, 245). She wrote of wonderful dinners and the seeming lack of repression in the three dictatorships.

ALBA never truly became secessionist or umbilical cord cutting. Like many other Bolivarian initiatives, it relied heavily upon Venezuelan largesse and crumbled when the funding faltered. In 2018, center-left Ecuadorian president Lenín Moreno said he was leaving ALBA because "it hasn't functioned for a while" (Rueda 2018). That generated squabbling, and ALBA's executive secretary argued that Ecuador's decision put regional integration "in severe jeopardy" (TeleSur 2018). Venezuela's economic and political crisis had consequential ripple effects. But that came later.

PETROCARIBE

Petrocaribe is one offshoot of ALBA. As the name suggests, it entails providing oil and petroleum products at preferential prices to Caribbean states.[11] Hugo Chávez developed it and Venezuela's state oil company Petróleos de Venezuela (PDVSA) was the supplier. Created in 2005, Petrocaribe was one element of Chávez's regional foreign policy, which was both Latin Americanist in orientation and multilateral in execution (Benzi and Zapata 2013, 69). It had deeper roots since the 1980 San José Accords, signed by both Mexico and

Venezuela, promised oil at favorable prices to Central America and the Caribbean. But this was on a new and grander scale.

Hugo Chávez and thirteen heads of state from Caribbean countries signed on to the 2005 agreement. Although mostly centrist or center-left, by no means was it a group of anti-US firebrands. Few were interested in antagonizing US policy makers. The agreement itself was peppered with Chávez's ideological references, so the official purpose of the fund was to acknowledge the "unjust international economic order, inherited from colonialism and imperialism and imposed by the rich and developed countries" (*Granma* 2005). Overall, the stated goal of the project was to foster socioeconomic development and integration of Caribbean countries.

The deal was good for the Caribbean. Governments could purchase up to 185,000 barrels a day with only a part of the cost up front, then pay the remainder in up to twenty-five years at 1–2 percent interest.[12] Further, in the original agreement Venezuela provided $50 million to create the ALBA-CARIBE fund for economic and social development projects. That the Venezuelan government funded the entire affair meant its success hinged on the price of oil. At that point, oil prices were on the rise and so it was an opportune moment. It was especially good for Cuba, which found new economic life from Venezuelan oil (first negotiated in 2000 for 53,000 barrels a day in exchange for, among other things, Cuban doctors, exported by Cuba to serve Venezuelan patients at no cost). Chávez and Fidel Castro created a shared company, Transalba, to ship the oil. That was intended to remove all intermediaries and make the endeavor truly humanitarian rather than profit-driven.

Echoing many sympathetic academic treatments, Benzi and Zapata (2013) argue that Petrocaribe represented South-South foreign policy that favored cooperation and resisted US efforts to destabilize the Chávez government. It wasn't about states seeking comparative advantage or using power. It was about one government with a scarce resource sharing it with fellow Latin Americans solely for the benefit of their citizens. Old national boundaries thus ostensibly became less relevant. It was a use of soft power at a time when Venezuela was at odds with the United States in the United Nations. But it was also an innovative project on its own merits without the strings normally attached by the United States government (Benzi and Zapata 2013).

The Venezuelan government made sure to publicize Petrocaribe's activities, and eventually it even put together Twitter (@Petrocaribe) and Instagram (petrocaribe_oficial) accounts. It touted the agreement's contributions to health care, energy security, solidarity, and economic development. Especially after Chávez's death in 2013, when Venezuelan oil production accelerated its downward trend, countries that had enjoyed years of privileged access to oil and money started to feel the pinch. In 2013, Guatemala pulled out of Petrocaribe, with the government accusing Venezuela of raising interest rates without notice (*El Nuevo Diario* 2013). Jamaica remained a willing partner but actually had to halt payments in 2019 because of US financial sanctions on Venezuela (Craham 2019). Meanwhile, in 2019 Haitians protested in the streets because of corruption charges against President Jovenel Moïse related to diversion of Petrocaribe funds (Marmouyet 2019). This obviously negated any goodwill the agreement originally generated. Its social media posts also dwindled.

But that gets ahead of our narrative. The mid-2000s were a time of triumph for Hugo Chávez. He was flush with oil money, as the price rose in the period between the 2003 invasion of Iraq and the 2008 financial crash. For Chávez, that period was a frenzy of international initiatives funded by oil that he hoped would break the imperialist US grip on Latin America and the Caribbean. Nonetheless, even the foreign policy element of his twenty-first-century socialism was careful not to go too far. Chávez wanted autonomy from the United States, but not enmity, or at least not too much of it.

The timing was propitious for Chávez for reasons other than just favorable oil prices. After the 2002 coup, he wanted to consolidate power by linking domestic politics and foreign policy more tightly (Serbin and Serbin Pont 2017). This involved personalizing his power even more than in the past. In foreign policy he restructured the Foreign Service by requiring candidates to participate in and learn Chávez's revolutionary ideals (Serbin and Serbin Pont 2017).[13] Over time, loyalty and nepotism trumped even ideological training. After his death in 2013, only seventy of eight hundred Venezuelan embassy and consular officials had even done diplomatic coursework, which required the creation of short courses intended to introduce the inexperienced with basic ideas of how an embassy functions (Miro 2014).

The ministry recruited with revolutionary compatibility in mind. Meanwhile, with military rebellion fresh on his mind, Chávez purged its ranks, put only loyalists in key positions, and began more closely controlling promotions. That served to co-opt senior officers and emphasize Chávez's personal leadership over them. The autonomy project suited Chávez's domestic goals nicely. The Foreign Ministry was now the People's Power Ministry for Foreign Affairs, and the military was the backbone of the people. The military's independence role expanded over time.

As noted in chapter 2, Chávez developed a relationship with Vladimir Putin, who had come to power at roughly the same time. In 2004 Chávez went to Moscow and negotiated an arms deal, which culminated in a 2005 contract for one hundred thousand Kalashnikov rifles and the creation of a rifle factory, which by 2012 had reportedly produced three thousand AK-103 assault rifles (*Telegraph* 2012).[14] Hugo Chávez reached out even more to China as well, and the Chinese government was keen on providing loans in exchange for oil. Increasing Venezuelan dependence on those loans only served to deepen the state's exclusive focus on extracting oil. Later, when global investors became skittish about risk in Venezuela, Chávez (and Nicolás Maduro after him) turned to China to serve as an economic stabilizer (Rosales 2016).

Chávez also maneuvered around existing regional institutions. The Comunidad Andina, or Andean Community, originally known as the Andean Pact, was formed in 1969. Its purpose was to bring together governments of the Andes in a customs union.[15] Its original members were Bolivia, Chile, Colombia, Ecuador, Peru, and Venezuela. Chile withdrew in 1976 both because the Pinochet government wanted to sign free trade agreements and therefore chafed under the restrictions of a common external tariff, but also because of Decision 24, which had set limits on how much foreign investors could repatriate (O'Keefe 1996).[16] Over time, the remaining members negotiated an expansion to become more integrated, and in 1996 they became the Andean Community (with a nod to the European Community). Such changes have been slow, as sectors in Ecuador and Peru in particular did not see sufficient benefits to integration (Hey 2003).

Under Hugo Chávez, Venezuela left the Andean Community, claiming he preferred anticapitalist principles found in ALBA (Malamud and Gardini

2012). In 2006, however, Chávez joined Mercosur, which was not anticapitalist in any sense. It was formed in 1991 when promarket governments in Argentina and Brazil signed an agreement, which would eventually also include Paraguay, Uruguay, and Venezuela. It was modeled loosely on the European Union, with free trade, a common tariff, and freedom of movement. Although other countries periodically took affiliate status or discussed possible membership, it tended not to expand. Chávez's shift from one to the other shows how difficult any regional unity project will always be. There are numerous subregional agreements that sometimes even overlap, and countries move in and out of them according to their own interests. As a result, none of them have been capable of moving the region any closer to hemispheric consensus. They can, however, serve as vehicles for greater autonomy.

THE RISE OF EVO MORALES IN BOLIVIA

Aside from Hugo Chávez (and of course Fidel Castro), one of the longest-lasting proponents of Latin American autonomy was Evo Morales, a coca union leader turned unlikely presidential candidate in Bolivia. He was elected in 2005 in the midst of severe economic crisis. Conservative governments in the 1990s had enacted stringent market reforms that were tightened in the early 2000s. The "Cochabamba Water War" in 2000 consisted of large protests against the privatization of water, which had quickly led to rate hikes. The World Bank considered Bolivia an excellent candidate for privatization as a way to increase efficiency and improve service, but the effect was the opposite.[17] Those protests were followed in 2003 by more, centered on privatization of natural gas. Gonzalo Sánchez de Lozada (popularly known as "Goni") became president in the middle of intense national debate over how much revenue the Bolivian state (versus private investors) should earn from the exploitation of its gas, whom the revenue should benefit, and where pipeline should be located. Those issues split a country already geographically and ethnically polarized. Indigenous organizations and unions laid blockades and launched strikes and protests. Goni responded with military force and martial law, and in October 2003 he was forced to resign.

As a labor leader and member of the Movement Toward Socialism (MAS) party, Evo Morales had been vocal in calling for Goni's resignation. Goni was an embodiment of Bolivian elite connection to the United States. He was born in Bolivia but grew up and was educated in the United States, to the point that his Spanish retained a noticeable accent. He was an advocate not just of US-proposed structural adjustment but also US-driven militarized antinarcotics policies. Evo Morales tapped deeply into national disenchantment with the economic model and the establishment political parties. He continued to lead protests and ran for president in 2005. He won 54 percent of the vote, a remarkable feat in a country that had not yielded a majority vote for president since the democratic transition from military rule began in 1978. That meant he took power with a high level of legitimacy.

Part of Morales's message was rejection of US economic policy and drug policy. Drugs in particular had been an irritant for more than two decades. For the US government, drugs were the highest priority because they affected US national security. In 1985, the Foreign Assistance Act required countries to be "certified" that they were combating narcotics adequately. Decertification entailed aid cuts, which placed enormous pressure on Bolivian presidents to comply. The United States wanted coca to be eradicated, preferably all of it but at least all of it save a small amount deemed for personal/traditional use. It was a policy of all stick and no carrot, with little to no understanding or even much interest in the local Bolivian social, economic, and political realities, which included chewing coca and using it in a host of other ways. For Bolivians, coca is also a tea, a medicine, a social connection, and a spiritual symbol. For the US government, it was cocaine.

The United States tended to conflate coca, Hugo Chávez's influence, and security threats all over the Andean region. In fact, Roger Noriega, assistant secretary of state for Western Hemisphere affairs, told reporters in 2005 that "Chávez's profile in Bolivia has been very apparent from the beginning. His record is apparent and speaks for itself" (MercoPress 2005). When asked if he actually had evidence of meddling, he coyly said, "I don't know." But his point could not be missed. Unrest in Bolivia was not about Bolivians. It was manufactured abroad for ideological reasons. When President-Elect Morales met with the US ambassador, he was pressed to clarify his reference to President

Bush as a "terrorist" and in part responded that he was unhappy that US government officials called him a "narco-terrorist" (Wikileaks 2006b). In that context of mutual distrust and even dislike, Evo Morales took office.

Morales's platform for foreign policy was based on certain elements that did not mention the United States by name but were obviously linked to it.[18] He advocated for national sovereignty, rejection of foreign intervention, regional integration, heterodox economics, and autonomy (Ceppi 2014). Canelas and Verdes-Montenegro (2011) argue that autonomy entailed a "postliberal" stance that refused to accept the primacy of free market principles. That orientation meant greater state control over oil and gas. Morales passed a decree sharply increasing the share the state took from extraction.

In practice, economic autonomy from the United States also meant a sharp and deliberate pivot toward China. Just days before he even took office, Morales visited China and met with President Hu Jintao. As the Chinese state media approvingly explained, Morales made a point of reaffirming Bolivia's commitment to the one-China policy and emphasized that expanding relations was a policy priority for him (*People's Daily Online* 2006). Morales wanted Chinese assistance with developing its natural gas industry.

During Morales's first presidential term (2005–2009), the export of raw materials increased from $12.5 million to $140 million.[19] It kept growing from there. The Chinese government, not unlike the colonial Spanish government centuries before, was interested largely in metals and minerals. In the same period, Bolivia's imports from China grew from $136 million to $371 million, and ballooned thereafter. Those were finished goods, including machinery and electronics. This is the same imbalance apparent across Latin America.

He aligned with fellow leftist leaders and become close to both Hugo Chávez and Fidel Castro, and also to Néstor Kirchner and Lula. He became one of the longer-lasting presidents of the twenty-first century, literally outliving the first three. At the time of his election, all these presidents were at their heights and the leftist political juggernaut appeared unstoppable even in the face of staunch opposition from the Bush administration.

But his economic policy was never anywhere close to as radical as Chávez's, or even Kirchner's. The Bolivian state increased its take from hydrocarbons and increased spending to tackle poverty, but within a measured framework.

He named Luis Alberto Arce (who much later became president) as his minister of economy and public finance. Working under a picture of Che Guevara, Arce oversaw a moderate approach to the economy that was careful to avoid overspending. He won accolades from radicals and conservatives alike. This was part of a long-standing pattern with Evo Morales and his government. The rhetoric was hot but the governing was sober and farsighted. For all the times Morales was a firebrand, he also worked behind the scenes in ways that were not radical at all. He wanted more autonomy but not at any price.

THE CRISIS BREWING IN HONDURAS

José Manuel Zelaya was elected Honduran president in 2005. His 2009 overthrow in Honduras offers a curious counterpoint to the question of regional political autonomy from the United States. The election itself did not offer any hints of radicalism. For the first time, the country had primary elections, which meant there was extensive debate about policy positions. Zelaya proposed greater "citizen power" (*poder ciudadano*) but nothing outside the bounds of establishment politics. He was an elite and at the time displayed no obvious signs of radicalism.

Zelaya was a business leader and establishment political figure who since the 1980s had held various positions in both the legislative and executive branches as part of the Liberal Party. He ran for president in 2005 on a typical probusiness platform, and after winning, he stocked his cabinet in the usual fashion of rewarding members of his party. With regard to the United States, he supported the Central American Free Trade Agreement and generally worked like his predecessors to avoid further deportations and to encourage foreign aid (Ajenjo Fresno 2007). But, particularly in his second year in office, he faced an energy crisis because Honduras's electricity production required oil and the price was rising (Cunha Filho, Coelho, and Flores 2013). The dire need for oil at a time when oil prices were high prompted Zelaya to court Hugo Chávez. In 2007 he participated in celebrating the anniversary of the Sandinista Revolution and announced that Honduras would join Petrocaribe. In 2008 he decided to join ALBA. His quick ideological switch angered both domestic elites and the United States. But it yielded cheap Venezuelan oil.

The historian Dana Frank, a longtime observer of Honduran politics, attributes Zelaya's conversion to influence from the left and center-left governments that had been taking power since 2000 (Frank 2018, 11). Honduras was consistently one of the poorest countries in the hemisphere. It was also one of the most unequal, and Zelaya's moves against elites, such as blocking privatization and increasing the minimum wage, made him a target.

We will return to Zelaya in chapter 5 and place him in the broader context of Latin American–US relations with a new president in the White House and the challenge of pursuing autonomous foreign policy in the context of political crisis. Zelaya had the firm support of leftist governments across Latin America, but verbal support never translated into much action. His fall from power and the central role of the United States threw a wrench into arguments that US hegemony was waning, at least in the Central American context.

THE IMPACT OF 9/11 ON MEXICO-US RELATIONS

Mexican president Vicente Fox wanted to maintain collaborative relations with the Bush administration, but the impact of the 9/11 terrorist attacks made that difficult. Both immigration policy and drug policy became ensnared in the politics of the "global war on terrorism." From a policy perspective, this meant the US government maintained a largely unilateral approach. As he would do several times during his presidency, Bush proposed immigration reform that would eventually founder on the shores of domestic polarization. The Mexican congressional opposition hammered at Fox for not doing more to advance the interests of Mexican immigrants and not adequately addressing the flow of xenophobic rhetoric coming from politicians in the United States (Velázquez Flores 2008). Although the 9/11 terrorists entered the United States legally, the right in the United States considered undocumented immigrants as potential (or even probable) criminals.

In 2004, Fox did propose a law that would decriminalize drug possession in small amounts and increase assistance to addicts. Yet under pressure from the United States, he would not sign that bill into law for another two years. As one government official put it at the time, the veto "took into consideration the observations of US authorities" (quoted in Becerril, Vargas, and Mendez 2004). The opposition took him to task. Fox approached the struggle against narcotics trafficking in the militarized manner that the United States preferred, with a role for the military and close collaboration with the US Drug Enforcement Agency. In all likelihood, he did so as a way to gain concessions in other areas, such as immigration. Although President Bush himself did favor immigration reform, he was a hard-liner when it came to drugs, and the United States pushed hard against Mexican autonomy on that issue.

Vicente Fox was a center-right politician, so we would not expect much push toward autonomy, especially at that time. Yet this was a fertile time for the political left in Latin America and for projects aimed at increasing autonomy from the United States. Hugo Chávez was an acknowledged regional leader in this regard. He emerged stronger after being briefly removed from power in 2002, and within a few years had like-minded colleagues in Argentina, Bolivia, Brazil, and Uruguay. Oil prices remained strong, which in tandem with Chinese investments meant the left had considerable reach in the region.

In different ways, the foreign policy change reflected a conscious shift away from a pro-US stance. This might be radical, as in Bolivia and Venezuela. But Brazil and Uruguay did so while avoiding hostility toward the United States. In Brazil's case, Lula's orientation was global, and although over time he would clash with the Bush administration, that was not a goal in itself. The hype surrounding Latin America's left turn, the endless (and sometimes breathless) press accounts both in the United States and in Latin American outlets, generally left unanswered the question of whether the policy shifts and initiatives were sustainable. Global recession was not yet on anyone's minds.

4. NEW INTERNATIONAL INSTITUTIONS (2006–2008)

IN HIS 2007 INAUGURATION speech, Ecuadorian president Rafael Correa proclaimed that "With its new political economy, Ecuador will start to become independent from the international organisms that represent foreign paradigms and interests" (*DemocraciaSUR* 2007). Greater autonomy from the United States and the international institutions it dominated increasingly seemed a real possibility. Funds were available from other sources, and fellow leftist governments could unite in useful ways. Proclamations like Correa's found fertile political ground.

The mid-2000s was a heady time for the Latin American left. The United States—always the left's antagonist—seemed in retreat, with an administration distracted by Middle Eastern wars and a "global war on terrorism." In a 2006 *Foreign Affairs* article, Pater Hakim asked, "Is Washington Losing Latin America?" His answer was affirmative, lamenting that "There is little reason to expect that US relations with Latin America will improve soon. More likely, they will get worse." This was a decidedly US-centric view, beginning with the assumption that Latin America was a sort of US possession that could be lost. Similar views sprouted and continue to do so. Not surprisingly, the Latin American view took a different angle. Instead of "loss" there was "erosion" of hegemony (Herrera Chaves 2006). The United States simply was no longer in a position to assert dominance in the region the way it used to. The US view was more binary: winning versus losing. From the Latin American angle, there was simply more space for maneuver without US backlash. The core of both arguments was that Latin American autonomy was expanding.

That belief rested in part on the extensive unpopularity of President George W. Bush, which by 2006 was deeply rooted. Middle Eastern wars, drug wars, counterterrorism policies, and a swaggering rhetoric generated backlash. The regional Latinobarómetro poll catalogued his steady drop in popularity over the years, which by the end of his presidency averaged a 4.2 on a 10-point scale, the lowest of any Western Hemisphere leader in 2005–2008 (Corporación Latinobarómetro 2008). South Americans were by far the least pleased with him, but no one was terribly happy.

In late 2005, Bush named veteran Foreign Service officer Thomas Shannon as assistant secretary of state for Western Hemisphere affairs, the State Department's point person for the region. His influence gradually toned down the administration's inflammatory language, which he made an explicit goal. In a 2008 speech, he laid out his desire to "create an authentic diplomacy in the Americas which is really about how you attempt to overcome rhetoric and ideology to focus on shared values and shared interests to build an agenda for the Americas that has broad consensus and that has a potential for success over time" (Shannon 2008). Shannon practiced this, and he refrained from using the various Nazi references preferred by Secretary of Defense Donald Rumsfeld in favor of, among other things, traveling to Caracas to advance dialogue with the Venezuelan government.[1] His efforts did not improve Bush's approval numbers, but they marked a change that would last through the Obama administration (in which Shannon remained an influential figure for Latin America policy).

With oil prices high and a keenly interested Chinese government flush with resources, pushing the boundaries of autonomy was a real possibility. The Bush administration was antagonistic toward governments it considered leftist adversaries, but the hostility was often largely rhetorical and stopped well short of the harsh tactics that were common during the Cold War. Blatant use of force, whether overt or covert, was no longer considered a viable option, which provided space within which any Latin American government could move if it wished.

Evo Morales was a prominent example of this autonomy expansion. He shifted the direction of Bolivian foreign policy, which involved reorientation of the long-standing friendly relationship with the United States and the region. In particular, for decades the United States government successfully pushed both market economics and antinarcotics operations in Bolivia. President Gonzalo Sánchez de Lozada became a victim of the former since he was ousted after repressing protests against privatization.

Changes under Morales were tied to broad domestic reforms as well, including nationalization (e.g., natural gas), revising the constitution, increasing the role of the state, ending hard-line antinarcotic policies, and above all focusing on the long-standing discrimination of the indigenous population. His predecessors' failed market reforms, pushed by the US government and international institutions, had deepened poverty in the country. That left an imprint on his Movement Toward Socialism (MAS) party, which emphasized sovereignty and mixed economic models of development.

Morales immediately embraced Hugo Chávez and was an enthusiastic support of ALBA. He also established close ties with Argentina and Brazil, both of which elected leftist leaders (Néstor Kirchner and Lula, respectively), and evinced interest in closer ties to China and Iran. This served to "recuperate the autonomy that previous governments had relinquished" (Ceppi 2014). Further, he routinely used the United Nations as a platform to expand Bolivia's diplomatic relations and to speak to a global audience, particularly about indigenous communities and climate change. He raised eyebrows in 2006 when he brandished a coca leaf in a speech to the UN, emphasizing the difference between the leaf and the cocaine derived from it. He even gave Secretary of State Condoleezza Rice a coca-inlayed *charango*, a traditional Bolivian instrument. In particular, he sought to counter US policy by showing the cultural and religious importance of the leaf to Andean indigenous communities.

Morales's stance on coca was jarring and annoying to Bush administration officials, who previously had worked with Bolivians willing to zero in on coca eradication despite how unpopular it was in the country. The State Department's 2009 International Narcotics Control Strategy Report reflected that annoyance (Bureau of International Narcotics and Law Enforcement Affairs 2009). It was written in the first months of the Obama administration but did not stray too far from its predecessor, lamenting the "increasingly hostile rhetoric" and recommending the US Drug Enforcement Agency be readmitted. At a minimum, the State Department wrote, the government should "improve the awareness of the Bolivian population regarding the danger of illicit drugs." Rejecting US assistance must mean they were unaware. For many Bolivians, that policy had almost entirely negative consequences, since a guaranteed cash crop was not replaced with anything else. Technical and financial aid for alternative crops were either slow or nonexistent, which frustrated farmers.

That frustration had deep roots. The United States had been in the anticoca business in Bolivia since the early 1980s. A 1993 report commissioned by the Office of National Drug Control Policy was blunt, pointing out that the impact of crop substitution had been "minimal" despite some hopeful signs of growing pineapples, and so the prospects were "murky at best" (Lee and Clawson 1993, 44). The report was pessimistic about the practice elsewhere in the Andes as well. The US approach to drug eradication, which tended to laud precisely such shaky efforts along with militarization, was broadly unpopular.

Nonetheless, Morales proved himself a pragmatic leader. He was initially cautious about criticizing the United States, though over time that changed. In a 2006 interview, he refused to criticize the Bush administration, saying only that "I hope we can improve relations with Bush's government" (*Democracy Now!* 2006). Four years later he said, "The thing is that there's permanent sabotage and blackmail from the US government" (*Democracy Now!* 2010), and it sharpened from there. At home, his economic policy included nationalization and increased spending on social projects, but always within a framework that invited foreign investment, kept inflation under control, and was mindful of debt accumulation. The Bush administration tended to view him as pragmatic when he took office (Constable 2006). As with Hugo Chávez, there was a kind of suspicious acceptance, ready to break at any time.

The distance between the governments with regard to approaching coca cultivation never provided much hope for friendly relations. The United States insisted on a militarized approach with little to no leeway for legal consumption of coca. The Bolivian government accepted the concerns about cocaine production but insisted there had to be an avenue for legal cultivation and use. Rejecting long-standing US demands, Evo Morales implemented community-based plans to reduce illegal planting of coca while providing social services to help those farmers. In 2008, Morales expelled the US ambassador and the

Drug Enforcement Agency, at which point relations bottomed out. Even so, he did not drastically alter the bilateral trade relationship, where the United States was Bolivia's third largest export destination behind Argentina and Brazil (Ceppi 2014). Those exports were primary products, such as tin, precious metals, and cereals.

Despite the name of his own party, Morales's global ambitions were less about socialism than they were about sustainability and equality. His interest in autonomy was about bringing like-minded allies together to highlight those issues, which in his opinion the United States refused to do because of its imperialist nature and lack of any global accountability. For all the piercingly critical rhetoric he used about the international capitalist system, Morales's foreign policy was cautious, and he often did not follow where Hugo Chávez led. He did not dive into the alternative regional currencies, for example.

Along those lines, ALBA dipped its toes into regional economic autonomy with the introduction of the Unified System of Regional Compensation, or SUCRE, created in 2008 to replace the dollar in regional commercial exchanges. It is a virtual currency based on the value of a basket of regional currencies, and it serves as a clearinghouse that allows countries to give and receive payments. When Venezuela and Ecuador conducted the first transaction (Venezuela bought roughly $1.5 million worth of rice in 2010) Hugo Chávez said that "it allows us to advance towards freeing ourselves from the dollar, decoupling ourselves from the international hegemonic system" (Mather 2010). Nicolás Maduro, then the foreign minister, was even more triumphant, asserting that it was the first step "that frees our countries from poverty, backwardness." More than a decade later, that goal remained unreached, and Maduro as president launched a national cryptocurrency to evade US economic sanctions.

Nonetheless, the vast majority of such exchanges were conducted just between Ecuador and Venezuela, and overall the system amounted mostly to Venezuelan imports (Pearce 2018, 77).[2] It was a mechanism largely for Venezuela, even if not necessarily intended that way. Further, the nature of Latin American economies constitutes an obstacle. Countries that focus largely on commodity exports need partners that export finished goods, which of course is the core of dependency theory. The SUCRE does not work well when countries are looking outside the hemisphere for their imports, which is key for Latin America. But the fact of the matter is that in the wake of the 2008 financial crisis, the reality that the SUCRE successfully got off the ground and was central to hundreds of millions of dollars' worth of trade demonstrated that Latin America *could* operate in autonomous ways.

Those were the salad days, when oil prices were high and revolutionary possibilities seemed endless. Later, the Venezuelan economic and political crisis, which went hand in hand with the drop in global oil prices, served to push the SUCRE aside. Indeed, over time the United States imposed financial sanctions on Venezuela that made alternative currencies potentially a matter of survival rather than simply a lofty goal. As with many policies aimed at regional autonomy, the realities of the Venezuelan context tended to get in the way of high aspirations.

CHILEAN AUTONOMY

In the twenty-first century, Venezuela is often the exceptional case. Chávez had grander goals, took bigger risks, and cared less about consequences than most Latin American presidents, leftist or otherwise. Most preferred to keep the costs of autonomy in mind. The complicated nature of the Latin American left is exemplified well in Chile. Michelle Bachelet was the daughter of an air force general who was put in charge of food distribution during the socialist government of President Salvador Allende (1970–1973). After the coup, that participation marked him for imprisonment and torture (which led to his death by heart attack). His daughter was also tortured, eventually getting released and fleeing to Australia. In exile and then later back in Chile, she pursued a medical degree and became a doctor. She was a member of the Socialist Party, which had a long history of activism in Chile and tended to be more radical than the Communist Party (though it became more moderate after the coup). After the return to democracy in 1990, she become more politically active and in 2000 President Ricardo Lagos named her minister of health. From then on, she retained a national political profile and Lagos named her minister of defense. In 2006 she won the runoff presidential election.

On the surface, she fit the "pink wave" that pundits loved to cite. She was a socialist who promised to focus on social policy. Summing up her first year in office, the US ambassador to Chile wrote in a cable that her foreign policy "is to adopt positions of brotherly solidarity, including those with an 'anti-imperialist' tint" (Wikileaks 2006a). Further, she was ambivalent about "too close ties to the American 'hegemon'" (Wikileaks 2006a). It was, he continued in textspeak, "Michelle & Hugo 4ever." Given the complicated relationship Chávez and Bachelet had, it is difficult to imagine a less prescient analysis. Further, "socialism" in Chile did not mean the same thing as elsewhere.

Members of the Socialist Party suffered terribly during the dictatorship, and many of its leaders (including Bachelet) were committed to moderation and dialogue. They accepted the inherited economic model as part of that calculus. Capitalism in Chile was more firmly established than anywhere else in Latin America, and perhaps more than in the United States as well. Social policy was debated within the framework and constraints of capitalism. For Bachelet it was, as Silvia Borzutzky (2010, 87) puts it, a "kinder, gentler Chile, a Chile where the market was going to be limited by social policies geared to reduce poverty and inequality."

Foreign policy centered on free trade and investment. By the time Bachelet left office, Chile had signed on to fifty free trade agreements, the most in the world, which gave it access to 81 percent of global gross domestic product (Borzutzky 2010, 93). Unlike Brazil, Chile did not seek a larger diplomatic role in other areas. Chile did get the spotlight when it resisted Bush administration demands that it support a resolution for use of force in Iraq, but that was following a tradition of Latin American nonintervention rather than any ideological line. And it was a spotlight Chilean policy makers did not choose or desire. Other than that, Chilean foreign policy was almost entirely economic (and capitalist) in orientation.

Following the model adopted with the end of the dictatorship, Bachelet's stated foreign policy priorities made no mention of Latin America, and certainly not of regional integration. Although the minister of foreign relations did speak approvingly of regional connectivity, Bachelet's administration made sure to keep expectations low, which meant repeated use of the word "realistic" whenever referring to integration (Jenne and Briones Razeto 2018).

Like other Chilean presidents, Bachelet showed considerably more enthusiasm when talking about bilateral agreements in the region. The logic was clear. Chilean policy makers looked askance at multilateral agreements that might tie them excessively to governments whose economic policies did not match theirs. They had no wish to be dragged down and instead could pick and choose bilateral deals that by themselves would not make or break them since they would just be one of dozens.

In Merke and Reynoso's (2016) study of Latin American foreign policy, Bachelet was "left-pragmatist" and equidistant between alignment with the United States and autonomy. She was more interested than Lagos in being involved in South American affairs (she later headed UNASUR, for example), and she never aligned herself with Chávez's hemispheric vision and definitely not his economic one. Bachelet might agree publicly with Chávez on some issues (raising people out of poverty with some state intervention, for example) but the methods and the style had little in common.

A relationship with China was consistent with Chile's global economic ambitions and had no ideological undertones. Over the course of the 2000s, Chile's economic connection to China was cemented with a number of milestones. The Chile-China Free Trade Agreement went into effect in 2006 and Chile was the first Latin American country to sign a free trade agreement with China. Ricardo Lagos had negotiated the deal with Chinese president Hu Jintao, which both signed in 2005. Bachelet then negotiated a supplementary agreement in 2008, which was later updated again in 2017. The agreement was structured to cover 97 percent of goods over a ten-year period. In a 2005 speech, Jorge Heine, the Chilean ambassador to China, pointed out that from 2000 to 2005, Chile's exports to China tripled and Chinese exports back had almost doubled, and he noted that Chile had come to realize it needed to move away from reliance on export markets in the United States and Europe: "Yet, in the early 1990s, it [Chile] realized the world's economic axis was shifting toward Asia, and that unless it became a partner in the process of growth and change sweeping across the Asia Pacific region, it would be left behind" (Heine 2006, 144). This was a message of autonomy, to change long-held economic assumptions and to diversify. But it came from the mouth of an establishment, center-left political scientist and not a bombastic leftist. Even under leftist governments, Chile never pushed the United States away. It just wanted to play the field.

THE TENSION BETWEEN AUTONOMY AND US AGREEMENTS

That many governments did not reject the United States complicated Chávez's efforts. As noted in chapter 3, the Andean Community was an example of a push for autonomy that long predated Hugo Chávez's election and developed in ways that reveal the complicated interplay between national self-interests and ideology. It began in 1969 with the Cartagena Agreement, which laid out a customs union between Bolivia, Chile, Colombia, Ecuador, and Peru. Through the remainder of the twentieth century its membership shifted a bit. Venezuela joined in 1973, while Chile (which was undergoing its own radical economic restructuring) left in 1976. The benefits of the agreement expanded, including open skies, a free trade zone (which eventually became the Andean Free Trade Area), a common external tariff, and removal of visas for travel.

In 2006, Chávez announced that Venezuela was withdrawing. For him, the core problem was that member countries Colombia and Peru were both negotiating free trade agreements with the United States, which was anathema.

> For years I've been saying that the Andean Community is dead. Right now, I'm president of the Andean Community. And what am I president of? Of a big lie. Above all now that Colombia and Peru have signed a free trade agreement with the United States, in this it's true that they finished killing it. (quoted in Baribeau 2006)

Most Latin American countries did not share Chávez's goal of avoiding all entanglements with the United States. Colombian president Alvaro Uribe was a staunch conservative who despised Chávez but nonetheless lamented the Andean Community decision because of the volume of trade with Venezuela. Peruvian president Alejandro Toledo had similar views of economic policy, favoring a market-led model. Chávez made clear his preference for the center-left Peruvian presidential candidate Ollanta Humala, insulting both Toledo and candidate Alan García as tools of the empire and "alligators from the same well" (*caimanes del mismo pozo*, more colloquially translated as "birds of a feather") (Rico 2006). Uribe and Toledo preferred not to cut anyone out of trade. As Chávez would discover, neither would Humala after he was elected, even though he was widely labeled as similar to Chávez.

Alligator or not, Toledo had made it publicly clear that he was a US ally, but even that included an element of autonomous pushback. For example, he said in a 2006 joint press conference with President Bush that the two countries were partners not only in free trade, but also "in the search of peace in the world" and that the two men would be friends forever (*Weekly Compilation of Presidential Documents* 2006, 448). Even while Toledo pushed forward with free trade (which went into effect in 2009), he faced a dicier situation with counternarcotics operations, where US interests and domestic politics clashed. The Bush administration, as always, wanted Peru to accelerate coca eradication, while Toledo faced major protests from coca growers (*cocaleros*) to limit or end the practice.

For years Toledo and his successor Alán García were wedged between organized coca growers and US demands, and they vacillated. The National Association of Peruvian Coca Producers was adept at blocking roads and marching into Lima. García did launch an offensive in 2007, not unlike the anticartel offensive the Mexican government initiated in 2006, but the militarized approach did not achieve any significant results. Fearful that rural Peruvians might turn to the remnants of the Shining Path guerrillas in response, Peruvian governments remained tentative about following US demands (Koven and McClintock 2016). But they never pushed autonomy much beyond what the United States government would accept.

The Colombian government negotiated a free trade agreement with the United States and became an enthusiastic partner. Colombia had been pursuing an FTA for several years, initially as part of a broader regional initiative that never got off the ground. Colombia was a member of the Andean Trade Promotion and Drug Eradication Act, which started in 2002 and provided privileged access for certain Andean exports as a way to incentivize production of legal agricultural goods.[3] The problem was that that agreement was narrower than a full free trade agreement and required reapproval by the US

Congress. President Uribe viewed the FTA as a way to maintain the Bush administration's support for his security policies (Pulecio 2005). For Uribe, free trade was another aspect of a privileged relationship with the United States, which funded his ambitious plans to destroy the Fuerzas Armadas Revolucionarias de Colombia (FARC) guerrillas and combat narcotrafficking. Those twin goals matched perfectly with US policy preferences. Uribe even pushed unsuccessfully to include language about Colombia being a "strategic ally" to cement bilateral ties as much as possible (Pulecio 2005, 20).

The two countries signed the agreement in 2006 but the US-Colombia Trade Promotion Agreement waited six more years before it was ratified and went into force. The Bush administration pushed Congress hard and framed ratification in security terms. United States trade representative Susan Schwab veered toward the apocalyptic:

> Leaders in the hemisphere and Latin America have said that the single most destabilizing factor in Latin America today may be the US Congress's failure to ratify the Colombia Free Trade Agreement. That is more destabilizing today than anything that Colombia's neighbor Venezuela is doing or threatening to do— and that is saying a lot. (quoted in Pethokoukis 2008)

But President Bush also couched it in self-interest terms. Even as the administration repeatedly hammered its security line, it also admitted there was a lot of self-interest. The president himself argued that the FTA was actually not as good for Colombia:

> Today almost all of Colombia's exports enter the United States duty-free. Yet American products exported to Colombia face tariffs of up to 35 percent for non-agricultural goods, and much higher for many agricultural products. Think about that. They export into the United States duty-free, and we don't have the same advantage. I would call that a one-sided economic agreement. (Public Papers of the Presidents 2001 2004, 495)

Overall, debates both in Colombia and the United States were about appealing to US interests in security terms. Starting with the Uribe years, Colombia hitched its foreign policy wagon firmly to the United States and kept it there.

THE 2008 FINANCIAL CRASH

The financial crisis of 2007–2008 was the worst economic crash since the Great Depression, and it had important implications not just for Latin America, but also for Latin American–US relations. It all started with the obscure practice of providing subprime mortgages in the United States. Subprime lending refers to the practice of giving loans to individuals who likely will have difficulty paying them back. During the 2000s, the housing market in the United States heated up as people bought homes with subprime mortgages. Through highly complex processes, these risky mortgages were bundled together with solid ones and sold as a package to investors. In 2006 the housing boom reached its end and the rate of delinquencies grew, a trend that accelerated in 2007. Since the bad loans were mixed with the good loans, nonpayment pulled everything down with it. Banks faced disaster and stock markets were spooked.

The 2008 crash involved a large number of global financial institutions that suddenly found themselves hemorrhaging money. Lehman Brothers, a major bank that had taken a lead in subprime lending, filed for bankruptcy in September 2008. Many others hovered on the brink. As confidence in banks and the stock market withered, wealth disappeared literally into thin air. Any financial disruption in the United States is almost immediately felt elsewhere. The crash hit Latin America, where gross domestic product across the region fell 1.5 percent in 2009 (ECLAC 2014). The global demand for oil dropped sharply, which multiplied the negative effects in Venezuela as well as Colombia, Ecuador, and Mexico. Demand for Latin American products fell across the board, poverty ticked up, and debt rose.

The crash itself therefore had a major economic impact on Latin America, but it also took US credibility down a peg. US economic policy during and after the Latin American debt crisis was predicated on the idea that governments must make politically unpopular and economically fraught decisions in the name of macroeconomic stability. Structural adjustment in the 1980s and beyond ended presidencies and even forced presidents into exile. People, not just the poor but also middle class, were desperate and angry, so they took to the streets, sometimes violently. The message from Washington, DC, was to stay the course. Reduction of government spending was the core of that message. Belt tightening, so the argument went, was better for everyone in the long term.

When it came to economic crisis in the United States, the government chose not to take its own advice. In particular, it spent tens of billions of dollars to bail out banks rather than let them fall, arguing that the ripple effect would destroy the economy (the "too big to fail" logic). A United Nations meeting not long after Lehman Brothers declared bankruptcy was brimming with criticism, both for the lack of oversight in the United States and for the hypocrisy of the bailout (MacFarquhar 2008). The contrast was glaring. In that case, why should Latin America listen to US policy advice versus finding alternatives elsewhere?

This point about the Latin American response should not be taken too far. The Bush and then Obama administration responses to the crisis did not radically tilt Latin America in a more autonomous direction. But it did coincide with other simultaneous factors. China was all over the region by then, no longer a possible influence but a clear one. Regional integration projects were proliferating, and even though many would not reach their goals, they presented alternatives to US economic retrenching. The US economic policy hypocrisy is just one of numerous factors encouraging Latin American governments to find new solutions that did not involve their northern neighbor.

THE RISE OF UNASUR

UNASUR is one such example. The Union of South American Nations, or UNASUR, has its origins in a 2000 presidential summit led by Brazilian president Fernando Henrique Cardoso, in no small part to serve as Brazil's own regional leadership project. It included discussion about how to mutually support democracy and encourage development. That differed from the FTAA or Mercosur, which were more narrowly centered on trade and investment. At a 2004 summit, regional leaders created UNASUR, which had three goals:

regional integration, creation of infrastructure, and eradicating poverty (Riggirozzi and Grugel 2015). This last point in particular distinguished UNASUR from previous models, and certainly from any model the United States proposed. For example, UNASUR included the South American Health Council in recognition of how living conditions affected economics.

From the Latin American perspective, this shift away from a narrow capitalist orientation was what made UNASUR an important symbol of autonomy. In that sense, autonomy allowed for a broader, more ambitious view of how Latin America could come together. It wasn't easily categorized either. Was it posthegemonic, postliberal, postneoliberal, or something else entirely? Regardless of the precise label, the idea was that Latin America was not simply rejecting the United States, but rather reorienting its political and economic priorities toward what South American leaders believed to be more crucial (Falomir 2013). The United States was not a member of UNASUR, not just because the left-leaning governments of the region wished to exclude it (though they assuredly did) but because it did not share the same priorities or even the same geographic space.

The 2008 Bolivian crisis was an early test for the new organization. Eastern departments (the functional equivalent of US states) in Bolivia protested the government's new tax policy on hydrocarbons, leading to violence between protesters and the Bolivian army, which defended government buildings. The conflict was rooted in long-standing political divisions and separatist sentiment in the eastern part of the country. Evo Morales saw the crisis as an effort to overthrow him and blamed the United States. By that time, bilateral relations were at a low point, as Morales expelled the Drug Enforcement Agency and the ambassador as well, whom he blamed for plotting against him (Constable 2008). As then-president of UNASUR, Michelle Bachelet convoked another forum during the already scheduled United Nations meetings. Contributing to dialogue in Bolivia gave UNASUR an auspicious start. For the time being, it kept the momentum going for a regional body that could—in theory—help nip political crises in the bud. The crisis ended through negotiations between the two sides.

UNASUR also became involved in infrastructure development. In 2000, South American presidents came together to create the Initiative for the

Integration of the Regional Infrastructure of South America (IIRSA). Ironically, it was first associated with the doomed Free Trade Area of the Americas, but later UNASUR took it on. The ideal of integration thus shifted sharply away from the United States. The idea was to develop strategic plans for sustainability and development with regional rather than solely national aspirations, making IIRSA a component of UNASUR's broader goal of unity. It in turn created the South American Council of Infrastructure and Planning (COSIPLAN) to coordinate. Over the years, COSIPLAN has overseen hundreds of infrastructure projects. China's increased loans facilitated them as well. The intended effect was to replace the decades-long relationship with the United States Agency for International Development (USAID), which many on the left viewed with suspicion.

But not without controversy. From the left came criticism that even leftist governments failed to take into consideration the social and environmental impacts of the projects, undertaken without any real regional goals in mind, which led to "carrying out projects for the sake of carrying them out" (Zibechi 2015). Using large-scale public works projects to further electoral gains was nothing new in Latin American history. Critics also pointed to IIRSA's accelerated pace as partially responsible for devastating fires in the Brazilian Amazon (Walker 2019). Roads, rail lines, and dams require extensive clearcutting.

Supranationalism, referring to the enforcement of rules and regulations of an organization outside individual states, has a checkered history in Latin America. New organizations overlap and occasionally compete, with nationalism blocking supranational authority. A more jaded view suggests that for "scholars, politicians, and bureaucrats, regional organizations offer attractive opportunities to make a living" as long as the funds keep coming (Malamud 2019, 56). Such organizations sprouted up in this period, with plenty of publicity but little attention to local political realities.

CRISTINA FÉRNANDEZ DE KIRCHNER IN ARGENTINA

Cristina Fernández de Kirchner served as first lady of Argentina from 2003 to 2007 with her husband Néstor. Unlike many other presidents in the region, who ran for re-election or even changed the constitution to do so, in 2007 Néstor Kirchner chose not to. Instead, his wife ran as the Peronist candidate. She spent a lot of her campaign traveling and talking about foreign affairs, though less on projecting Argentina abroad (or asserting independence from the United States) and more on promoting human rights. Between the two of them, they were in office from 2003 until 2015.

Morasso (2016) puts the two foreign policies of the two presidents together and labels them an "autonomist orientation," characterized by a statist economic model that limits foreign influence, combined with pushing for deeper regional relations. The reduction of foreign influence over decision making was part of the very public decision to end automatic partnership with the United States. Cristina Fernández negotiated some long-standing debt repayments, but fought back against other holdouts (those who previously refused the government's offers) who had the support of the US government. A *Congressional Research Report* dryly noted that under the Kirchner governments "there were periodic tensions in relations" (Sullivan and Nelson 2017, 1).

Fernández was a vocal supporter of Hugo Chávez, which was problematic for US-Argentine relations. In 2007, a US-Venezuelan dual citizen was caught bringing $800,000 in cash to Argentina, ostensibly to bribe government officials on behalf of Venezuela or perhaps to help Fernández herself. Various heads rolled while the presidents themselves denied any knowledge, all the while lambasting the US government for its investigations into the matter.[4] But their bond was tight, in no small part because of their mutual disgust with the United States. In Argentina's case, this remained centered on its debt default. In a ceremony honoring Chávez after his death, Fernández lauded him for being the person who "helped in difficult moments," since without his help Argentina could not have endured the default (TeleSur 2016).

Initially, like Kirchner she emphasized integration within Mercosur, which could also be a vehicle for economic ties outside the region, especially the European Union. Later, she focused more on UNASUR and coordinating with Venezuela and mentioned Mercosur less (Zelicovich 2011). As she would later tweet upon hearing of Chávez winning an election in 2012, she considered his victory one for South America, Mercosur, and UNASUR as well (Kirchner 2012). In that sense, her vision was that Argentina's global role and autonomy project more generally did not rest primarily on Mercosur. She signed the treaty for UNASUR's constitution in 2008 and remained a proponent even as it slowly disintegrated.

Fernández's relationship with Lula was more complicated. Argentine-Brazil relations were historically rocky and in recent years had been exacerbated by trade and currency disputes. Therefore, neither she nor any Argentine president was prepared to embrace Lula completely, but the relationship had evolved in a positive direction. Argentine elite perception of Brazil moved from suspicion to a sense that it was an "inevitable" and even occasionally "indispensable" neighbor (Russell and Tokatlian 2016, 28). Tensions did not evaporate—especially with regard to tariff barriers—but they did not become obstacles to bilateral relations. Naturally, Lula saw Fernández as an ideological ally but also as someone whose partnership could help Brazil solidify and legitimize its regional leadership.

Whatever the state of Argentina's relations with its neighbors, Fernández firmly believed in a future that reduced US influence. She courted China, though as with Brazil, disputes emerged quickly about antidumping restrictions that Argentina applied against Chinese goods, which jeopardized Argentina's lucrative soy exports to China. Fernández sought loans from China, since financing elsewhere was unavailable and indeed was actively blocked by the United States. The result was to shift the traditional reliance on the United States toward China.

Overall, her various South American relationships highlights the strong and widely held belief at the time that there was a real regional initiative underway that would increase its independence from the United States and its role globally. The weak foundation undergirding it was not yet apparent.

THE ELECTION OF RAFAEL CORREA

Ecuador became part of these initiatives as well. Rafael Correa was elected president of Ecuador in 2006 after a period of domestic political chaos. Between 1996 and 2006, Ecuador had eight presidents, one of whom (Rosalía Arteaga) served five days and another (Abdalá Bucaram) who was popularly known as "El Loco." Jamil Mahuad, three presidents after El Loco, pushed through dollarization in 1999 and 2000 in the midst of economic contraction and inflation around 60 percent. Naturally, US influence became a major national topic for debate since dollarization is difficult to reverse and by design involves loss of economic autonomy. Correa, a US-trained economist, was finance minister in 2005 and vocally critical of US policy and World Bank stipulations for economic development projects. Those criticisms found an eager audience in the country and he rode economic discontent to victory.

Correa was popular and outspoken. He quickly became a core voice among the growing group of left-leaning governments in Latin America. To consolidate his vision of a new era of Ecuadorian politics, he successfully convinced voters to approve the election of a constitutional assembly. That body finished in 2008, producing a mammoth document of 444 articles.[5] Tucked inside were clear references to autonomy from the United States. Article 3 forbids the "establishment of foreign military bases or foreign facilities for military purposes." Article 416 lays out foreign policy principles and "condemns the interference of States in the domestic affairs of other States and any kind of intervention, whether armed raids, aggression, occupation or economic or military blockade." For Correa, pushing back against the United States was part of Ecuador's institutional structure. The entire constitution was Correa's "citizen revolution" (*revolución ciudadana*).

An attack in March 2008 showed that his antimilitarist orientation was timely. For years, FARC guerrillas had camped on the border with Ecuador, routinely crossing into it. With intelligence assistance from the United States, the Colombian government attacked a camp, which included bombing Ecuadorian territory. The attack was successful, yielding a wealth of information on laptops, killing the FARC's second-in-command, and capturing others. The response from Ecuador (and Venezuela), however, was vocal indignation about the violation of sovereignty. After all, Colombia had bombed its neighbor. The Organization of American States passed a resolution labeling the action a violation of sovereignty, though it did not condemn Colombia. Venezuela sent troops to the Colombian border to counter "the expansionist designs of the empire," viewing it as a US-driven operation (Romero 2008). The Colombian government, knowing Venezuela intended the action as a show but that further belligerence could lead to unwanted consequences, did nothing. Rafael Correa broke relations and warned Colombia but also did not want escalation. All involved understood that the US government was deeply involved, which only deepened hostility and distrust.

With Ecuador and also Bolivia, the US government made a decision that further served to push them away. The Andean Trade Promotion and Drug Eradication Act was enacted in 2002, replacing the 1991 Andean Trade Preference Act, and its purpose was to provide preferential trade access for Bolivia, Colombia, Ecuador, and Peru to encourage the export of goods other than narcotics. The name change reflected an increase in the number of eligible goods. The agreement never generated huge export boosts, but at least it was a way to access the US market.

In 2008, the Bush administration announced suspension of Bolivia's designation as a beneficiary country, for its "demonstrable failure to cooperate in narcotics efforts over the past 12 months" (United States Trade Representative 2008).[6] Morales had declared his opposition to US policy numerous times, and just prior to the Bush administration's announcement, he ordered the US ambassador to leave the country, accusing him of conspiring with the opposition.[7] It was a delicate time in Bolivia, with violent opposition protests, though losing the agreement's benefits did not seem to have much adverse political effect for Morales.

But resistance to US drug policies was not universal. Felipe Calderón became Mexico's president in 2006 and promptly launched a drug war, which entailed large-scale military and police operations against drug cartels. US diplomats in Mexico were enthusiastic, writing even before the election that Calderón "shares our point of view on everything ranging from migration to competitiveness to border security" and that "His security efforts are designed to reassure foreign investors and Mexicans worried about drug-related crime and lawlessness" (quoted in Hunt 2019). A central aspect of Calderón's foreign policy was to develop a closer relationship with the United States, a change from twentieth-century Mexican practice (Chabat 2013).

The primary fruit of that relationship was the creation of the Mérida Initiative in 2007. The US Congress appropriated roughly $1.5 billion for its initial 2008–2010 phase, with the vast majority of the funding going to military, police, and intelligence services. From its beginning, the Mérida Initiative emphasized the use of force, a measure simultaneously being rejected in Bolivia. In late 2007, President Bush praised Calderón and expressed his optimism:

> The United States is committed to this joint strategy to deal with a joint problem. I would not be committed to dealing with this if I wasn't convinced that President Calderón had the will and the desire to protect his people from narco-traffickers. He has shown great leadership and great strength of character, which gives me good confidence that the plan we'll develop will be effective. (quoted in United States Department of State 2007)

In 2008, Mexican foreign minister Patricia Espinosa praised the initiative as "a system of bilateral cooperation that will allow both countries – that is, in fact, already allowing both countries to expand their exchange in terms of combating organized crime" (United States Department of State 2008).

Thus, with regard to fighting drugs, Mexico aligned itself with US policy preferences. Mérida's success, meanwhile, was hard to pinpoint. As a 2015 *Congressional Research Service* report put it:

> With little publicly available information on what specific metrics the US and Mexican governments are using to measure the impact of the Mérida Initiative, analysts have debated how bilateral efforts should be evaluated. How one evaluates the Mérida Initiative largely depends on how one has defined the goals of the program. While the US and Mexican governments' long-term goals for the Mérida Initiative may be similar, their short-term goals and priorities may be different. (Seelke and Finklea 2015)

It also raised serious human rights concerns, which always accompany programs that bring the military or highly militarized police forces into domestic law enforcement. Mexico's National Human Rights Commission received thousands of reports detailing killing, torture, and rape. But Mexican officials shared US goals and were funded to achieve them.

President Calderón de-emphasized immigration during his time in office.

He was much more interested in stemming the flow of drugs and in security more broadly, and in getting the United States to accept its own responsibility as a major consumer of drugs as well as an exporter of guns (Durand 2013). He therefore had no intention of alienating potential political allies in the United States with any shift toward autonomy with regard to immigration. He treated immigration as a problem that economic growth could help fix. During his time in office, the number of undocumented Mexicans in the United States hit a peak of 6.9 million in 2007, then began to fall. At the same time, the number of state and local level anti-immigrant laws mushroomed in the United States, and Calderón criticized them. But he kept his policy focus largely elsewhere.

The fight against drugs was more complex in Colombia, but it also reflected close cooperation with the United States. Alvaro Uribe was re-elected in 2006 and agreed completely with the US-preferred militarized approach. Colombia simultaneously fought a civil war with the FARC, which Uribe intensified with the goal of breaking the stalemate and forcing surrender. That outcome would in fact occur, but it took years and thousands of lives. Officially, the United States funded only the counternarcotics policies, but in practice they were difficult, if not impossible, to disentangle. Helicopters, weapons, and other military purchases were used interchangeably.

Uribe fought narcotics on all fronts, pulling coca out of the ground, spraying it with herbicides from the air, destroying drug laboratories, tracking boats and planes, and constantly using intelligence fed to him by the US government. Unlike Bolivia, Colombia had no large and politically organized indigenous population that used coca for cultural or religious purposes, and so the policy was relentless. This was one of many reasons he and Hugo Chávez vocally and publicly hated each other so much. Uribe accused Chávez of genocide for supporting the FARC, while Chávez called Uribe a puppet (McDermott 2008). Neighbors could not agree about autonomy.

EXTRA-HEMISPHERIC ACTORS

China continued to expand its presence in Latin America. In Venezuela, it established what was known as the Heavy Investment Fund, with $6 billion in

2007 and another $6 billion in 2008 (Ellis 2009, 109). Venezuela borrowed the funds, which were managed by China, and paid Chinese companies (in yuan, not bolívars) contracted for specific projects. Venezuela got needed infrastructure financing, though it went into deep debt. The projects involved petroleum, naturally, but also telecommunications and transportation. Between 2004 and 2008, Venezuela's oil exports to China went from almost zero to 80,000 barrels of crude (Ellis 2009, 112). Chávez's professed long-term goal was to reduce dependency on the United States. In the same 2004–2008 period, U.S imports of Venezuelan oil dropped from 568,944 barrels to 435,029 barrels and continued declining thereafter.[8] Although it looks dramatic, that reduction took place within a broader context of the gradual decline of overall oil production, which was at its peak when Chávez took power. Venezuela did reduce its dependence on the United States but simultaneously found itself starved of hard currency. Over time, its oil exports to Russia and China were simply repaying loans rather than generating new revenue.

For Chávez, China's expanded position in Latin America meant the "construction of a new geopolitical world order." The United States was a unipolar power after the Soviet Union fell, and China created a new pole that undermined the "power of the empire" (*La Vanguardia* 2009). Dan Burton, the US representative from Indiana whose last name is forever attached to the Helms-Burton Act, was similarly concerned. Calling China a superpower, Burton quoted the movie "Cabaret" about money making the world go around and said that China was "producing products" with cheap labor, which allowed them to buy ideological alliances (United States House of Representatives 2008, 31). The notion that China challenged the United States with its economic might was widely shared.

Because of its historic relationship with Cuba, Russia always had a presence of some sort in Latin America. The leftist governments of Daniel Ortega in Nicaragua (already familiar with Russia because of his first presidency) and Chávez in Venezuela offered more avenues for Putin to keep his foot firmly planted in the regional doorway. The new era of Russian interest was launched in 2008, when President Dimitry Medvedev toured the region just before Barack Obama took office, announcing new deals as he went. "Russia is looking to consolidate its relations in Latin America, largely forgotten since the fall of the Soviet Union," he said in Peru (Kraul and McDonnell 2008). Consolidation, however, never became truly regional.

In 2000, Russia exported $7.5 million to Nicaragua and imported a mere $270,000, which by 2017 grew to $33.7 million and $16.1 million.[9] In 2000 Russia exported $80.6 million to Cuba and imported $304.4 million, while by 2017 it exported $269.5 million and imported $11.9 million. Finally, in 2000 it exported $10.3 million to Venezuela and imported $57.4 million, whereas in 2017 it exported $67.6 million and officially imported only $731,000. The low amount of Venezuelan exports to Russia reflect the fact that the two governments worked out oil-for-debt swaps that brought oil to Russia as payment rather than as a regular export.

Putin offered no ideological kinship. As Medvedev pointed out, the Cold War was long over. The Russians were not much interested in Latin American revolutionary identities. But Putin was keenly interested in power projection, in answering what he perceived to be encroachments into Russia's own sphere of interest. Putin also possibly took President Obama's announcement of a "reset" of Russian relations as a signal that Russia could expand its reach (Boersner and Haluani 2011). Over time, Venezuela made significant arms purchases and signed agreements on oil and energy. Similarly, Nicaragua bought weapons and in 2008 hosted a Russian warship as a public challenge to the United States while signing a variety of bilateral agreements.

From then on, and especially after the 2008 economic crash, Russia's influence strengthened in Cuba and Venezuela as they reached out for economic assistance denied from the United States. That influence extended to Nicaragua but not much elsewhere. Putin established friendly relations, especially with governments that tended to be adversarial with the United States. That strategy served to maintain a visible connection the United States could not possibly miss.

US Southern Command's 2008 posture statement, the last of the Bush presidency, made no mention of Russia (United States Southern Command 2008).[10] It crept into the 2009 statement, just with an ominous-sounding quote from Vladimir Putin about how he would "pay more and more attention to this vector of our economic and foreign policy" (United States Southern Command 2009). Under the Obama administration, the US Army shifted from viewing Russia as interested in the region to considering it a threat. As with China, this shift in perception was gradual but clear, and it reached a crescendo during the Trump presidency years later.

Ironically, this period of autonomy expansion coincided with the decline of the figure in Latin American history who most defied the United States. At age seventy-nine, Fidel Castro underwent intestinal surgery—likely for diverticulitis—in 2006 and almost died. He shifted power to his younger (by five years) brother Raúl, who had commanded the military since the early years of the revolution. Fidel formally stepped down as president in 2008, and in true revolutionary fashion Raúl was elected unanimously. Hugo Chávez was already an iconic figure by that time and took on the mantle of Latin America's antagonist. Raúl himself never sought or took on such a role. Like Fidel, his speeches criticized US policy and were constantly couched in terms of sovereignty but lacked his brother's conscious bite. Nonetheless, the State Department spokesperson responded to his calls for dialogue by calling him "Fidel's baby brother" and "Fidel Lite" (LeoGrande and Kornbluh 2014, 366). Fidel himself remained in the background, writing occasional essays for the state newspaper *Granma*, sometimes about weighty topics and sometimes just wherever whimsy took him, including expressing his frustration that no one told him a famous Cuban volleyball player had died (Castro 2014).

In 2009, the ideological shifts taking place in Latin America coincided with a change of US president. During the campaign in 2007–2008, Barack Obama did not offer any radical changes in Latin America policy, but his statements showed clear differences with Bush. He argued that the United States should reject the idea of not meeting with adversarial governments like Cuba and Venezuela; that immigration policy should be made in concert with the Mexican government; and that the United States ought to promote social justice in the hemisphere. On the issue of Cuba, he was even combative, fighting back against the long-standing policy of isolating the island: "It's time for more than tough talk that never yields results. It's time for a new strategy" (Schor 2008). It was a winning strategy that especially resonated with the left and center-left governments that wanted more independence and more flexibility. Chapter 5 addresses that change in more detail.

5. MATURATION OF AUTONOMY (2009–2015)

THE GLOBAL FINANCIAL CRASH of 2008 marked the beginning of what we might call the maturation of autonomy in Latin America. The notion of freer rein and successfully pushing boundaries was no longer novel. The US image as a partner had been dented. At least for the time being, the Latin American left still rode high. Hugo Chávez, Evo Morales, Rafael Correa, and others won elections easily. The Bush administration was nearing its end, with a president who was unpopular at home and abroad. Academics and pundits alike wrote countless analyses about the successes of the so-called "pink tide."[1]

The financial distress was severe, and Latin American leaders scrambled for solutions. As a report by the United Nations' Economic Commission for Latin America and the Caribbean pointed out, economic recovery in Latin America was driven in large part by investment from and trade with China (ECLAC 2010). In 2009, Latin American exports to the United States dropped by 26.5 percent whereas with China they increased 5 percent (ECLAC 2010, 9). India also showed demand for the region's primary goods, but China was by far the most dynamic economic partner, helping to pull Latin America out of a deep recession.[2]

China continued its Western Hemisphere expansion. In 2010, Hugo Chávez announced that China had agreed to $20 billion in loans, with repayment at least partially in oil. The deal also included the formation of a joint venture for oil exploration in southern Venezuela (Romero 2010). The same year, an economic counselor in the US embassy cabled that a member of PDVSA's board of directors revealed that in some cases China was paying only $5 a barrel in some deals and then reselling the oil for a profit.[3] The market price in 2010 fluctuated within the $70–$80 per barrel range, then rose to over $100 before falling to roughly $50 in 2015. There were a variety of reasons for the fall, including growing inventories at a time of slowing economies. The price decline was accompanied by rapid democratic erosion, as President Nicolás Maduro fought back against an opposition-controlled legislature. That same year, Maduro claimed China agreed to invest another $20 billion.

There were, however, geographical differences. Central America and Mexico, historically deeply embedded in the US economy, tended to import more from China than they exported. South American countries were much more likely to boost their own exports of primary goods. But the overall effect of the recession was to expand China's presence, which meant Latin American countries had more options other than the United States. For Hugo Chávez, the rebound of oil prices provided new momentum, albeit only for a few years.

In 2013, Chinese president Xi Jinping launched the Belt and Road Initiative. The name referred back to the Chinese building trading routes along the "Silk Road" more than two thousand years ago. Now, the "belt" refers to land routes and the "road" refers to moving overseas. In all, Xi viewed it as a way to increase Chinese influence globally through trade, investment, and the building of infrastructure. Given the favorable conditions this book has laid out, Latin American countries were logical partners and within four years became a formal part of the initiative.

Russia took a different tack. It still did not expand its reach much beyond Cuba, Nicaragua, and Venezuela. With Cuba, of course, there was a long history. In Venezuela, the relationship was relatively new but Vladimir Putin saw in Chávez the perfect ally in his quest to remind the United States of Russia's power and its ability to meddle in the Western Hemisphere if the United States did the same in what Russia considered its own sphere of influence. In 2009, the Russians announced that Chávez had offered them access to the air station on La Orchila, an island off the northern coast, not far from Caracas. The Venezuelan government denied that the offer was ever made, but the gamesmanship was clear.[4] Both Chávez and Putin enjoyed poking the United States and emphasizing its weakened position. It came up again in 2018, and once again was a public relations tweak at the US government. Eventually it was obvious that there was no such plan, but the Russian government played into the autonomy theme.

That same year, Russia loaned $2 billion to Venezuela, which was followed by the presidents visiting each other, both in Caracas and in Moscow. The governments announced a wide variety of projects, most notably a nuclear power plant. That, like many others, never actually developed. Nonetheless, other deals did go through, like a 2011 loan of $4 billion to purchase Russian weapons. Over time, Venezuela accumulated a significant stock of jets, helicopters, and rifles. From the perspective of Latin American–US relations, whether or not all the deals necessarily came to fruition was secondary to the notion that they *could* potentially do so. Chávez was forging ahead with plans the Obama administration viewed with suspicion. Obama himself said that Venezuela had every right to build a power plant "but we do think Venezuela needs to act responsibly" (BBC 2010). But Secretary of State Hillary Clinton opposed arms purchases, citing the potential for a regional arms race (Quinn 2009).

Meanwhile, Iran continued its low levels of engagement. An Iranian lawmaker argued that Iran inspired Latin America with its "freedom-seeking, revolutionary and anti-imperialistic thoughts," which "is unbearable to the United States" (KhabarOnline 2012). That is both hyperbolic and distant from the truth, but the same year the US Congress passed the "Countering Iran in the Western Hemisphere Act of 2012," a largely symbolic measure that involved requiring threat assessments. As far as Iranian influence goes, though, trade was relatively light. But this is difficult to measure because, like Russia, Iran tended to announce lots of agreements (e.g., a deep-water port and hydroelectric plants) that never actually got off the ground. Further, it concerned mostly imports rather than exports. Latin America was not looking to Iran for any particular goods and needed it largely as a market for commodities, which is not hard to find elsewhere. Iran's presence in Latin America consistently alarms US policy makers, but its role remains limited. As we shall see later, its main influence was to assist Venezuela after imposition of oil sanctions.

THE OBAMA ADMINISTRATION

Changes occurred in the United States as well when Barack Obama became president. In the eyes of Latin American leaders, the shift was dramatic.

Obama was not just moderate, but was also the first person of color to be elected President of the United States. That fact resonated in a region where only gradually did people of indigenous or African descent more commonly get elected president. As Lula said right before the election: "In the same way that Brazil elected a metalworker [referring to himself], Bolivia an Indian, Venezuela a Chávez, and Paraguay a bishop, I believe it will be an extraordinary thing if in the biggest economy in the world a black is elected president" (quoted in Erikson 2008, 101). That was the most common view, though Hugo Chávez, perhaps overly accustomed to verbal sparring, soon said that "If he doesn't obey the orders of the empire, they'll kill him" (quoted in Forero 2009). Chávez kept up this sort of message until he died, with the premise that Obama was not such a bad person but was caught up in an imperial machine that constrained or even controlled his actions.

Importantly, Obama asked Thomas Shannon to stay on as assistant secretary of state for Western Hemisphere affairs (in 2010 Obama named him ambassador to Brazil). Shannon had overseen the gradual toning down of the inflammatory rhetoric that was prevalent during President Bush's first term. He served as a bridge. Near the end of 2009, Obama named Georgetown political scientist Arturo Valenzuela to the position. Valenzuela was well known in his field and had published extensively on both Chilean politics and Latin American democratization, a far cry from the highly politicized predecessors before Shannon. Overall the message to Latin America was that subject matter expertise and diplomacy were priorities.

Obama was the first president born after the Cuban Revolution (two years after, in 1961) and in fact was born just one year before the United States imposed its embargo against Cuba. He held no ideological attachment to traditional Cold War policy. In 2007, during the presidential campaign, he published an op-ed in the *Miami Herald* criticizing the Bush administration and calling for greater freedom of travel (Obama 2007). But he also made a broader campaign promise.

> I will use aggressive and principled diplomacy to send an important message: If a post-Fidel government begins opening Cuba to democratic change, the United States (the president working with Congress) is

prepared to take steps to normalize relations and ease the embargo that has governed relations between our countries for the last five decades. (Obama 2007)

This was not typical Cuba rhetoric for serious presidential candidates. During the 1992 campaign, Bill Clinton courted Cuban Americans by promising the exact opposite, namely, tightening the embargo and, as he put it, to "hammer down on Fidel Castro and Cuba" (Rohter 1992). To be sure, Obama's promise was heavily qualified and simply followed the dictates of the 1996 Helms-Burton law, which put control over the embargo entirely in Congress's hands. Yet the tone was new.

Obama's overall message was one of nonideological engagement. At least for Latin America, to the extent there was an identifiable "Obama Doctrine," it was a willingness to engage even with adversaries, and to prefer soft power over hard, diplomacy over force (Kassab and Rosen 2016). It was pragmatic, which at times angered both the right (who, for example, believed he was soft on Cuba and Venezuela) and the left (who believed that his pragmatism outweighed commitment to democracy, as in Honduras). Obama did not oppose the new autonomous regional organizations, praised democratic elections regardless of who won, and in general melted the ice that had crusted around Latin American–US relations.

But he did not come into office seeking radical change in those relations. The drug war remained highly militarized, though with more emphasis on the social context. Military aid overall remained high (though smaller than other types of aid), but it shifted away from Colombia and Mexico and more to Central America, modeled on Plan Colombia. In 2015, then vice president Joe Biden heralded the aid, saying "security makes everything else possible" (Biden 2015). During Obama's term, imprisonment and deportation of Latin American immigrants soared, earning him the label of "deporter-in-chief." During his two terms, the administration deported some three million people.

Immigration reform in the United States required a level of legislative consensus that never emerged. In response to gridlock, in 2014 President Obama did enact the Deferred Action for Childhood Arrivals (DACA) by executive action. It protected US citizen children of undocumented immigrants. It immediately came under legal attack (which it withstood) but in any case was only a drop in the immigration bucket. Change did not come from within the United States, and there were few ways that Latin American countries could carve out autonomous space on immigration.

Despite periodic calls from Latin America to discuss potential decriminalization of drugs, Obama demurred. In 2009, a distinguished group of Latin Americas, including former presidents, published an essay openly criticizing US drug policy. They wanted a shift in emphasis toward demand (in the United States) versus supply (in Latin America) and a greater focus on public health. It even noted hopefully, "the inauguration of the Barack Obama Administration offers a unique opportunity to reshape the failed strategy and engage in the common search for more efficient and humane policies" (Latin American Commission on Drugs and Democracy 2009, 11).

Countries where voices for rethinking the drug war were loudest were sometimes allies most heavily affected by its effects, such as Colombia and Mexico. In these countries the question of autonomy was not ideological, but pragmatic. President Felipe Calderón was waging a controversial war that would take many lives during his six-year presidency (2006–2012). The homicide rate spiked and by 2019 some 200,000 people had died. In Colombia, aerial herbicide spraying of coca plants continued and generated intense domestic opposition.[5] Farmers complained of legal crops dying, while the guerrillas of the Revolutionary Armed Forces of Colombia (FARC) fought back, shooting down two planes (one of which had a US-citizen pilot) in 2013. After initially suspending spraying, the Colombian government ended the practice in 2015 (though restarting it was always a topic of conversation). All US administrations supported the spraying, seeing it as core to reducing coca acreage.

This Latin American reaction, including those in the 2009 report, did not necessarily call for more autonomy from the United States. Instead, the goal was a mutually acceptable shift in policy toward something less militarized. Nonetheless, it reflected the clear belief that the optimal model for addressing the narcotics crisis was in Europe rather than in the United States. The commission wanted the US government to admit its policy was a failure and then work together with Europe to develop more effective and humane policies.

THE HONDURAN COUP

The year Obama took office also saw a stress test of Latin American autonomy that revealed the challenge of exerting autonomous foreign policy in times of crisis. In chapter 3 we saw that José Manuel Zelaya was elected president in Honduras, then moved away from his oligarchic roots and toward leftist policies and allies like Hugo Chávez. This quickly generated resistance among Honduran elites and conservatives both in the region and in Washington, DC.

Political crisis cascaded from there. With less than a year in his presidency, Zelaya told the country that he wanted a popular consultation to decide whether there should be a referendum to consider creation of a constituent assembly. He called it a mere "public opinion poll" but the Supreme Court ruled it illegal because the constitution forbade amendments (Weeks 2009). On June 27, 2009, the day Hondurans went to vote on what was essentially a referendum on a possible referendum, Zelaya was arrested by the army and whisked off illegally to Costa Rica. Zelaya's own account brings home the terrible absurdity of the crisis: "They took off, and there I was. The democratically elected president of Honduras, standing in my pajamas in the middle of a runway in Costa Rica," Zelaya says. "I said to myself, 'So this is that great new future everyone is talking about for Latin America?'" (quoted in Murphy 2012). The prevailing procoup argument was that Hugo Chávez was behind it all. Even the Honduran Catholic Church did not bother to label itself an impartial arbiter. Without any evidence to support the position, Cardinal Oscar Rodriguez Maradiaga said publicly that Zelaya was "just trying to impose Hugo Chávez's project at all costs" (Trotta 2009). The following six months provided signs of how difficult it was to establish political autonomy from the United States.

The legislature named the president of Honduras's congress, Roberto Micheletti, as interim president until regularly scheduled elections could be held in December 2009. Political elites were adamant that Zelaya could not return to the presidency and would be arrested if he returned to the country. There was extensive condemnation from across Latin America, but the way the crisis played out demonstrated the paper-thin regional commitment to going much beyond rhetoric to counter US policy.

The Obama administration sought a middle ground that labeled the action a "coup" and illegitimate, but they did not insist on Zelaya's return or call for sanctions against the interim government. OAS head José Miguel Insulza tried and failed to get governments to act in addition to making pronouncements. UNASUR condemned the coup and announced it would not accept the results of the 2009 presidential election, which eventually it would back down from.

Other Central American countries enacted an embargo but abandoned it after forty-eight hours because it was too costly (*Reuters* 2009). Lula agreed to harbor Zelaya in the Brazilian embassy in Tegucigalpa and vocally defended him but did not go beyond that. Zelaya had left Costa Rica, camped out in Nicaragua on the border, then managed to sneak back into the country with help from the leftist Farabundo Martí National Liberation Front (FMLN) government in El Salvador. Perhaps the best example of apathy is that a month after the coup, Hugo Chávez was left simply to say, "Do Something. Obama, do something!" (Meyer 2009). Even the most radical of all Latin American leftists was reduced to asking the United States government to cut the Gordian knot and resolve the problem. The Obama administration, meanwhile, had no intention of changing the status quo.

In the end, inertia won. Real and rumored negotiations started and floundered with regularity, which served the purposes of Micheletti, whose goal was simply to make time pass until the election. Since the presidential election was already scheduled just six months after the coup occurred, disinterest on the US part to act and inability of Latin American countries to unite meant that despite violence and protests, a new president was elected. Porfirio Lobo, who had lost to Zelaya in 2005, won and assumed the office in January 2007. Lobo eventually met with Zelaya and allowed him to return two years later.

With differing degrees of vehemence, there was broad condemnation of the coup from Latin American leaders. Even conservative Colombian president Alvaro Uribe expressed concern, generally aligning himself with the Obama administration. Hugo Chávez put his troops on alert and claimed that if a new government was sworn in, "We will bring them down, we will bring them down, I tell" (quoted in the *Telegraph* 2009). Venezuela temporarily cut off oil supplies, which hurt because Honduras was getting it at preferential prices. The problem was that Zelaya himself noted that Honduras got only 15 percent of its oil from Venezuela. The rest came from the United States, which meant leverage was limited. In the midst of crisis, Latin America mostly looked to the United States.

The response underlines the point that Latin American autonomy is not synonymous with unity. Many Latin American countries were painstakingly diversifying their economies and developing new diplomatic relationships, but they did so individually and not collectively. Venezuelan political scientist Carlos Romero referred to the Honduras crisis as a "morgue" where regional norms and ideas went to die (Romero 2010, 86). Seen from a different perspective, it may well be that some ideas do indeed thrive but encourage inaction. The principle of nonintervention is central to most Latin American governments. Repeated invasion by the United States and Europe had the effect of making Latin American leaders skeptical and suspicious of intervention, specifically in terms of using leverage and pressure to force a certain outcome in another country. That attitude is shared across ideological lines. The 1902 Drago Doctrine was an important marker in international law, drafted by Argentine jurist Luis Drago and sent to the US government. It claimed that the use of force to collect debt was a violation of sovereignty. The US resisted the logic, though gradually felt compelled to accept it (Schoultz 1998, 180). On the Latin America side, it meant often preferring not acting to possibly violating sovereignty.

Cooper and Legler (2006) analyze the Organization of American States's effectiveness at resolving conflict in Latin America. They demonstrate that its great strength is *facilitating*. Using a dialogue approach, the OAS can foster intraelite discussion about solutions and emphasize the need to protect democracy. This becomes action without intervention. That ceases to be useful when one or more of the parties are intransigent, as was the case with the Micheletti government in Honduras. So, for example, the head of the OAS, José Miguel Insulza, spoke with the government and was rebuffed, which was followed by the OAS suspending Honduras. The Micheletti government declared it would rather leave the OAS than reinstate Zelaya, which left Insulza with no option other than to assert unspecified "pressure" to be applied. At that point the OAS was no longer much of a player.

Of course, the OAS includes the United States, so it cannot be used as a direct example of autonomy, but it remains the most visible regional entity. None of the organizations that Hugo Chávez spearheaded is built to include all countries.[6] The only way to resolve a crisis without the United States is through ad hoc dialogue, which has a long history in the region. A major example is Costa Rican president Oscar Arias's mediation of the Central American civil wars in the mid-1980s, for which he won the Nobel Peace Prize. The particular challenge in the Honduran crisis was that a deadline—the election—loomed. If no decision could be reached within that time, Zelaya's term would simply end and someone else would become president.

The response to the Honduran crisis highlights the fragility of autonomy in times of crisis. Lula, who as we have seen consciously expanded Brazil's regional and global reach, took the most action by far but he was virtually alone. Hugo Chávez's passivity is especially noteworthy given his endless exhortations for collective action and balance against the empire of the north. The roots of Latin American autonomy remained shallow. Honduras was, and continues to be, a small and economically dependent country with close historical ties to the United States, dating back to O. Henry's coining of the phrase "banana republic" in 1904. Its own political elites, whose fortunes are tied to the United States, instinctively looked north for a solution. Unlike many of its Central American neighbors, Honduras had never shown an independent streak in this regard.

Yet Chávez had been in power a decade by that point and had already launched numerous initiatives to counterbalance the United States. Although he could give a good speech, he did not try to bring the hemisphere together in the heat of the crisis. He talked vaguely of military action, which no one took seriously. José Miguel Insulza was effective in quickly getting hemispheric consensus condemning Zelaya's overthrow, but he failed completely in terms of going beyond statements and convincing Latin American governments to use whatever leverage they had. He went to Honduras, demanded action, and was ignored. Before long he became a peripheral figure. Since Insulza failed to achieve anything through the OAS, the Obama administration was freer to push whatever solution it preferred. Oscar Arias pushed for talks outside the auspices of the OAS. He stayed in close communication with the administration. By late August he was telling US officials that "the U.S.

had played the game exactly right, with the appropriate mix of carrots, sticks, toughness, unified message, even-handedness and above all, good timing."[7]

One conclusion to take from the Honduran crisis is that Latin American governments are not—and indeed never have been—unified in any real manner and that their interest in autonomy varies greatly. Acting quickly and decisively was therefore close to impossible. Given the historically central position of the United States, governments found it simpler to follow along. A similar dynamic would manifest itself in 2019, when another US president took the lead in the long-unfolding political crisis in Venezuela. There too, Latin American governments chose to follow rather than lead.

Although it never generated unity that could spark consensual action, one outcome of the Honduran coup crisis was the creation of the Community of Latin American and Caribbean States, created in 2010. It was intended to replace the Cold War–era Rio Group, which provided a counterweight to US policy. CELAC's stated purpose was to foster integration, but it never advanced much in that direction. It has, however, provided a forum for discussion and continues to hold summits, and it is a platform upon which the region can collectively meet with governments beyond the hemisphere, especially with China and the European Union.

THE DIVERSITY OF LEFTIST PRESIDENTS

Brazil is a useful example of how foreign policy in a country can change in important ways with a change of government. Dilma Rousseff won the Brazilian presidential election in 2010 with 56 percent of the votes in the second round. She had a long political history, both from her personal history (like Michelle Bachelet, she was imprisoned and tortured by a dictatorship) and her experience, as she served both as minister of energy and chief of staff. She was Lula's protégé, but her view of Brazil's global role was different. Although she was widely labeled the chosen heir of Lula, Dilma Rousseff had different foreign policy priorities that were more inward-looking and less attuned to autonomy.

Although she kept autonomy-minded foreign policy advisors she inherited from Lula, she quickly abandoned his global pretensions (Miriam Gomes Saraiva 2014). She cut the foreign ministry's budget, reduced payments to the United Nations, and limited her trips abroad (Marcondes and Mawdsley 2017). She tended to see relations with other Latin American countries more in terms of potential markets than of a group to be led. In this regard, she was more attuned to Brazil's economy than to global leadership. As Brazil's economy stumbled after 2010, it became Rousseff's overriding priority, and her inability to counter it eventually became a factor in her ouster from power.

International relations literature in the United States tends to downplay individual leaders because they are embedded within constraining structures. Latin American scholarship has much more to say, focusing on the lack of a stable, long-term set of foreign policies that do not change drastically from one president to the next.[8] What we see in Brazil is clearly a sharp turn away from diplomatic activism. Being an independent and autonomous regional leader was de-emphasized. Lula built what he hoped would be a model for broader Brazilian leadership, but Rousseff ignored it, or at least much of it. For example, she did not follow Lula's example of trying to make Brazil a player in Middle East negotiations.

Like many other presidents, she combined critique of US policy with professed personal respect for Barack Obama. When in 2013 reports came out about the United States spying on Brazilian leaders, including her, Rousseff cancelled a state trip, but within months downplayed the controversy: "I do not believe the responsibility for the spying habits lay with the Obama administration," she said (Reuters 2014). She was not interested in being part of the anti-US left.

Dilma Rousseff's foreign minister, Antonio Patriota, publicly praised Barack Obama and Secretary of State Hillary Clinton in 2012 for the Global Partnership Dialogue, noting that leaders of the two countries were meeting regularly on global issues (United States Department of State 2012). Vice President Joe Biden went to Brazil and invited Rousseff for a state visit. In fact, by incredible coincidence, one of Biden's top aides was the uncle to one of Rousseff's top aides. As Rousseff said, "That man could sell an icebox in Canada" (quoted in Winter 2015).

The same year Obama took office also saw a bumper crop of left or center-left presidents elected in Latin America. The 2009 election of Mauricio Funes in El Salvador was especially historic because he was the first president in the country's history who even leaned left. During the 1980s, the United States had backed right-wing governments fighting guerrillas in a devastating civil war that left more than seventy-five thousand dead. After the negotiated end to the war in 1992, the right dominated the presidency. Like Zelaya in Honduras, Funes became president of a country that was tightly bound to the United States. In particular, the flow of Salvadoran migrants fleeing the civil war eventually became a core source of revenue through remittances. Although relatively more industrial than its Central American counterparts, by and large El Salvador was a model case for dependency theory. Unlike Zelaya, Funes never had any intention of seeking much autonomy from the United States.

Funes's party, the Farabundo Martí National Liberation Front (FMLN), was formed as a guerrilla coalition in 1980. Composed of the Communist Party and four others, it sought to emulate the success of the Nicaraguan Sandinistas and overthrow the military-dominated government by force. After the war ended, the FMLN successfully shifted to become a political party. The party's own account of its evolution is frank, noting the difficulties of changing its mindset that was "designed for war" even though it was fighting "the same enemy" (i.e., the right) (Institute de Iberoamérica 2006). It was a party born of Marxist revolution, but in power it proved pragmatic, and that included a strong relationship with the United States.

Funes emphasized his desire for a partnership among equals, but he had no intention of pushing the United States away. To the contrary, in 2010 he met President Obama in the White House and made it clear he was no radical:

> [W]e definitely cannot blame the United States for the situation that we are in. And instead, we are looking for the United States to become a strategic partner, as President Obama so well said; not a bigger partner or a lesser partner but an equal partner and an efficient partner. (White House 2010)

Funes and Obama got along well, and he simultaneously worked pragmatically with Hugo Chávez. The two met in 2009, with Funes talking of "solidarity" but eschewing any more radical rhetoric as he negotiated for Venezuelan oil (AFP 2009).[9]

Likewise, Funes criticized Zelaya's removal in Honduras. Zelaya even came briefly to El Salvador and met Funes. But when Porfirio Lobo won the presidential election later that year, Funes recognized him and that was the end of the crisis as far as he was concerned, whereas Hugo Chávez boycotted an EU–Latin America summit in 2010 because of Lobo's presence. Despite the constant media and academic talk of a pink tide, there were actually many different shades of pink, and many of them worked with the United States when it suited them.

The more anti-US left, however, remained strong for the time being. In 2009, Evo Morales easily won re-election with 64 percent of the vote (and his Movement Toward Socialism party won both chambers of the legislature). His election came on the heels of the successful referendum to ratify a new constitution earlier that year, which served to make his socialist-leaning political project more durable. The word "sovereign" appears twenty-two times in the document, and natural resources were carefully protected from foreign domination.[10] From the perspective of bilateral relations with the United States, this result cemented a drastic shift away from decades of close and not always fully voluntary cooperation. Drug policy often clashed with economic development or democracy and took precedence over them. In the past, US policy makers dictated policies to an extensive degree, to the point that autonomous Bolivian efforts were unsuccessful in no small part because they received too little support from the United States and international economic institutions (Lehman 2006).

Morales was a consistent critic of US policy globally and a close ally of Hugo Chávez. He did reduce dependence on the United States, though Bolivia never aimed to shift away from a reliance on primary products, which it sold in large quantities to China and elsewhere. Just in 2009, China loaned Bolivia $60 million to purchase natural gas drilling rigs, sold Chinese light military aircraft for $58 million, and planned a $300 million sale of satellites (*Reuters* 2009). Even if Bolivia did not restructure its economy away from commodities, China's presence provided Evo Morales with economic space to continue condemning the US government without fear of economic backlash. In fact, trade with the United States grew.[11] Playing the field did not mean giving up the original partner.

A Cuban scholar frames Morales's foreign policy in 2009 as a shift from "dependency diplomacy" to "diplomacy of the people" (Hernández Bermúdez 2020). This meant breaking with past governments' "total subordination" to the United States, which in practice entailed speaking forcefully in international fora, expelling US officials from Bolivia, and establishing the country as an anti-imperialist ally. Given the strength of trade, however, there was also behind-the-scenes diplomatic maneuvering to ensure that difficult political relations would not interfere with economic ones.

Morales's re-election was mirrored in Ecuador, where Rafael Correa similarly won election, oversaw the writing of a new constitution, then was re-elected under that new document. One difference was his smaller margin of victory, 52 percent. Correa faced more opposition both from the left (concerned about his commitment to the indigenous population) as well as from the right. Correa used the same "twenty-first-century socialism" rhetoric as Hugo Chávez, though he supported the maintenance of dollarization. Autonomy is a messy and complicated project.

Even more than Evo Morales, Correa embraced China. In 2008, he announced that Ecuador was defaulting on two bonds, arguing they were issued illegitimately by a previous government. In the past, that option was not on the table because there was no alternative to going along with US demands. With China willing to loan massive sums, in 2009 Correa was able to secure a $1 billion loan, repayable in oil (just as China would do with Venezuela). This gave Correa distance from the United States, which Correa could use to be vocal with little to no fear of retaliation, but which of course also tied Ecuador much more closely to China economically.

In some ways, the United States actively, if unwittingly, contributed to Latin American governments looking elsewhere for trading partners. The Andean Trade Preference and Drug Eradication Act was enacted in 1991 to give Andean countries—Bolivia, Colombia, Ecuador, and Peru—preferential access to US markets. The logic was to encourage legal trade versus narcotics; all but Ecuador are coca-producing, though Ecuador suffers from transshipment. The Obama administration chose to let the agreement expire in 2013 to punish the leftist governments of Bolivia and Ecuador (Colombia and Peru had by then signed free trade agreements with the United States). Losing preferential treatment became greater incentive to find new partners.

Chapter 4 discussed how Bolivia was dropped from the Andean Trade Preference and Drug Eradication Act, with the Bush administration accusing it of not sufficiently fighting drugs. The end for Ecuador came in 2013, when President Rafael Correa chose to grant asylum to Julian Assange and to discuss doing so with Edward Snowden. Assange founded Wikileaks, which obtains declassified documents and publishes them on the web. Snowden, a CIA contractor, worked with Wikileaks to published thousands of sensitive US government documents. In short, the US government did not look kindly upon them or anyone who assisted them. Correa saw a way to assert his foreign policy independence, further arguing that Ecuador rejected trade agreements from countries that pressured it and that he would not "submit to commercial interests, however important they might be" (*La Nación* 2013). Ecuador withdrew from the agreement, which the US Congress let expire at the end of the year.

That shift away from the United States, along with the US push out the door, served to deepen Ecuador's relationship with China. It seemed clearly to be a negative for the United States since it prompted Ecuador to seek new markets, which has a ripple effect with partners, suppliers, and the like.

The Obama administration's reaction remained measured. The president called Correa to congratulate him on his re-election, which prompted a conservative critic to argue that "Obama should pick his friends in Latin America more carefully" (Hidalgo 2009). Although the US right criticized Obama for phone calls, handshakes, and positive comments, they were well-received in Latin America. For the time being, the left was ascendant in the region, and Obama largely accepted that fact.

Although much has been made of the so-called "pink wave" of leftist presidents elected in the first part of the century, this period highlights their diversity. José Mujica was elected president of Uruguay in 2009, and from his roots as a Cold War guerrilla (he was arrested and tortured by the military government more than once) he advocated more social democratic views, and for him autonomy did not mean seeing the United States as adversarial. Dilma

Rousseff, who as we have seen had a similar background and outlook, was re-elected the following year. Meanwhile, Cristina Fernández, who was firmly in the Chávez camp, was re-elected easily in 2011. And even the right was diverse. Juan Manuel Santos was elected in Colombia in 2010 as well. He was a conservative vice president in the far-right government of Alvaro Uribe, but he showed himself to be highly pragmatic (which earned the scorn of his former president).

Chile is a case featuring both the left and the right. Michelle Bachelet, the pragmatic socialist president, was replaced in 2010 by Sebastián Piñera, a billionaire candidate of the right. Nonetheless, that shift was not accompanied by a wholesale change in foreign policy. Ever since the transition from military to civilian government in 1990, both the left and the right had maintained the fundamentals of global reach and a focus on free trade. They both expanded Chile's global economic reach and maintained a free trade agreement with the United States.

The 2011 Peruvian presidential election demonstrates further how the Latin American left tended to be lumped together. Ollanta Humala defeated Keiko Fujimori (daughter of former dictator Alberto Fujimori) with just 51.5 percent of the vote in a runoff. Humala was cast as a Chávez clone, a leftist populist agitator. US ambassador Michael McKinley asserted in 2009 that Chávez was funding Humala (Kozloff 2011). To be fair, Humala seemed a wild card, someone who had led an unsuccessful coup attempt against Alberto Fujimori in 2000, which gave him a superficial similarity to Chávez. Plus, Humala had met Chávez in Caracas, and Chávez had praised him.

The conservative *Financial Times* noted that Humala's election had "sent chills down investors' spines," but maybe he wasn't so bad after all (Mapstone 2012). In 2013, he even met with the US Senate Foreign Relations Committee. He went to the White House, where President Obama welcomed him with, "Peru is one of our strongest and most reliable partners in the hemisphere" (White House 2013).

Indeed, Ollanta Humala was one of four presidents (along with the presidents of Chile, Colombia, and Mexico) to launch the Pacific Alliance in 2012. Ollanta's predecessor Alán García got the project going as a way to gather free-trade-minded countries with an emphasis both on integration and with trade and investment with Asia. Although it does not actually include all the countries with Pacific coasts, several other Latin American countries, including Costa Rica and Colombia, expressed interest in joining (but thus far have not). Over its first ten years, countries such as Australia, New Zealand, and South Korea became associate members. Singapore signed a free trade agreement with the group in 2022.

It was a self-conscious response to the proliferation of left-leaning blocs. As such, it represented countries coming together in pursuit of something the United States favors but is not directing. Briceño-Ruiz, Legler, and Prado Lallande (2021) argue that US competition with China may well prompt the Biden administration to make overtures to the alliance. In other words, autonomy does not require rejecting the United States, which can still act as a strategic partner. Meanwhile, leftist governments in Latin America were far from a bloc, and they forged ahead in diverse ways. There was no regional ideological consensus.

At the same time, the US government continued policies that frustrated Latin American leaders. Since Fidel Castro and his fellow revolutionaries forcibly removed the US-backed dictatorship of Fulgencio Batista in 1959, Cuba had been the main example of Latin American autonomy. It was dependency theory come to life, especially after the United States imposed its economic embargo and Cuba's economy became socialist and shifted toward the Soviet Union. Politically, Fidel Castro defied the United States at every turn, from the United Nations to proxy (and sometimes direct) guerrilla fighters. Administration after administration in the United States kept Cuba cut off, to the point that autonomy was partially forced.

Especially as the number of elected center-left and left governments in Latin America increased, the counterproductive nature of US policy became more evident. The United States was the only country in the hemisphere calling for Cuba's isolation, and its unilateral sanctions were rejected not only in Latin America but across the world. Like clockwork, every year starting in 1992, Cuba introduced a United Nations resolution condemning the embargo. Over time, the number of countries opposing the resolution dwindled until the only two consistent opponents were the United States and Israel, with a scattering of small, usually Pacific island countries joining. Nonetheless, as the political and economic situation in Venezuela deteriorated, the US response gradually echoed that of its famously ineffective Cuba policy.

HUGO CHÁVEZ'S DEATH

The vociferous anti-US policy perspective took a blow when Hugo Chávez died of cancer in March 2013. He announced he had cancer in 2011 and traveled periodically to Cuba to receive treatments and surgeries. Going to Cuba ensured total privacy, though the dearth of information also fueled conspiracy theories. He ran for re-election in 2012 and won, though he was often in pain and not always visible. Returning to Cuba in December 2012, he had surgery and did not recover, seeing only a handful of people and making no public appearances. He died several months later.

Chávez's death marked the beginning of the end of region-wide autonomy initiatives. The ones he created stalled or withered, while no other political leader took the helm. Leftist presidents who had been in power for some time already, like Rafael Correa and Evo Morales, made comments on regional and global issues (for the former, typically via Twitter, a practice Morales later embraced as well) but did not do the extensive traveling, cajoling, and negotiating that Chávez had thrived on.

His death also shifted Venezuela's political and economic trajectories. Nicolás Maduro, who had just been named vice president only in October 2012, assumed the presidency and (following the constitution) also scheduled a new presidential election, in which he barely defeated opposition candidate Henrique Capriles. Maduro was a loyalist, an ardent Chávez supporter since the early 1990s, when Chávez tried to overthrow the government of Carlos Andrés Pérez.

Several factors worked against Maduro exerting the same type of regional leadership as Chávez. According to the US Energy Information Administration, Venezuela's oil production was flat at the time he took office at just under 2.5 million barrels a day, but began falling in 2015, so revenue also fell sharply under his administration.[12] Years of mismanagement and accelerated corruption within the state oil company Petróleos de Venezuela (PDVSA) took its toll. In 2013 Maduro announced that he would cut foreign aid, including Petrocaribe, a mainstay of Venezuelan soft power. That meant changing the terms of the agreement to make it less favorable than before (Fieser 2013). Oil had fueled—so to speak—almost all Venezuelan policies, domestic and foreign.

As Venezuela became more indebted, it also sent increasing amounts of oil to China and Russia to service that debt. The government was no longer in a position to fund autonomy-related initiatives. But Maduro also lacked Chávez's charisma and struggled to gain anywhere near his predecessor's popularity. Instead, he contributed to Chávez's posthumous rise to near deification to bolster his own position. Michelutti (2016) refers to Maduro's need to cultivate "quasi-charisma" largely by channeling Chávez's image on a constant basis. Yet all the reverent references to the "eternal commander" could not make up for his lack of connection with Venezuelans. Lastly, because of the drop in oil revenue, corruption, inflation, an almost worthless currency, and then also sanctions from the US government, Maduro was overwhelmed by domestic crises and played almost no international role at all. But with military backing and increasing repression, he stayed in power nonetheless.

Later in the same year he was elected, Maduro decreed that Christmas would come early (Agencia Venezolana de Noticias 2013).[13] This was, he said, the best way to respond to his political opposition. But it also conveniently included an early Christmas bonus to come in the midst of December municipal elections. He struggled to extend any sort of political honeymoon despite invoking the "eternal commander" Chávez, and from that point forward Venezuela retreated significantly from its global initiatives. Maduro never showed the same interest as Chávez in building international coalitions or asserting Venezuela's global authority.

Venezuela's already tense relations with the United States worsened as Maduro increasingly turned to authoritarian means to counter the growing calls for his removal. In 2015, the Obama administration declared a national emergency with regard to Venezuela for "erosion of human rights guarantees, persecution of political opponents, curtailment of press freedoms, use of violence and human rights violations and abuses in response to antigovernment protests, and arbitrary arrest and detention of antigovernment protestors, as well as the exacerbating presence of significant government corruption" (Administration of Barack Obama 2016). That action allowed for targeted sanctions against Venezuelan officials. Presidents Obama, Trump, and Biden all continued to renew the executive order each year.

Later in 2015, Maduros's Socialist Party (the PSUV) lost its majority in the National Assembly to the Democratic Unity Roundtable (MUD) coalition, despite widespread accusations of government manipulation. In fact, the MUD won a supermajority that the Supreme Court effectively annulled by suspending three MUD members. Stung and threatened, Maduro would allow no more free elections. The MUD's legislative proposals, and its effort to launch a recall referendum, were also blocked either by the Supreme Court or by the National Electoral Council. As Maduro dismantled what was left of Venezuelan democracy, the bilateral relationship became even more hostile.

Despite Venezuela's economic and political collapse, institutions like UNASUR did continue on. Its twelve members met in late 2014 and approved the idea of a South American citizenship that would include a single passport (Robertson 2014). These ideas, like many that were generated over the years, were brought up periodically as proposals but never made much headway. In 2012, the Paraguayan legislature removed President Fernando Lugo in a speedy impeachment process that allowed him just two hours to defend himself. Left-leaning governments called it a coup, and UNASUR held emergency talks. Meanwhile, the Obama administration recognized Lugo's vice president, who was sworn in to take his place. UNASUR suspended Paraguay's membership in the organization but was unable to change the outcome. The organization had little leverage, especially since it rejected the use of sanctions. Nonetheless, "it is clear that UNASUR actions were important for the exercise of regional autonomy, as the organization was the main interlocutor between the parties" (Martinez and de Lyra 2018, 117).

As the Venezuelan political crisis heated up after Maduro took office, the government called for UNASUR to serve as mediator for talks with the opposition. Opposition leaders resisted the idea. The Obama administration preferred using the Organization of American States, which some allies like Panama echoed, to Maduro's great disgust (BBC 2014). Maduro increasingly viewed the US and like-minded governments as part of a fascist plot to overthrow him. That built on Chávez's own inclination to use conspiracy theories strategically. As Venezuelan political scientist Hugo Pérez Hernáiz argues, conspiracy theories served to create a "political religion" and to produce a loss of political agency in the population (Pérez-Hernáiz 2008). Maduro became adept at selectively rejecting fora for mediation and dialogue, which generally meant choosing those that did not involve the US government.

CHINA'S CONTINUED INFLUENCE

China's influence was by then well-established. This period is when the notion of "dependency" started emerging to describe China's economic relationship with Latin America. In Latin America, there was plenty of scholarly debate about it.[14] A similar discussion occurred in the United States, but editorials and opinion pieces included a sense of anxiety about the United States losing its traditional position. As one journalist put it, "Washington wouldn't be facing this China syndrome in its own hemisphere if it had simply taken 'high-level engagement on Latin America' more seriously a decade or more ago" (Padgett 2013). Among US pundits, this line of argument built on the foundation of "losing Latin America" arguments that went back years. A simple Google search of "losing Latin America" reveals the rich history of the seemingly permanent idea that the United States government is doing too little to "win" the region, whatever that means.

The Chinese government's own statements on trade sometimes even unintentionally reinforced the dependency angle. For example, in 2012 it touted its ties to Uruguay: "China is now the largest buyer of Uruguay's wood, soy and cellulose. It also imports frozen fish, leather, meat, gemstones and dairy products from Uruguay. Meanwhile, Uruguay imports trucks, motor vehicles, computers, screens and telephones from China" (quoted in Weeks 2012). The main thrust of dependency theory is that less developed countries export primary products and import finished goods, to the point that they become structurally unable to produce the latter themselves. Swapping frozen fish for trucks is an example fit for a textbook. Indeed, between 2009 and 2013, 69 percent of Latin American exports to China consisted of iron ore, soybeans, copper, and petroleum (Ray and Gallagher 2015).

Up to this point, China's engaging with the region consisted mostly of trade rather than loans or foreign direct investment (FDI). But that changed quickly. CELAC held a meeting in Beijing in 2015 attended by Chinese president Xi Jinping. The outcome was mostly pronouncements, with Xi saying that such a forum was "just like a young shoot sprouting out of the earth, whose sturdy growth into a towering tree needs meticulous cultivation of both sides" (Ministry of Foreign Affairs 2018). The level of interchange, and perhaps in some cases also the level of dependence, thus gradually increased and deepened over time. Chinese loans to Latin American governments increased from $3.8 billion in 2012 to $22.1 billion in 2014 (Ray and Gallagher 2015).

AUTONOMY AND THE DRUG WAR

During the Obama administration, the US media and Latin American leaders alike became more vocal about the inability of the US drug war to achieve results. It got to the point that Janet Napolitano, the secretary of homeland security, felt compelled to say the use of police was not a failure (BBC 2012). No matter how many narcotics the US governments claimed to interdict, how many cartel members it arrested, or how many hectares of coca were eradicated, drugs flowed into the United States almost unabated and Latin American countries suffered violence from the never-ending battles they fought.

In 2011, Colombian president Juan Manuel Santos called for the legalization of marijuana (Hidalgo 2011). Otto Pérez Molina, a conservative retired military officer who became Guatemala's president, called for a broader legalization of drugs. His assertion that "We are not doing what the United States says, we are doing what we have to do" was not something commonly heard coming from the mouth of a hard-liner (*Salon* 2012). But it reflected a deep dissatisfaction with what the drug war produced in Latin America, namely increased violence and the spread of organized crime, which also brought corruption. The decriminalization cat was really out of the bag.

In addition to broader (though still controversial) calls for legalization or at least decriminalization, Bolivia expelled the US Drug Enforcement Agency in 2008 and turned instead to neighboring Brazil and to the European Union for counternarcotics assistance. As time went on, the Obama administration was not sure how to respond. When asked directly about the issue, the State Department spokesperson creatively evaded the question.

> **QUESTION:** Bolivia. New reports suggest that Bolivia's efforts to fight drug trafficking without the assistance of the DEA or other US authorities may be having some bit of an impact, although it is considered controversial. Has the US seen these reports? And what does the US think about the efforts to deal with illegal drug trafficking, coca growing in distribution, outside of a Merida-type relationship?
>
> **MS. NULAND:** I didn't get the vector you were coming at from the beginning, Roz, that they are making improvements or that they're not making—
>
> **QUESTION:** Apparently they have made some progress—
>
> **MS. NULAND:** Yeah.
>
> **QUESTION:** —in stopping the trafficking, particularly of coca and its byproducts.
>
> **MS. NULAND:** Let me get you a fuller report on this. You know that we've had longstanding concerns about the narcotics situation in Bolivia. That said, I think we do agree that they have made some progress in 2010, 2011, but there is a whole lot more to do. But let me get you a more subtle sense of that directly later today (United States Department of State 2013).

The promised subtlety—or vector—did not materialize.[15] Nonetheless, the Obama administration decertified Bolivia, which meant claiming it was not cooperating sufficiently with US drug policy. President Bush had first decertified in 2008, and the Obama administration followed suit every year. Such an action potentially threatened foreign aid, US opposition to development bank loans, and even trade sanctions, though all these were often lifted with a waiver. Otherwise, it was a high-profile slap in the face intended to punish governments that did not combat drug trafficking the way US officials preferred.

Yet Bolivia was succeeding. A 2016 report from the United Nations Development Programme used Bolivia as a case study of successful balance between the needs of subsistence farmers and the need to prevent export of coca for cocaine production. Coca farmers participated in closely monitored government programs to grow coca for local consumption while destroying any excess. It reduced violence and improved the relationship between the state and some of its poorest citizens.

Colombia also moved away from traditional US-led drug policy when in 2015 President Juan Manuel Santos announced he was ending the aerial spraying of coca. Spraying in practice meant using small planes to drop glyphosate onto coca plants. US officials countered that coca cultivation would increase, which in fact did happen after 2012 (from 2012 to 2020 it went from 78,000 hectares to 245,000 [White House 2021b]). But what works against cultivation has real human consequences, which the Colombian government resisted incurring.

For the time being, US-Mexican relations with regard to drug trafficking remained positive. After President Felipe Calderón announced a drug war in 2006 and expanded the military's role in combating Mexican drug cartels, those cartels splintered and multiplied. Further, the traditional illegal exports of drugs like marijuana, cocaine, and heroin were being supplanted by synthetic drugs, like meth and fentanyl, which were smaller, easier to produce and hide, and much more addictive. When Enrique Peña Nieto became president in 2012, he promised to place drug trafficking high on his list of priorities, and indeed eventually successfully worked with the United States to capture the infamous drug kingpin "El Chapo." He captured other high-level members of different cartels as well, some of whom were extradited to the United States.

Peña Nieto supported the Mérida Initiative, which expanded to focus on strengthening the criminal justice system in addition to providing security aid. President Obama enlisted his help on immigration, such as dealing with unaccompanied children arriving at the border and on pushing Cuba to improve its human rights record. Both issues remained a serious problem, but the bilateral relationship was generally friendly. Yet despite his support, Peña Nieto also declared in a 2016 speech at the United Nations that priority should be "to shift from prohibition alone to effective prevention and regulation" (Gobierno de México 2016). Amidst the deep cooperation, there were always seeds of pushback.

THAWING RELATIONS WITH CUBA

When he took office in 2009, Barack Obama did not make substantive changes to George W. Bush's Cuba policy. During the campaign he expressed support for the embargo and sought marginal changes to "empower" the Cuban people, which mostly meant allowing Cuban Americans to send more money and visit their families on the island (King 2007). For even those minimal proposals, he was pilloried from the right for appeasement. He made no signal that he saw Cuba policy as a priority, though over time he was more critical of the embargo. Behind the scenes, however, his administration engaged in talks with the Cuban government about the normalization of diplomatic relations (there had been no US ambassador since 1961) and a general thawing of hardline policies about travel and the movement of money.

Then in late 2014, the administration announced that it was re-establishing relations, reviewing Cuba's long-standing presence on the "State Sponsor of Terrorism" list, and easing travel and business restrictions. This would, the president said, "end an outdated approach that, for decades, has failed to advance our interests" (White House 2014). Just engaging in formal diplomacy was a groundbreaking change in US policy, which meant it was controversial. Given the influence of Cuban American legislators like Sens. Ted Cruz and Marco Rubio, Obama's policy announcement generated loud condemnation.

No US president can unilaterally end the embargo, which is codified into law through the 1996 Helms-Burton Law. That law contains highly detailed and lengthy requirements required for the embargo to be lifted, which include not only a transitional government but also giving back property to US citizens.[16] From a policy perspective, this meant that without congressional support (which he lacked) Obama could only tinker at the edges of Cuba policy. It also meant that whatever he did was easily reversible if a future president chose to reverse it, which indeed happened within a short time.

He did take the significant step of ending the decades-old "wet foot, dry foot" Cuba immigration policy. Unlike any other migrants, if Cubans successfully reached land in the United States, they could remain in the country. If picked up at sea, they were returned to Cuba. In 2017, the administration announced that Cubans would be treated the same as other migrants.

One effect of the Obama administration's shift on Cuba policy was actually to reduce its radical autonomy, which had served largely to make Cuba dependent on US adversaries. Venezuela became a lifeline to the Cuban government after severe economic depression in the 1990s. Venezuela provided badly needed oil to Cuba, while Fidel and then Raúl Castro sent military and intelligence advisors, who were central to Chávez's ability to eliminate enemies and to consolidate control over the armed forces, especially after the 1992 coup attempts. For decades, the United States punished Cuba, and in return had very little influence.

When Obama left office, Latin American–US relations were cordial after a period of considerable turbulence. After Hugo Chávez's death, the strident anti-US rhetoric was less evident. Nicolás Maduro did not attract the same kind of regional attention as his predecessor, and he lacked the same level of state revenue. Over time, his economic mismanagement and human rights abuses earned him the criticism even of leftist leaders (most notably Michelle Bachelet, who in 2018 became the U.N. high commissioner for human rights). Yet the embrace of autonomy was as strong as ever. The next chapter will examine how Donald Trump's election in the United States accelerated Latin American processes of autonomy.

6. LATIN AMERICA PLAYS THE FIELD (2016–2020)

FOR YEARS, US ADMINISTRATIONS came and went, and although their approaches to Latin America varied, there was a certain predictability. In the early twenty-first century, for example, you could count on a push for free trade, talk of partnership, and an emphasis on shared values. That blew up with the 2016 presidential election in the United States. When Donald Trump took office in 2017, Latin American autonomy was extensive when compared to the twentieth century. China had a presence everywhere, which would have been close to unthinkable a few decades prior. US officials were certainly not pleased about the situation, but their options were limited. They could sanction Latin American countries or threaten China, which risked serious backlash. They could court those governments, but that was never a hallmark of Trump policies. Instead, he oversaw a period of heightened belligerence.

Long before the election, Trump's message about Latin America was already unfriendly, laced with racism, nationalism, isolationism, and verbal abuse. His inaugural address was apocalyptic, where "American carnage" required policies based on "America First" principles to "protect our borders from the ravages of other countries" (CNN 2016). The speech was intense enough to prompt George W. Bush to remark, "That was some weird shit."[1] Trump opposed free trade agreements, especially the North American Free Trade Agreement, and he wanted to build a wall on the border with Mexico and to restrict migration of all types from the region. His supporters whooped and cheered in enthusiastic approval. Those messages made Latin American leaders uneasy about what concrete policies would emerge from them.[2] That uncertainty never fully dissipated and Latin American–US relations evolved as a consequence.

To be clear, this evolution did not necessarily entail the growth of regional leadership in counterpoint to the United States. As previous chapters have noted, Hugo Chávez played a leadership role undergirded by oil revenue, but it was always limited by its ideological fervor. In the absence of Chávez, Latin America returned to its default, which was heterogeneity and skepticism of unity.

One aspect of Trump's foreign policy that prompted never-ending consternation was his use of Twitter. He dropped rhetorical bombs without warning, often leaving his own advisors scrambling to explain what he said and meant. His social media habit was further complicated by his proclivity to make things up as he went. He alternated between praising and attacking the Mexican government, and his ire occasionally also shifted to Central America, Venezuela, or Cuba. Tweets would sometimes, though not always, be followed by a punitive policy announcement. Even those, however, were not necessarily carried out. President Trump's style of diplomacy tended toward harsh threats aimed at forcing concessions, then backing off. One result was the generalized sense in Latin America that the United States was not a reliable partner, given that agreements could change on a dime without warning based on the president's whim.

Trump's ire always came back to free trade, which he believed to be unfair to the United States. Opening new markets abroad was a long-standing project for US presidents, and, as mentioned in chapter 3, even included a failed attempt by President George W. Bush to create a hemispheric Free Trade Area of the Americas. Hugo Chávez and Donald Trump disliked free trade for opposite reasons, each believing it disadvantaged them. Chávez viewed it in dependency terms, while Trump seemed to believe that poor US negotiating skills consistently led to an imbalance.

All of Latin America responded by looking to new economic and diplomatic partners or simply deepening relationships with existing ones other than the United States. We know from previous chapters that China was already in the mix, but other countries jumped at the opportunity as well. Even countries like Australia, which did not have strong historical ties to Latin America, negotiated a free trade agreement (FTA) with Peru specifically in response to Trump's protectionism (Weeks 2018). Peru then did the same with China. Ecuador developed an economic partnership agreement with the European Free Trade Association, which went into effect in 2020.

The Trump administration's approach opened up new, even unprecedented opportunities for autonomy. Trump quickly withdrew from the Paris Agreement on climate change, which the Obama administration signed in 2016. Trump claimed it damaged the United States since climate change was a hoax, leaving Latin America free (or resigned) to pursue its own climate agreements. Although governments navigated their own policies for carbon neutrality, emissions reductions, and other areas, regional coordination did not emerge. Governments in Brazil (Jair Bolsonaro) and Mexico (Andrés Manuel López Obrador, or AMLO) were climate skeptics, which further hampered regional coordination. Eleven countries did sign the Escazú Agreement in 2018. Its full name is the Regional Agreement on Access to Information, Public Participation and Justice in Environmental Matters in Latin America and the Caribbean, but it is thankfully known by the city in Costa Rica where it was written. It centered on public participation in promoting environmental human rights. The agreement entered into force in 2021, but it did not (at least yet) include Brazil, Colombia, or Peru. Former president Temer actually already signed in 2018, but Jair Bolsonaro refused to send it to Congress for final approval.

China did not step in as a new extra-hemispheric force for environmental issues. It did invest heavily in electric vehicles, wind turbines, and solar panels to generate badly needed energy in a region historically tied to oil. Yet those investments were overshadowed by China's voracious interest in extraction and fossil fuels (Cote-Muñoz 2019). There was ample space for Latin America to take coordinated action on the environment, but no regional consensus or interest from wealthier countries that might help with the resources required to combat the myriad problems wrought in particular by climate change.

Climate change is an increasingly serious problem for Latin America because, for example, shifts in weather patterns increase hurricanes and drought. In turn, they generate crop destruction, flooding, and inevitably emigration, especially to the United States. The United States-Mexico-Canada

Agreement (USMCA) that replaced NAFTA included some commitments to environmental protection. For example, it protected flora and fauna, imposed standards for fishing, and created obligations for marine litter. Overall, though, the Trump administration's message was that the phenomenon was a hoax or at least overstated.

The Pacific Alliance, founded in 2011, represented another avenue of trade that went beyond the United States. Its original intent was aimed at greater trade with Asia, which intensified in the scramble immediately after Trump took office. As Mexico's economy minister put it, "It is in the best interest of Mexico to be linked to the Asian economies" (quoted in Jegarajah 2017). Its four countries—Chile, Colombia, Mexico, and Peru—met in 2018 to discuss ways of cooperating with Mercosur. They also set their sights beyond the region, however, including a 2019 declaration about deepening ties with the European Union and growth in trade with India in 2020–2021.

In this regard, Trump's election did not create the Latin American inclination to play the field more, but it certainly accelerated it. What once was an ideological mission or a pragmatic shift became necessity. If the United States became protectionist in the long term, which would be even more likely if Trump were re-elected to a second term, then Latin American governments needed more options. Throughout his term, Trump and his surrogates never let up on the basic "America First" message, so Latin American leaders became more intent on finding new partners. It may well be that the Pacific Alliance could shift its emphasis on engaging more globally, depending on the ideology of participant governments (Ramírez, Cadena, and Martínez 2021). But it opened doors outside the hemisphere that will not easily or quickly close.

Meanwhile, some older efforts at autonomy began falling apart. In 2018, the Colombian foreign minister dismissed UNASUR as something "created by late Venezuelan President Hugo Chavez to fracture the inter-American system and to create a sounding board for his regime" (Deutsche Welle 2018). Earlier in the year, half of all the countries (Argentina, Brazil, Chile, Colombia, Peru, and Paraguay) suspended their memberships because the organization seemed paralyzed (Paraguassu 2018). The initiatives of the century's first decade, largely initiated by Venezuela, faded away. Lack of leadership and traditional fractured hemispheric unity put UNASUR in the same category of countless failed attempts at regional institutional cooperation.[3]

Hopes of regional unity did not die with UNASUR, but they changed ideological flavor. In 2019, Iván Duque and Sebastián Piñera, conservative presidents of Colombia and Chile respectively, proposed the creation of the Forum for South American Progress (PROSUR) to replace UNASUR. Shortly thereafter, the governments of Argentina, Brazil, Colombia, Chile, Ecuador, Guyana, Paraguay, and Peru signed the Santiago Declaration to become founding members. Venezuela was not invited because it was not democratic. The declaration was broad, with a call for integration but also for flexibility, respect for human rights, and respect for national territory (Ministero de Relaciones Exteriores 2020).[4] It was less ambitious than most of Hugo Chávez's projects, noting that integration should move forward according to each state's "own national realities."

In 2020, Paraguayan president Adbo Benitez met with Duque and discussed the matter (Agencia de Información Paraguaya 2020). Meanwhile, Duque and Piñera announced that they wanted to raise PROSUR to a treaty level, to be ratified by national legislatures (*Seguimiento.co* 2020). Duque's own words, though, showed even more clearly the ideology embedded in the new institution. It would, he said, be aimed at promoting "liberty" and "free trade" while remaining "non-bureaucratic (*Seguimiento.co* 2020). This makes it more difficult for it to serve as a long-term vehicle for generating lasting investment and trade connections that strengthen South America without the presence of the United States. They depend on the continued election of like-minded leaders, which in a democratic context can never be counted on.

Another problem with an effort like PROSUR was that it had no long-term vision. As Argentine political scientist Alejandro Frenkel (2019, 1) put it, PROSUR was the "latest Frankenstein of South American integration." Its founders just wanted to replace UNASUR, and in a way that demonstrated close ties to the United States. Frenkel also viewed PROSUR as an explicit rejection of autonomous projects. An organization that deeply attached to ideology faced the same challenges that its predecessor did.

VENEZUELA'S RADICAL AUTONOMY

During this period, Venezuela joined Cuba as an example of radical autonomy. In practice, the extremely high level of autonomy was economically disastrous. Bilateral trade with the United States took place, but because of US sanctions, it was at a level far below what it could be. US sanctions also disrupted economic transactions with other countries, which exacerbated domestic economic woes. In practice, radical autonomy meant greater suffering, especially after the Trump administration placed sanctions on oil, which was Venezuela's source of foreign currency. A combination of economic mismanagement, kleptocracy, authoritarianism, and US sanctions immiserated Venezuelans.

In early 2019, Nicolás Maduro was scheduled to be inaugurated after being elected the previous year. The election was marred by calls of fraud, imprisonment of opposition political leaders, intimidation, and media harassment. The opposition chose not to participate and called the election illegitimate. Juan Guaidó, the little-known president of the National Assembly, announced that Maduro was a "usurper" and called for an interim government and new elections. This was actually shaky from a legal perspective, since the constitution did not include provisions for interim governments and had no language for deciding that the president was illegitimate (as opposed to, say, incapacitated). The constitution certainly did not anticipate the legislative and executive branches labeling each other illegal and illegitimate. A constitutional crisis blew up.

January 23 was the anniversary marking the uprising that ultimately overthrew the Venezuelan dictator Marcos Pérez Jimenez in 1958. On that day Guaidó went before a crowd and proclaimed himself to be president of Venezuela. Not long after, Donald Trump recognized him as such. Following the US example, Canada recognized Guaidó and a slew of other countries followed suit. The United States and Venezuela traded accusations and threats, and from there the situation settled into stalemate. The Trump administration believed—incorrectly—that the moment was a sign of impending collapse.

President Trump and members of his administration periodically hinted at invasion, claiming that "all options were on the table." John Bolton, who had been a strong supporter of the Iraq invasion to overthrow Saddam Hussein in 2003, was national security advisor and an advocate for doing the same in Venezuela. Sometimes he was even melodramatic, as when he went to a press briefing with a yellow pad with "5,000 troops to Colombia" scrawled on it, which went viral. In his memoirs, he said that talking of invasion "was solely to keep Trump interested in the objective of overthrowing Maduro, without actually wasting a lot of time on a nonstarter" (Bolton 2020, 255). Bolton's ambivalence seemed to mirror Trump, who wanted credit for ousting Maduro but chose neither force nor dialogue as a means of doing so. Instead, US policy toward Venezuela took on the same hues as old school Cuba policy, where the United States applies sanctions on the assumption that the economic pain will generate armed opposition within the country. Even if it doesn't work, it is at least punishing an adversarial government.

The Trump administration brought in Elliott Abrams to coordinate Venezuela policy. Abrams was an infamously old hand at Latin American–US relations, having served in the Reagan administration, where he defended the human rights records of pro-US dictatorships and ultimately was convicted in 1991 (and pardoned presidentially the following year) for withholding information from Congress when testifying about the Iran-Contra affair. As with Bolton's appointment, the administration was signaling an old-fashioned approach to relations that always carried the threat of force behind it.

The Trump administration rejected multilateral coordination. In 2017, twelve countries from across the Western Hemisphere, including Venezuela as represented by Juan Guaidó, joined to apply multilateral pressure to the Maduro government. It became known as the Lima Group (for the city where it first convened). The group periodically issued responses to events in Venezuela, such as condemning clearly unfree elections. Its purpose was to find peaceful and negotiated solutions to restore democracy in Venezuela, especially through free and fair elections. It also reiterated sovereignty and sought "to urgently commit to supporting a process, shaped and driven by themselves, to establish an inclusive transitional government" (Government of Canada 2020).

The Lima Group did not represent a Latin American initiative intended to exclude the United States. The exclusion was self-imposed. The Trump administration did not agree with the Lima Group's rejection of armed force or of its support for dialogue, though the administration periodically praised the group publicly when its policy preferences converged (generally meaning condemnation of Maduro). The Lima Group was launched in large part by Peru, and Brazil's role was much smaller. Barros and Gonçalves (2019) argue that this marked a shift toward the fragmentation of regional governance. Whatever cohesion Chávez once achieved had disintegrated, and Brazil showed no interest in filling the gap. Further, Mexico under AMLO did not support any Lima Group action that it considered interventionist, a shift that found echo under the new Argentine government of Alberto Fernández. AMLO objected to any declaration on Venezuela (Dinatale 2020). Fernández actually pulled out entirely in 2021. Chávez was gone, but political differences remained a roadblock for hemispheric unity. In his memoir, John Bolton provides considerable detail about events in Venezuela, but mentions the Lima Group only in passing. The Trump administration did not pay it much attention.

In December 2020, Venezuela held legislative elections that the opposition boycotted and in which only about 30 percent of Venezuelans bothered to participate. Since he did not run, Juan Guaidó's role was ambiguous. Was he still a legislator (and recognized by many as president) by virtue of the last free elections, or was he a former legislator? The Trump administration insisted the former, but the Latin American response, as always, varied. The Lima Group issued a statement saying it did not recognize the "legitimacy or legality" of the new National Assembly, though it did not refer to Guaidó as president (Lima Group 2021). Once again, however, both Argentina and Mexico refused to sign.

Under these conditions, Venezuela became what Escudé (2014) labeled a "rebel state," a situation he believed in general was both avoidable and self-destructive. The Venezuelan government faced high costs for almost any action it took, so it acted however it could to survive. For example, in January 2019, President Trump issued an executive order imposing sanctions on PDVSA, which is the only vehicle for the import and export of oil. US companies could therefore not engage in any transaction with PDVSA without approval. Maduro therefore turned to Russia and also India. Two months later, the administration applied sanctions to a Russian bank, Evrofinance Mosnarbank, that worked with PDVSA to elude the sanctions. Individually applied sanctions continued thereafter, but they did not stop the flow of oil. Later, Maduro worked with Iran, which of course was near the top of adversaries for the Trump administration. Like Cuba, Maduro had near total autonomy; the United States was already punishing the country as much as it could short of military invasion.[5] Short of using armed force, however, the Trump administration found itself unable to isolate Venezuela fully. Russia and Iran managed to find ways to ship Venezuelan crude.

This level of autonomy entailed considerable suffering for Venezuelans. Venezuelan economist Luis Oliveros (2020) estimated that US sanctions directly caused a decrease in oil revenue of between $17 and $31 billion from 2017 to 2020. Those came on top of long-standing economic mismanagement and corruption, which left more than 90 percent of the population in poverty. As in Cuba, the irony was that access to dollars—the currency of the sanctioning country—was a lifeline for many. Chávez originally viewed autonomy as a means to generate greater equality and enhanced sovereignty. For Maduro, autonomy became a difficult and unwanted consequence of US wrath. By necessity, it meant Venezuela's ties to countries outside the hemisphere became stronger than ever, even as its dependence on the US dollar deepened.

Cuba's situation was similar, though of course not new. The Trump administration called the Obama administration soft and then tightened sanctions. His reasoning repeated the rhetoric commonly heard since the early 1960s. Saying that he was "canceling the last administration's completely one-sided deal with Cuba," he worked toward ending the "reign of suffering" because "I do believe that end is in the very near future" (White House 2017). Mere days before Trump left office, the State Department placed Cuba on the State Sponsor of Terrorism list, which it shared with Iran, North Korea, and Syria. From 1982 to 2015, Cuba had been on that list, with the evidence for sponsoring terrorism becoming increasingly tenuous. By 2015, when Obama removed it, the rationale was centered mostly on relations with the Fuerzas Armadas Revolucionarias Colombianas (FARC) guerrillas. The Trump administration also cited Colombia, though no longer focusing on the now demobilized FARC and centering instead on the Ejército de Liberación Nacional (ELN), who had leaders in Havana engaged in peace talks with the Colombian government. That was enough to get nailed. Being on the list entails sanctions not only on the country but on anyone trading with them, thus complicating commercial relations. The designation was aimed primarily, if not entirely, at courting conservative Cuban American voters in Florida, whom Trump viewed as loyal supporters.[6] Crafting Cuba policy to please that audience dated back to the 1980s.

This was a situation with which Cuba was deeply familiar. In 2018, Miguel Díaz-Canel became president of the Council of State and the Council of Ministers, which is Cuba's executive. Fidel was gone and Raúl Castro, at age eighty-seven, transitioned to secretary of the Communist Party. Being twenty-nine years younger than Raúl, Díaz-Canel brought the Castros' long-standing message to Twitter for the first time. Instead of hours-long speeches a la Fidel, Díaz-Canel tweeted about Donald Trump's message being "arrogant, cynical, immoral, offensive, interventionist, hypocritical, war-like, and dirty" (Díaz-Canel 2019). Cuba and Venezuela, tight for years, became even more close.

Despite its historically close relationship with Cuba and its new one with Venezuela, Russia never became a significant part of Latin American autonomy more broadly. In 2016, the Russian government published its "Foreign Policy Concept of the Russian Federation," a sprawling document outlining Russia's global position (Embassy of the Russian Federation 2016). It did mention "comprehensive strengthening of relations" with Latin America, though it focused largely on multilateral organizations like CELAC. While it marketed its COVID-19 vaccines, trade remained modest, and Russia did not follow China's strategy of engaging (and spending) across the entire hemisphere. Vladimir Putin's gaze was aimed primarily at Cuba and Venezuela, with some interest in Nicaragua given not only its historical ideological connection from the Cold War, but also because under Daniel Ortega, it had evolved into the type of authoritarian and anti-US government that Putin appreciated. Russia did not have the resources or indeed even sufficient interest to become a serious competitor to the United States in most of the region. It did view Cuba as a traditional ally, but the times of pouring resources into it were old history.

The US approach to Cuba remained idiosyncratic and largely self-defeating. In 2016 the Obama administration chose to abstain from the annual vote in the

United Nations condemning the embargo on Cuba, demonstrating support for the notion that the embargo was not a useful policy and a slap at Congress for not repealing it.[7] That was a major shift because it is obviously unusual for a country not to oppose a resolution criticizing its own laws. Not surprisingly, the Trump administration reversed that choice in 2017 and went back to the vote the United States had cast for almost a quarter-century before that. Again, the rationale was domestic politics, a way to show conservative Cuban Americans that the administration would reject everything about the Cuban government.

The Cuban case is an example of policy continuity. The core of the embargo remained firmly in place no matter who was US president, and Cuba remained defiant. Yet in some cases, the rise of Donald Trump yielded unexpected foreign policy shifts within Latin America. Brazil and Mexico, historically fiercely independent, showed an obeisance in place of foreign policy entrepreneurship. Neither one challenged Trump administration initiatives.

BRAZIL: AUTONOMY REVERSAL

Brazil serves as a vivid reminder that presidential changes can presage major shifts in foreign policy and interest in autonomy as a goal. Lula's cabinet member and chosen successor, Dilma Rousseff, was elected in 2010 and won re-election in 2014. As time went on, however, the economy sagged and she faced charges related to the accounting of her 2014 campaign. Through 2015 and 2016, she was impeached by the Chamber of Deputies and then convicted in the Senate. The evidence was thin, and the entire process tended to work more like a no-confidence vote than a presentation of evidence for impeachment.[8] Indeed, many lawmakers cited the infamous "Lava Jato" corruption investigations even though her name was not linked to them (Burges and Chaga Bastos 2016).[9] She labeled her removal a "coup" but did not contest the result, choosing instead later to run (unsuccessfully) for the Senate.

Vice President Michel Temer took over and for his entire truncated term was dogged by corruption charges, as he was clearly tied to Lava Jato in a way Rousseff was not (he was in fact arrested after leaving office). His foreign policy was antagonistic toward governments Lula had favored, and he reconsidered Lula's regional policies (Marcondes and Mawdsley 2017). Temer had no interest in countering US influence and for the most part worked on cost-cutting measures the United States supported. Lula's initiatives fell from sight.

The 2018 presidential election was controversial and contentious. Lula, still a popular political icon, was in prison on corruption charges and not allowed to run. The Worker's Party candidate Fernando Haddad lost to Jair Bolsonaro, a member of the Chamber of Deputies who ran a campaign eerily but also self-consciously similar to Donald Trump's. His message was unabashedly nationalist, racist, homophobic, and authoritarian.

Bolsonaro's foreign policy made a drastic turn toward the United States, and Trump in particular. He prioritized aligning Brazil with the United States with regard to recognizing Jerusalem as the capital of Israel, and he rejected the Paris Agreement on climate change, for example. His style was even similar, as he casually offended other presidents (most notably France). He professed an antiglobalist worldview, replete with conspiracy theories about climate change and other "hoaxes." Two of his first three trips abroad were to Israel and the United States. He showed no interest in continuing the Brazilian tradition of exerting leadership in South America.

At times, even sovereignty gave way to signaling support for the United States. In 2019, Bolsonaro announced he was open to the idea of having a US military presence if necessary, which alarmed his own military, especially in the context of the Venezuelan crisis (Brooks and Paraguassu 2019). This is the sort of thing no one would ever expect to hear coming from the mouth of a Brazilian president, but there it was.

An even more head-turning shift came from Andrés Manuel López Obrador (AMLO) in Mexico. In 2017, a year before he was elected, he published a book, *Oye Trump* (Listen Up Trump in English) and even presented it to audiences in the United States. Speculation ran wild on both sides of the border about what direction US-Mexican relations would take. He had a pugnacious tone, which when combined with traditional Mexican suspicion of the United States, suggested a rough bilateral relationship. But there was something else at play as well. Former Obama official Mark Feierstein said he had heard

Trump refer to AMLO as "Juan Trump," a Mexican version of himself (Tan 2018). AMLO's critics accused him of authoritarian tendencies like Trump's. AMLO actually felt compelled to say, "We're not authoritarian," in a press conference in response to a letter signed by 650 intellectuals, artists, and others who accused him of trying to limit freedom of expression (*El Universal* 2020).

AMLO's foreign policy toward Latin America was hesitant. Mexico's immigration policy toward Central America traditionally was aggressive even while the government publicly complained of how Mexicans were treated at the northern border. Yet under AMLO, Mexico accepted US demands without complaint. In early 2019, the Trump administration implemented the Migration Protection Protocols (MPP), which became popularly known as the "Remain in Mexico" policy. The policy stipulated that anyone hoping to cross the US-Mexico border to seek asylum would be required to stay in Mexico while US courts decided their fate. For months or years, they faced harsh conditions in unfamiliar areas. By 2020, only 4 percent even had access to legal representation, less than 1 percent had been granted asylum, and almost a thousand reported kidnapping, rape, torture, or assault while they waited (Human Rights Watch 2020). Part of AMLO's response was to demand the resignation of the commissioner of the National Institute of Migration and replace him with someone who had spent the bulk of his career as an administrator of prisons, even while framing his acceptance of Trump's policy as seeking a humanitarian solution to the migration crisis (Gutiérrez 2020).

AMLO remained a firm admirer of his US counterpart, going so far as to say that Trump had been good for Mexico (Domínguez 2021). It seemed rather that Trump had been good for *him* politically, insofar as Trump never criticized AMLO for corruption, for example, or for his opposition to renewable energy. AMLO navigated around Trump's foreign policy, accepting what he couldn't change and appreciating US lack of interest in Mexican governance. Trump also remained quiet as AMLO courted China for COVID-19 vaccines. Through the pandemic, Mexico's trade with the United States dipped while China's rose. Mexico renegotiated NAFTA but never lost sight of China, something that the Trump administration was helpless to stop.

At the end of Trump's presidency, the Mexican and Brazilian presidents shared the dubious distinction of being the only Latin American presidents not to congratulate Joe Biden and recognize his 2020 election victory, preferring to wait until Trump's string of unsuccessful and conspiracy-laden electoral lawsuits ended. By mid-November, only they, along with the Russian and North Korean dictatorships, still refused to acknowledge Biden's win. That fact highlighted the historically unprecedented deference to a US leader, to the point of tacitly accepting an outlandish and clearly fictitious narrative about voter fraud. Such admiration reached absurdist peaks, such as when Jair Bolsonaro's son Eduardo put Trump's face on his Twitter account to protest "TWITTER'S AUTHORITARY [sic] ACTS," referring to Twitter banning the US president from its platform (Bolsonaro 2021). They were all in for Trump.

During the Trump administration, Central American governments also faced intense, even overwhelming pressure to accept harsh US immigration policies. In 2019 the US government announced the negotiation of "asylum cooperative agreements" with Guatemala, El Salvador, and Honduras. Their purpose was to send asylum seekers to those countries rather than allow them to enter the United States. The US Department of Homeland Security (2019) claimed the intent was to "allow migrants to seek protection within the region," even though, of course, their original goal had been to leave the region. Guatemala implemented the agreement and El Salvador announced its intent to do so in 2020, but the Biden administration quickly suspended the program and began a process to terminate it.

US pressure prompted Mexico and Central American countries to use their militaries to stop migrants from moving northward. Threatened with tariffs, the Mexican government deployed its military to the Guatemala border when so-called "caravans" of Central American migrants arrived there. They would wait with riot gear to repel those migrants, even though the Mexico-Guatemala border is more than five hundred miles long, so the long-term impact of such high-profile measures is doubtful. In the last days of the Trump administration, Guatemalan president Alejandro Giammattei declared a state of emergency and sent soldiers and police to the border. The Guatemalan military continued this kind of work after Joe Biden became president. The Guatemalan government preferred accepting lack of autonomy than antagonizing the United States.

US influence in Central America is also notable with regard to corruption.

Guatemalan elites felt squeezed by the United Nations' International Commission against Impunity in Guatemala (CICIG), which had been a Bush-era creation. Similarly, in 2016 the Organization of American States sponsored an anticorruption initiative in Honduras, called the Support Mission Against Corruption and Impunity in Honduras (MACCIH). Although its mandate was narrower than CICIG (for example, it relied more on the executive branch and was only an advisory body) it uncovered considerable wrongdoing on the part of Honduran elites (Perelló 2020). Those elites predictably wanted it gone, and with Trump in office they felt no external pressure to renew MACCIH's mandate when it expired in early 2020. The inclinations of the US president were central to the very existence of independent anticorruption commissions in Central America. Support served as pressure to political elites, while signals of a lack of interest prompted quick demolishing of anticorruption institutions and threats against prosecutors.

THE IMPACT OF COVID-19

COVID-19 was first identified in Wuhan, China, in December 2019, and by March 2020 it had compelled countries to impose lockdowns and close their borders. Like the rest of the world, Latin Americans watched in alarm as the virus spread through their communities and overwhelmed their already badly strained health care systems. The impact of COVID-19 on Latin America was quickly devastating. By the latter half of 2020, the region had 28 percent of the world's cases and 34 percent of deaths, while only constituting 8.2 percent of the world's population (IMFBlog 2020). That led to a GDP contraction of 8.1 percent over the year prior. With large informal economies, weak safety nets, and poorly resourced health care systems, people defied lockdown orders in order to survive. Tens of millions of jobs were lost, and recovery was slow.

The impact on Latin American–US relations followed a similar pattern as the first three years of the administration. By and large, the Trump administration sent financial and/or material aid while simultaneously maintaining a highly public skepticism and even hostility toward basic precautions such as wearing masks to prevent spread.[10] Billions were made available to the region through the Inter-American Development Bank, the Development Bank of Latin America, the World Bank, and the International Monetary Fund, in addition to more direct government aid (Congressional Research Service 2021).

COVID-19 did, however, show that opportunities for greater autonomy do not necessarily yield results. There was no coordination, and neighboring countries squabbled. The Trump administration left a leadership vacuum that no one moved to fill. When Jair Bolsonaro contracted the virus in 2020, Argentine president Alberto Fernández sent a message wishing him well but he also poked Bolsonaro with "the virus does not distinguish rulers from the ruled" (Berti 2020). Argentina had locked down, whereas Brazil remained more open, with the president contemptuous of safety measures. López Obrador shared much the same attitude, which put both leaders right alongside Donald Trump. The Organization of American States opened an information portal on its website and issued various proclamations, but it had no noticeable influence on national policies.

Importantly, the virus also served to deepen bilateral ties with China throughout the region. In July 2020, the Chinese and Mexican foreign ministers copresided over a virtual meeting, attended by their counterparts from across the region. Foreigner Minister Wang Yi told the group that China would provide access to the vaccine it was developing (Gobierno de México 2020). China sent masks, ventilators, test kits, and other COVID-related medical supplies. The Chinese government also participated in CELAC meetings to discuss the epidemic. Nicolás Maduro talked of help from the Russians, but that assistance was not region-wide like China's.[11] On the other hand, COVID-19's economic effects did bring Chinese development loans to a halt in 2020, for the first time in fifteen years (Goodman 2021).

The US response was to declare that it would not join a global effort to create and distribute a vaccine because President Trump believed the World Health Organization, which coordinated it, was too "China-centric" (Rauhala and Abutaleb 2020). The clear irony was that avoiding a supposedly "China-centric" organization led to enhanced Chinese influence on Latin America. The United States did send aid to individual countries, for example through the US Agency for International Development, but chose not to spearhead any regional response or to assume a leadership position in the hemisphere. The playing field was left open for China and to a lesser extent India and Russia. These countries had vaccines available, and Latin American governments were interested in both. India, for example, sent vaccines to Argentina, Brazil, and Mexico (Seshasayee 2021).[12] US companies producing vaccines, such as Pfizer, offered vaccines for sale, but no Latin American country looked exclusively at the United States. There was plenty of competition, often with lower costs. The United States was not a leader in this area. In fact, although US-produced vaccines were available privately, the US government itself provided no vaccines to Latin America, and would not do so until several months after Biden took office.

After Trump left office, the Biden administration did try to reassert itself vis-à-vis China with vaccines. For example, it encouraged Paraguay to obtain vaccines through Taiwan (Reuters 2021). Since Paraguay was one of only fifteen countries in the world to maintain diplomatic relations, Taiwan jumped at the opportunity. In 2017, Panama switched its recognition from Taiwan to China as Chinese investment grew. El Salvador and the Dominican Republic followed in 2018. These shifts were a major diplomatic victory for China, which promised large infrastructure projects through its Belt and Road Initiative. Vaccine diplomacy (or more accurately the lack thereof) therefore represented another way that Donald Trump's presidency accelerated the long-standing trend toward deeper Latin American ties to China. Latin American governments needed vaccines badly and quickly, so US reluctance meant almost instant turns elsewhere.

China's activity coexisted with Donald Trump's indifference to the point that in late 2020, an Argentine official said, "I think China has more interest in Argentina than the United States has in Argentina. And that is what makes the difference. Trump did not show any interest" (Garrison 2020). China's interest was comprehensive and even intricate, dividing Latin America into ten categories based on the nature of the relationship (Myers and Barrios 2021). Seven countries are at the top with "comprehensive strategic partnerships."[13] The lowest level is reserved for countries that recognize Taiwan. China's strategy is to push revocation of that recognition as a precondition for relations. The gradations are fine enough to include both "friendly" and "friendly cooperative." Cuba enjoyed the status of "good brother, good comrade, good friend." The exact nature of these categories is not easy to pin down, but China had far more detailed strategies and plans for Latin America than Trump ever did.

As the nonpartisan Congressional Research Service (2020) reported, China had become the top trading partner of Brazil, Chile, Peru, and Uruguay and was the second largest trading partner for most other countries. Chinese banks had become the largest lenders to the region, and the top recipients—Argentina, Brazil, Ecuador, and Venezuela—followed no particular ideological proclivity. Politicians from across the political spectrum worked closely with China, sometimes more closely than with the United States. Even Jair Bolsonaro, who openly admired and emulated Donald Trump and his anti-China stance, walked a fine line. For example, he simultaneously criticized the Chinese Huawei telecommunications company (claiming it stole data) and courted access to China's large agricultural market and its broadband capabilities (Moak 2020).

When Trump left office in January 2021, his successor, Joseph Biden Jr., faced what Azpuru (2021) called a "different Latin America."[14] Trust in the United States had dropped in eleven out of seventeen Latin American countries compared to when Biden left office as vice president in 2017. To add insult to injury, trust in China had increased as compared to the United States. Again, this trend did not begin with Trump, but he exacerbated it. China's trade relationship with Latin America was strong and not likely reversible, while it also gradually gained trust.

Nonetheless, not everything was coming up roses, as positive Latin American relations with China did face obstacles. The most serious revolved around fishing. Chinese ships made their way some nine thousand-plus miles to the western side of South America, turned off their tracking systems, and fished illegally, mostly for squid (Agence France-Presse 2020). The Ecuadorian government complained, which prompted Beijing to ban ships from going there, but the problem persisted elsewhere. In 2020, Chile, Colombia, Ecuador, and Peru issued a joint statement condemning the practice, "to prevent, discourage and jointly confront" illegal fishing (MercoPress 2020). In late 2021, Colombia, Costa Rica, Ecuador, and Panama signed an agreement to protect their exclusive economic zones (EEZ), the areas over which states have rights. It is a high-profile and unresolved issue.

Latin Americans also showed concern about increased economic dependence on China. Giraudo (2020) points to China's expansion of influence over different stages of soybean production, which is an important South American crop. That effort includes buying or leasing land and using its market share as leverage for other issues (such as diplomatic recognition or preferential access for Chinese companies). In 2020, the chair of the Brazil Foreign Trade Association lamented that "there was already a dependency on China, which has increased. The market for manufactured products in Brazil, South America, and Argentina is in crisis" (Brazilian Report 2020).

This perception pricked the cultivated image of the Chinese government as more strings-free than the United States. The basic skeptical view of the United States, such as that found in most variations of dependency theory, was of a rapacious and profit-driven state uninterested in the sovereignty of other states. China's own actions seemed simply to replicate that model. Laufer (2020) writes that Latin American countries did not experience any change to their socioeconomic structures, so using the phrase "heterodox autonomy" a la Puig was inaccurate because the international division of labor remained intact. Nonetheless, Latin America did see more freedom of movement from the United States. The question was whether that autonomy benefited Latin Americans in concrete ways. It's open for debate.

Toward the end of the Trump administration, the US International Development Finance Corporation partnered with Ecuadorian president Lenín Moreno to help the country repay billions of dollars of Chinese loans in return for excluding Chinese companies from telecom work (Sevastopulo and Long 2021). This was a drop in the financial bucket, but it marked a long-delayed realization in the US government that it was no longer the go-to source of resources.

The structure of Ecuador's economy did not change, but greater autonomy meant it could play the field. Since the Ecuadorian government could reach out to China without incurring US wrath, then it could also play one side off the other for economic or political gain. From Moreno's perspective, the deal allowed him to send a negative signal to China about its fishing practices and was consistent with his general strategy of shifting away from Rafael Correa's wholehearted embrace of China. Ecuador's stance toward the United States and China was strongly correlated to whether the president leaned left or right.

A notable pattern in recent years is that Latin American leaders are not looking for regional options. Moving away from the United States tended to mean bilateral agreements with new countries rather than moving toward each other. Quirós (2017) points to an impasse in what she calls the posthegemonic, postliberal era, where there was an opening for greater regional integration but too many obstacles were in the way. One of these obstacles was Brazil, where political and economic crisis under Dilma Rousseff made regional leadership even less likely, and then later Bolsonaro's lack of interest and proclivity for insults meant Brazil would not serve in any regional leadership capacity. Venezuela was no longer in a position to be a leftist leader either. No other government took up the slack.

Further, China did not consciously contribute to Latin American autonomy. Its foreign policy was not ideological in any left-right sense, so it forged agreements and formed partnerships as it deemed strategically useful. But the Chinese leadership did not encourage or facilitate any regional counterbalance to the United States and had no interest in creating any broad alliance that the United States might view as a security threat. Instead, Latin American countries needed to take advantage of whatever autonomy China helped generate. Yet despite indifference from the Trump administration, regional unity did not manifest itself, and no government stepped forward to push it.

Ideological divides continued to serve as obstacles as well. Although Cuba continued to tout the value of ALBA and CELAC, they were clearly never going to be vehicles for integration. CELAC did continue meeting, though calls for a "Common Front" to forge a unified solution to corruption (ironically called by Mexico) and criticisms of neoliberalism did not go much beyond rhetoric (Infobae 2020). Meanwhile, Brazil pulled out of the organization in 2020. Alvarez (2021, 56) point to the declining interest/ability of Brazil and Venezuela as an essential reason: "post-hegemonic proposals lose dynamism and support once the regional leadership responsible for promoting them weaken."

TRADE AS A VEHICLE FOR AUTONOMY

One of Donald Trump's signature campaign promises was to renegotiate NAFTA because he claimed it had been unfair to the United States. He kept the promise by completing a replacement deal in 2019, which was ratified in 2020. It had the less than mellifluous name of United States-Mexico-Canada Agreement (USMCA).[15] The Trump administration touted its improvements, noting among other things better copyright protections, better access of US cheeses to Mexico (dairy was a point Trump brought up repeatedly), more efficient customs rules, fewer restrictions on US financial services suppliers, and new rules on how goods are sourced (United States Department of Commerce n.d.). At the time of the signing, AMLO praised the new agreement and also the US president, saying on his website that Trump had been "prudent and tolerant," intervening when understanding seemed far away (AMLO 2019).

The concrete impacts of the USMCA will take time to assess. But as Mexican academics pointed out, its core tenets contradicted the open regionalist approach being encouraged by the United Nations Economic Commission for Latin America and the Caribbean (Acua Popocatl, Gómez, and Bautista 2020). That approach involved greater attention to regional accords. Bilateral rather than regional strategies were also evident, however, for Central America, Chile, Colombia, and Peru, all of which also implemented free trade agreements with the United States. Those governments could still look to other countries for other trade opportunities (Chile is particularly active in this regard), but a regional agreement remained a remote possibility.

AMLO moved slowly to implement labor rights components of USMCA (Felbab-Brown 2020). The Trump administration, never much interested in the topic, did not push him on it, but the incoming administration signaled that it would. The Biden administration looked favorably at the USMCA and included some of the people who helped craft it, but it is too early to know how hard the administration will push AMLO to implement it.[16] We will need years to ascertain the impact of the changes to NAFTA and, like the original agreement, "where you stand depends on where you sit." That is, trade agreements do not affect a country in a singular manner. Their impact is mediated by many factors, such as geography or types of industries and workers.

DRUG POLICY

Drug policy under the Trump administration continued with the Obama administration's gradually increased emphasis on treatment rather than interdiction. As with so many things, Trump himself seemed indifferent to the details of antinarcotics policy, with the exception of touting his border wall as a deterrent and periodically tweeting insults at individual countries. In a visit to the Mexico-Texas border right before he left office, he bragged that drug smuggling had plummeted "in every region we've built the wall" (White House 2021). The fact that drugs typically come through established border crossings rather than open space did not bother him. For example, the vast majority of opioids go through land border crossings (of which there are forty-eight across the country), typically hidden in cars and trucks (Isacson 2017). Drugs come through doors, not walls.

In 2017, a bipartisan law created the Western Hemisphere Drug Policy Commission, which was to assess US antinarcotics policies and make recommendations for the future. The commission, composed of experienced analysts, released a report in late 2020. Its core recommendations entailed eliminating the controversial drug certification process, making greater use of the State Department to coordinate "whole-of-government" policies, and to establish clear metrics to determine whether a given policy was succeeding (Western Hemisphere Drug Policy Commission 2020). The report emphasized working with civil society in Latin American countries to determine what policies might in fact be counterproductive (e.g., aerial spraying in Colombia). It was also blunt at times, such as criticizing former Guatemalan president Jimmy Morales for shutting down CICIG in 2019 (Western Hemisphere Drug Policy Commission 2020, 67). When he found himself accused of corruption, he decided CICIG was a threat to the country.

Overall, the report called for significant policy shifts. A Colombian presidential advisor asserted that the government was already working toward the report's recommendations, especially in focusing on economic development in highly affected rural areas (*El Nuevo Día* 2020). Reality on the ground called that into question because the government's peace accord with the FARC was shaky, uncertain, and unpopular with Trump administration officials. State presence in rural Colombia remains minimal and land ownership is highly concentrated, which represents a serious obstacle to providing land for the internally displaced and generating real peace and economic development (Ahumada 2020).

Latin America saw prominent calls for decriminalization of narcotics, especially from former presidents. Juan Manuel Santos (Colombia) and Ernesto Zedillo (Mexico) coauthored an op-ed to argue that the drug war was "futile" and governments needed to take more control over the market (Santos, Zedillo, and Dreifuss 2019). That built on past public statements by Cesar Gaviria (Colombia) and Fernando Henrique Cardoso (Brazil). Vicente Fox (Mexico) supported legal use of marijuana. Even Otto Pérez Molina, the hardline president of Guatemala from 2012 to 2015, favored legalization. The use of medical marijuana is legal in eight countries, while Uruguay legalized recreational use in 2013. Other countries have moved in the same direction.

Public presidential support for recreational use initially remained largely confined to former presidents because it meant going out on a limb, and the US government was vocally opposed (though US governors were signing similar policies into law). Despite minimal gains in the "war on drugs," both Republican and Democratic administrations preferred tweaking the status quo rather than seeking substantial reform. Further, there was no regional consensus about the issue, either at the elite or popular levels. Lastly, outside powers like China or Europe had no incentive to become involved with such a touchy issue.

The US government remained opposed to decriminalization. Under Obama, Vice President Joe Biden was a drug war hawk, favoring more militarized solutions—such as Plan Colombia—and vocally opposing decriminalization. The Trump administration was even more opposed, and in 2017 even threatened to decertify Colombia as a partner in fighting drug trafficking, which would have entailed cuts in aid, which as we saw in the last chapter already happened to Bolivia. President Santos pushed back, saying that it was a "shared responsibility" that must also be borne by drug-consuming countries like the United States (Inzunza 2017).

Even AMLO pushed back, even while accepting many US demands on immigration. He insisted that his government would focus on corruption rather than using the military and police to combat drug traffickers. Mexico's relationship with the US Drug Enforcement Agency—often controversial—frayed more. Overall, AMLO seemed to distrust US technology and even its motives, given how broad US training (including police, prosecutors, and prison officials) had become (Sheridan and Miroff 2022). Around 2019, just after AMLO took office, is when the smuggling of the highly addictive drug fentanyl increased. Previously, most fentanyl came from China, but in 2019 the Chinese government officially labeled it as a class of drugs, which then led to greater enforcement. Mexican cartels shifted from transshipment to more production.

The radical, anti-US streak in Latin America had ebbed. Rhetoric in that vein came predictably from Cuba and Venezuela, but was less common elsewhere. Take Luis Arce, who served as Evo Morales's finance minister and was elected president in 2020. In that capacity, he was viewed as pragmatic, and once he became president he talked favorably about working with the United States. The Latin American left has never been uniformly antagonistic toward the United States, but the higher levels of vitriol from the 2000s was now mostly gone. The result was that the appetite for intentionally excluding the United States was mostly absent.

As Donald Trump left office, Latin America had more autonomy from the United States than perhaps at any time in its history. Its ability to negotiate and maintain diplomatic and economic relations with extra-hemispheric powers was broad. China's economic and diplomatic reach was vastly expanded since the century began. Across the region, it reached a status of "privileged relation" (Laufer 2020). The United States expressed alarm at China's presence but was slow to articulate any way to limit its growth that went beyond rhetoric.

There were limits. US power and influence certainly had not disappeared. Especially in Central America and Mexico, the Trump administration successfully forced governments to take actions they otherwise almost certainly would not have undertaken. Autonomy was connected to geography. Smaller, closer, and more economically dependent countries had less leeway, though not none. Argentina, where the concept had been developed, was far away and more autonomous.

China's position had substantial roots and it was no longer the outsider it had once been. Wise (2020, 240) argued that the "big China boom is over," though COVID-19 demonstrated that such a conclusion is complicated. To be sure, loans and investment fell, but vaccine diplomacy was front and center. Latin America's economies struggled, but there were other ways China remained engaged. The US response often was to criticize China's approach as detrimental, but the United States was slow to offer concrete alternatives.

Donald Trump did leave office, but only reluctantly. He left a legacy of insults, unpredictability, and punitive measures. The next chapter examines that legacy and how the Biden administration dealt with it even as he faced severe problems, which included a global pandemic of staggering magnitude. Re-establishing more positive relations and reducing the Latin American impetus to seek extra-hemispheric partners was a priority, but a tall order.

7. THE EMBRACE OF AUTONOMY CONTINUES (2021–2023)

WHEN DONALD TRUMP LEFT office in January 2021, increased Latin American autonomy was evident across most of the region, though unevenly. The Trump years had left a clear sense in the region that the United States could no longer be counted on. Long-standing agreements might be discarded and promises ignored. The administration was openly, and even proudly, hostile, dismissive, and arrogant. That simply deepened Latin American policy makers' commitment to reaching out more to the world outside the hemisphere. Trump accelerated the Latin American embrace of autonomy, albeit unwittingly.

Joe Biden took office in early 2021 amidst a global pandemic, false claims of electoral fraud, and an increasingly antidemocratic right wing, which meant his most pressing immediate issues were domestic. Nonetheless, Biden had extensive foreign policy experience and interest to draw upon. He was first elected to the US Senate from Delaware in 1972 and started serving on the Senate Foreign Relations Committee in 1997. He chaired that committee from 2001 to 2003 and from 2007 to 2009. Biden was a strong supporter of Plan Colombia, and in 2000 wrote a report to the committee arguing not only for the aid package, but also noting that he had suggested to the Colombian people that they hold a referendum "in which they will vote for a change for honesty and transparency in the way of doing politics" and claiming that more than 90 percent of Colombians supported that initiative (United States Senate 2002b). Offering friendly advice to a country about which he had mostly superficial knowledge was consistent with anyone who had been immersed in the US foreign policy establishment for decades.

Nonetheless, he was known as someone who paid attention to and was interested in Latin American politics, albeit with a hawkish edge. Just as Latin American–US relations improved when Barack Obama replaced George W. Bush, Biden was a relief after Donald Trump, judging both by public opinion polls and the enthusiastic reaction by Latin American presidents (Gedan 2021). But times had changed in the four years since he had been vice president. There was more pushback than ever, from across the region.

Biden was immediately confronted with crises on multiple fronts, all of which impacted Latin America in some way. Given its severity, the pandemic was especially pressing. Shortly after Biden assumed the presidency, the United States reached 900,000 deaths from COVID-19, with more than two million worldwide. Around the same time in 2021, after years of tension and violence, Russia sent troops to its border with Ukraine, demanding that it never become a member of the North Atlantic Treaty Organization (NATO). Russia invaded Ukraine in February 2022.

Biden faced domestic political insurrection that impacted the entire region. He took office just two weeks after January 6, 2021, when Trump cheered on his supporters as they assaulted the Capitol building in Washington, DC, which reverberated in Latin America and brought to mind similar coup attempts in the region's history. As three Latin American analysts put it, "For Latin America, and for Central America specifically, this episode signifies the rupture of the myth of democratic exceptionalism in the United States. It reveals US fissures and defects that are characteristic of the hemisphere's weakest democracies" (Sánchez, Kerche, and De Gori 2021). The Venezuelan government issued a statement, mirroring the routine type of rhetoric the US government typically uses, indicating its "concern" with the violence in Washington, DC, and how it "condemns the political polarization and spiral of violence" (Gobierno Bolivariano de Venezuela 2021). The United States, it added, "suffers the same that it has generated in other countries with its policies of aggression" (Gobierno Bolivariano de Venezuela 2021).

That political crisis carried with it echoes of the 2008 economic crash, when the US government chose not to take the austerity path it forced on Latin

American countries in the 1980s. The US government traditionally held itself up as a model (even if it chose to ignore its own democratic deficiencies, especially with regard to slavery and segregation), but a coup attempt made that difficult, if not impossible. The United States was struggling to keep its own democracy alive, just like many other countries.

Biden became president in a regional political context that had shifted just in the four years of the Trump presidency. Even in Central America, long an area where US power and influence was deep and long-standing, presidents pushed boundaries. For example, the Biden administration held a global Summit for Democracy in Washington, DC, in late 2021. The usual suspects of Cuba and Venezuela were not invited. But Salvadoran president Nayib Bukele was not invited either, nor were the presidents of Bolivia, Guatemala, Honduras, or Nicaragua.

That came not long after Bukele announced that bitcoin would become an official currency alongside the US dollar. Such a move could potentially be seen as a major step toward autonomy, because people could conduct business of any kind in a nondollar currency. Bukele had dreams of making El Salvador a tourist destination where bitcoin payments were the norm.

US policy makers opposed the move, and they made that known. In 2022, Senators Jim Risch (R-Idaho) and Bob Menendez (D-NJ) introduced the Accountability for Cryptocurrency in El Salvador (ACES) Act, which would require the State Department to analyze El Salvador's decision and "the risks for cybersecurity, economic stability, and democratic governance in El Salvador" (United States Senate Committee on Foreign Relations 2022). Bukele (2022) responded on Twitter by using the popular "OK boomers" insult and telling them to stay out of El Salvador's affairs. From the Salvadoran perspective, this was the usual kind of US interference, questioning internal decisions and seeking to impose punishment for what seemed out of line with US interests. Even the word "accountability" explicitly referred to the US government judging Salvadoran decisions.

That legislative push in the United States came just as doubts arose about whether bitcoin was even taking root in El Salvador. A national survey in early 2022 revealed that only 20 percent of Salvadoran firms accepted bitcoin, despite its status as official currency (Alvarez, Argente, and Van Patten 2022).

Firms that did were typically large, while more educated, banked, younger, and male Salvadorans were the most likely to use the technology. That profile represented only a small sliver of the population. Many people downloaded the required "Chivo Wallet" because doing so guaranteed the government would send you $30 (approximately 0.7 percent of annual income per capita), but 60 percent did not use the wallet after spending the bonus. The government revealed that in January 2022, only 1.8 percent of remittances came through bitcoin, and then announced that data from September 2021 through January 2022 was confidential (Agencia EFE 2022). Meanwhile, credit raters downgraded the country, sparking fears of default. Thus there were signs that hype and reality were not necessarily meeting.

Whether or not that trend continues remains to be seen, but it highlights the limits to Bukele's quest for financial autonomy. US pressure is a constant challenge, of course, but those limits come from within as well. Salvadorans are accustomed to conducting their business in cash, which for two decades has been officially been the US dollar. Doing so in a digital form that relatively few people are fully conversant with is a hard sell.

With regard to autonomy, Bukele's courting of China, Russia, and Turkey and his use of Twitter to criticize US policy are, according to one Salvadoran scholar, "audacious and risky," as they show how much Bukele is willing to do to demonstrate his independence from US influence (Hernández 2022). In late 2021, the Biden administration imposed sanctions on two Salvadoran officials for their role in negotiating a truce with gangs, and others were sanctioned for corruption. Further, the International Monetary Fund, over which the US has considerable influence, delayed a roughly $1 billion loan after the announcement about bitcoin. These US responses certainly have impact, but not enough to derail Bukele's quest for greater autonomy.

Its neighbor Nicaragua was in an unusual position. The government of Daniel Ortega had destroyed democratic institutions in the country and as a result faced targeted sanctions from the United States. The Organization of American States's Inter-American Commission on Human Rights issued a report in October 2021 detailing abuses and concluding that Ortega's goal was "indefinite perpetuation in power and maintenance of privileges and immunities, in a context of repression, corruption, electoral fraud, and structural impunity" (Inter-American Commission on Human Rights 2021, 10–11). This was no diplomatic mincing of words, and within a few months the government announced it was leaving the OAS.

Nicaragua, however, remained a member of the Central America Free Trade Agreement and routinely ran a trade surplus with the United States. In 2021, it was $2.5 billion and into 2022 showed the same pattern (United States Census Bureau 2022). Indeed, the last time the United States had a surplus was in 1995. Nicaragua's trade with the United States is an essential component of its economy, so in fact US consumers (especially when they bought clothing) were helping keep Daniel Ortega on an even economic keel. Unlike Cuba or Venezuela, Ortega did not deal with negative effects of radical autonomy despite his antagonism.

Indeed, Ortega even reached out openly to China. In late 2021, he broke off relations with Taiwan and seized its embassy, announcing that his government recognized China. That came after the Nicaraguan government had flirted for years with a Chinese billionaire to build a canal, harking back to the country's dreams in the nineteenth century. The project has yet to go anywhere, and for now there are no signs that it will.

In this context, in 2021 President Biden signed the RENACER Act, the stated intent of which was to "To advance the strategic alignment of US diplomatic tools toward the realization of free, fair, and transparent elections in Nicaragua and to reaffirm the commitment of the United States to protect the fundamental freedoms and human rights of the people of Nicaragua, and for other purposes" (Congress.gov 2021–2022). It included targeted sanctions, coordination with diplomatic partners, and the production of a variety of reports, including Russian activities. But it also called for reviewing Nicaragua's continued participation in the Dominican Republic–Central America Free Trade Agreement (DR-CAFTA). As of this writing, the Biden administration had not made such a review, at least not publicly.

At least for the time being, then, Nicaragua was in the unique situation of ignoring the United States with both domestic and foreign policy, while the retaliation it received from the United States was clearly bearable. Under both Republican and Democratic presidents, the US response was gradual and did not involve armed force. The primary kind of pressure consisted of sanctions, which in the Nicaraguan case have yet to expand beyond individuals. As in Cuba and Venezuela, US sanctions negatively impacted the average citizen but did not change regime behavior or effect prompt regime change.

CHINA'S CONTINUED ROLE

China remained a voracious consumer of Latin American raw materials. Excluding Mexico, which increased its trade with the United States, Chinese trade with Latin America by the end of 2021 was roughly $100 billion more than that of the United States (Jourdan, Aquino, and Spetalnick 2022). China was the largest trading partner with the vast majority of South American countries, with the exceptions of Colombia, Ecuador, and Paraguay. This was neither new nor surprising. China was willing to invest billions in infrastructure to facilitate its consumption, and for Latin America, that money was not easily available elsewhere.

China has gradually extended its cultural connections across Latin America as a way to improve its image, but even after years of engagement, these remain nascent and cautious. Vaccines certainly constitute an important example. Nonetheless, given regional polls showing more negative responses to China's political influence, Chinese gains seem limited (Ellis et al. 2022). By 2022, China had established Confucius Institutes in twenty-three Latin American and Caribbean countries, largely (like elsewhere in the world) at universities. Their essential goal is to increase familiarity with Chinese language and culture, though their impact remains more assumed or asserted than actually measured.[1]

When he came to office, Biden identified China as the key challenge for US foreign policy, but he soft-pedaled the issue in Latin America. His administration sensed correctly that although many Latin American leaders had specific concerns about China's actions, that was far from identifying it as a threat. The rhetoric from US administrations about the threat of China does not resonate in the region. So, for example, when Secretary of State Antony Blinken traveled to several Latin American countries in late 2022, he publicly criticized Russia but not China. In any case, those in the United States who view China's role with alarm do not have much in the way of specific recommendations for countering it. Into the foreseeable future, China represents an avenue for greater Latin American autonomy from the United States. The extent to which that generates political or economic dependence will certainly be the topic of future research projects.

RUSSIA'S INVASION OF UKRAINE AND LATIN AMERICAN REACTION

Russia's invasion of Ukraine revealed the complexity of Latin American foreign policy autonomy. Over the years, Russia did make diplomatic inroads with a handful of countries—especially those who were more hostile toward US policy—and there was still plenty of Latin American skepticism about US policy. Yet the invasion itself called up images of past US imperialism, with use of armed force, occupation, and political demands. Even the Cuban government, which was close to Vladimir Putin, avoided referring to the invasion at all. Instead, the Ministry of Foreign Affairs issued a statement blaming the United States and NATO for threatening Russia, and vaguely calling for peace (Ministerio de Relaciones Exteriores 2022).

One unexpected consequence of the Russian invasion of Ukraine was the Biden administration sending a delegation of high-level officials to Caracas to meet with President Maduro about the possibility of lifting oil sanctions. The goal was both to pluck off one of Putin's Latin America allies and to keep oil prices down. After that meeting, Maduro said that he would renew dialogue with his domestic opposition. Nothing came of these initiatives, but the Biden administration clearly viewed Venezuela in strategic terms that raised the possibility of rapprochement. And at least rhetorically, Maduro was willing to follow the money.

In March 2022, the United Nations General Assembly voted to condemn the invasion. Latin American abstentions included Bolivia, Cuba, El Salvador, and Nicaragua.[2] In April 2022, the Organization of American States voted unanimously to suspend Russia's observer status. Eight countries did abstain, but they had little interest in blocking the measure.[3] Even Nayib Bukele, famously vocal about everything, maintained silence about Ukraine. Brazil and Mexico were more vocally neutral, not supporting the invasion per se, but not condemning it either. There were four different types of Latin American responses: condemnation, neutrality but with some votes against the invasion in international organizations, silent neutrality (just El Salvador), and support (Sanahuja, Stefanoni, and Verdes-Montenegro 2022). In short, there is significant diversity of reaction, and these reflect sometimes highly complex domestic debates. Latin American countries may be uncomfortable with invasion, but they are also hesitant to situate themselves firmly into what they tend to view as a larger power conflict.

Argentine president Alberto Fernández had visited Moscow shortly before the invasion, and afterward the Russian new agency TASS approvingly noted that although the Argentine government had condemned the "special operation," it did not approve of applying sanctions to Russia (*Tass Russian News Agency* 2022). But there weren't many opportunities for Russian propaganda victories.

The Biden administration was initially critical of governments that failed to condemn the invasion, then softened that language, at least publicly. The calculation appeared to be that alienating governments over Russia ran the risk of pushing them even more toward China (Osborn 2022). In March 2022, the commander of US Southern Command gave a statement to the Senate Committee on Armed Services, where she argued that China "continues its relentless march to expand its economic, diplomatic, technological, informational, and military influence in LAC and challenges US influence in all these areas" (United States Southern Command 2022). Overall, her statement was a litany of China's evils across the region, and SouthCom's goal was "to illuminate, disrupt, degrade, neutralize, and defeat our adversaries," mostly China.

Yet despite the aggressive language toward China, the Biden administration was willing to swallow more Latin American autonomy, both with regard to Russia and to China. The administration's condemnation was aimed at the extra-hemispheric powers, not toward Latin American governments. That was actually just a continuation of the Obama and Trump administration policies. These days, Latin America had other options.

For the time being, Russian influence in Latin America remained limited. After 2000, Russia and Mexico had presidential visits and optimistically worded initiatives, but trade went up and down, and has not been a consistent priority for either country (Kosevich 2021). Brazilian president Jair Bolsonaro, who also happened to visit Moscow not long before the invasion, chose not to condemn the invasion and continued to trade with Russia, especially agricultural goods like fertilizer, for which it relies heavily on Russia. Oddly, Brazilian vice president Hamilton Mourão said Brazil opposed the invasion, which Bolsonaro quickly contradicted. But it is notable that Lula, once again running for president, agreed with Bolsonaro's stance: "We are not interested in a new Cold War" (Sanders 2022). But neutrality, which is not unexpected given Brazil's foreign policy independence from the United States, and trade in an essential good are not the equivalent of Russian influence.

Russia continues to broadcast its state-owned network RT, where, for example, Latin Americans heard that Ukraine bombed its own cities and blamed Russia (Chiba 2022). Disinformation is a long-standing Russian tactic, and RT sends it out on a daily basis. We do not know the depth of its reach, and recent studies suggest that preconceived notions about Russia or China color the consumer's view of those outlets (e.g., Morales 2021). Thus far, however, it has not seemed to affect Latin American governments' policies in any discernible way to benefit Russia.

THE EFFECTS OF COVID-19

The previous chapter discussed the delayed US response to the pandemic and how both Russia and China moved quickly to provide vaccines. Although Pfizer and Moderna, and to a lesser extent Johnson & Johnson, have been distributed around the region, they are often in the minority. Chile, for example, is a highly vaccinated country but mostly from Sinovac, a Chinese vaccine (Harrison, Horwitz, and Zissis 2022). In 2022, China even began building a Sinovac vaccine factory in Chile, which followed a similar endeavor in Ecuador.

India continued its brisk trade of pharmaceuticals, exporting even more than China in the twenty-first century, with the exception of 2021, when China exported more COVID-19 vaccines (Seshasayee 2022). The Indian private sector trades extensively across Latin America, and pharmaceuticals represent a major part of that. Nonetheless, the Indian government has yet to formulate any specific policy toward Latin America. The region is almost entirely off the foreign policy radar, and despite signing free trade agreements in other parts of the world, India has signed none in Latin America.

Domestic COVID-19 vaccine production does exist, most notably in Cuba and Mexico. Regionally, however, there is no sign that dependence on external sources will change appreciably. In 2022, the Pan American Health Organization coordinated with Argentine and Brazilian companies to receive training in South Africa to eventually increase domestic production of the vaccines (Pan American Health Organization 2022). Such advances, of course, will not develop quickly.

REGIONALISM AND AUTONOMY

The 2022 Summit of the Americas is another example of how times had changed. Since the first meeting in 1994, it had represented a forum for the region (sometimes, as in 2015 and 2018, even including Cuba) to discuss common challenges and offer a place for heads of state (or their delegates) to communicate directly. The 2022 meeting was held in Los Angeles, and the Biden administration excluded Cuba, Nicaragua, and Venezuela because they were not democracies. Cuba had been excluded from a majority of previous meetings (as it had from the OAS) and there was always criticism about its exclusion. Adding more countries to the forbidden list in an era of expanded autonomy made the response louder. Yet another problem was the possibility that the administration might invite Juan Guaidó, who was not universally recognized as president. Ultimately, Biden had a phone call with Guaidó but did not invite him.

Caribbean Community (CARICOM) leaders suggested they had not yet decided whether to attend, and they mentioned Guaidó specifically (and eventually they did attend) (*The Gleaner* 2022). AMLO said no country should be excluded and that he would not attend, though he would send a representative. One Mexican scholar pointed to this as an example of autonomy, as AMLO put Mexican interests before the United States's (Ramírez 2022). The presidents of the three countries of the Northern Triangle (El Salvador, Guatemala, and Honduras) chose not to attend, but sent representatives. Jair Bolsonaro announced he would not attend, then changed his mind. The Biden administration was left in the unusual position of needing to reach out personally to leaders in Honduras, a small and economically dependent country whose government had suggested it might follow AMLO's lead (Spagat, Goodman, and Megerian 2022).

Yet the situation once again highlighted the lack of regional consensus. As former Chilean president Ricardo Lagos put it, "As long as we don't speak with a single voice, no one is going to listen to us" (Spagat, Goodman, and Megerian 2022). Chinese government media, always happy to exploit any perceived weakness, claimed the exact opposite, claiming that a new wave of leftist governments "are more united and keen to rid the continent of US control and make more independent decisions based on their interests" (*Global Times* 2022). Of course, according to China, those interests would lead Latin American logically toward China, where cooperation was "truly mutually beneficial" while US efforts to disrupt those relations "is actually challenging the relevant countries' autonomy" (*Global Times* 2022).

Latin American scholars pointed to other problems. Juan Gabriel Tokatlian (2022) argued that Joe Biden simply represented "Trump soft," with mostly a continuation of the same policies but without the insults. Further, he noted, regional fragmentation ended up leaving countries looking individually toward China. Flavio Darío Espinal argued that the total absence of regional consensus on just about anything made such summits pointless (Espinal 2022). Overall, Latin American governments moved in many different autonomous directions, but rarely in concert with each other.

Tussie (2021) sees promise in "post-hegemonic regionalism," where Latin American governments can come together pragmatically in specific thematic areas. From that perspective, regionalism can prosper when tightly focused, rather than the creation of institutions with grandiloquent claims. Those were often the case with Hugo Chávez–era initiatives. Further, those also had exclusion of the United States as an explicit goal. These newer, more focused efforts were not conceived as anti–United States, but rather as an organic development of solutions to common challenges.

Nonetheless, persistent divisions complicated even such a modest variant of regionalism. Consensus never emerged around a regional response to the Venezuelan dictatorship. As a consolation prize for not being invited to the Summit of the Americas, President Biden spoke with Juan Guaidó and expressed support for negotiations and a willingness to "calibrate sanctions policy" accordingly (White House 2022a). Not long after, the administration also extended temporary protected status for Venezuelan migrants, which gave them another eighteen months of legal immigration status. Nonetheless, a group of Latin American and European countries found the Venezuelan government resistant to continuing negotiations that had started in Mexico in 2021. The Russian invasion of Ukraine also strengthened the Venezuelan government because sanctions on Russian oil increased scarcity and therefore price.

Another regional organization, CELAC, did at least start meeting again. After a sparsely attended presidential summit in 2017 and the cancellation of a CELAC–European Union meeting the same year, internal conflict prevented another presidential summit from being held until 2021. That rebirth can be attributed to Mexican president Andrés Manuel López Obrador, who distrusted the Organization of American States and wanted it replaced with "a truly autonomous body, one that is nobody's lackey" (*Al Jazeera* 2021). Brazilian president Jair Bolsonaro pulled out of CELAC in 2020, but Lula promptly returned when he took office in 2023.

Regionalism did not resonate with regard to immigration, where governments came to bilateral agreements with the United States. The Regional Conference on Migration, created in 1996 and comprising the United States, Canada, Mexico, and Central American countries, does allow for dialogue but does not create policy. No other institution or organization does either.

For Calderón (2021), Andrés Manuel López Obrador used humanitarian rhetoric with regard to immigration, but in truth he did not have immigrants in his vision for Mexico's development. As a result, his policies were just as pragmatic as any of his predecessors and involved compromising with the United States. The last chapter discussed his response to the hectoring of Donald Trump, and those policies did not change much when Biden took office. Despite spurning Biden's invitation to the Summit of the Americas, AMLO's government continued detaining twice as many migrants in the first third of 2022 compared to the same period in 2021 (Sheridan 2022).

The Summit of the Americas did produce a document with proposals for how different countries would respond to immigration (White House 2022b). Its intent was to "mobilize the entire region around bold actions" with "deliverables" and included initiatives that were "unprecedented in scale." It was a series of unilateral initiatives, aimed at refugee resettlement, guest worker programs, human rights protection for migrants, and asylee processes at the border. Promising words, certainly, though of course many previous meetings over the years produced similarly promising words.

Meanwhile, immigration from Cuba soared as economic conditions on the island worsened. For example, in August 2020, US Customs and Border Protection came into contact with 65,707 Cuban citizens. In August 2022, that number increased to 251,155.[4] In 2022, the Biden administration eased back on some of its predecessor's harsher policies. These included allowing Cuban Americans to apply to bring family members to the United States, improving capacity at the US consulate, expanding the number of approved flights, and removing a cap on remittances. As noted in chapter 5, the Obama administration had ended the "wet foot, dry foot" policy, so it faced the deportation of tens of thousands of Cubans, some of whom it sent to Mexico under Title 42.

Further, the administration restarted bilateral dialogue between the US State Department and its Cuban counterparts on immigration, which Trump had halted. US immigration policy remained as jumbled as ever, and Latin American governments continued to navigate the rough terrain in mostly bilateral terms.

Climate policy is another example of weak regionalism. As discussed in the previous chapter, the Escazú Agreement on the environment moved forward, albeit slowly. Chile ratified it in 2022 (becoming the thirteenth country to do so), but new Costa Rican president Rodrigo Chaves said he would not even though the very name is a Costa Rican city. As of this writing, Colombia signed the agreement but had not ratified it because of congressional opposition. Neither Peru nor Brazil showed signs of ratifying either. Overall, twenty-five countries have signed the agreement and thirteen of those ratified it as well. Its first meeting took place in 2022.

Given the crisis of attack of environmental activists all over Latin America, the agreement has the potential to serve as a global example (indeed, African human rights activists called for their own regional version). Not too surprisingly, the most dangerous countries for activists are precisely those that are not ratifying.

DRUG POLICY

The Bolivian case once again highlights how changes of government can lead to quick shifts toward or away from autonomy. Bolivian president Evo Morales was ousted from power under highly questionable circumstances in 2019, and the newly installed interim president, Jeanine Áñez, was a conservative who moved quickly to dismantle his policies. That included drug policy, where she shifted to the kinds of hard-line policies the US government favored, which included greater use of the army and police. In 2020, her government announced its new "United, Free of Drugs" strategy, claiming that Morales's government allowed drug trafficking to flourish in the country (Estado Plurinacional de Bolivia 2020). Coca farmers were referred to as narcotraffickers (Tedesqui Vargas 2020).

Presidential elections were held in late 2020, and the new president, Luis Arce, who was from Morales's party, shifted once again back to the community-based approach. His government criticized the Biden administration for continuing to assert that Bolivia was failing to combat narcotics, and they argued that the United States "lacked legitimacy and moral authority" because its citizens consumed drugs in such large quantities (Agence France-Presse, 2021). In a presidential address, he emphasized the government's commitment to cooperating with neighboring countries and the United Nations, while asserting that large amounts of cocaine disappeared under the previous government (Estado Plurinacional de Bolivia, 2021). In a polarized political environment, policy lurched back and forth.

The Biden administration's approach to curbing drug trafficking moved decidedly away from militarization and toward a holistic approach. The 2022 National Drug Control Strategy report outlined that approach and recognized both the importance of treatment in the United States and underdevelopment in Latin America (Executive Office 2022). That stood in contrast to the Trump administration's 2019 report, which had a more aggressive tone, criticizing Colombia for halting its aerial spraying of coca and asserting that countries who "aligned with U.S. interests" would be prioritized (Executive Office 2019, 14). Biden had shifted back toward the Obama administration's approach.

In 2021, the administration designated Bolivia and Venezuela as having failed to make sufficient effort to combat drug trafficking, which echoed both Trump and Obama. US policy had moved away from a strictly militarized position, albeit glacially. But it still centered on prohibition and on US-generated solutions. Countries that considered other options risked retaliation. Yet pushback had become more common.

As noted in the previous chapter, AMLO did resist US pressure on the drug war in Mexico. Nonetheless, despite his own rhetoric about ending the drug war, in many ways he continued an approach consistent with US policy, including an extensive role for the Mexican army (Linthicum 2022). He met with his Colombian counterpart, Gustavo Petro, to discuss how to change regional drug policy, but that dialogue remains nascent. Nonetheless, the absence of any US representation shows the autonomous bent of the endeavor.

In 2021, the United States and Mexico agreed to a new Bicentennial Framework for Security, Public Health, and Safe Communities, which was intended to replace the Mérida Initiative and cement a bilateral shift toward "health and safety" (White House 2022c). In the short term, not much has actually changed (Correa-Cabrera 2022), but it offers more emphasis on public health and arms trafficking. For years, the latter has been a bone of contention for the Mexican government and inevitably got tangled up and stalled by the US domestic debate on gun control. How much drug policy in the two countries continues to move toward a less militarized solution remains to be seen.

CONCLUSION

This book began with Hugo Chávez first getting elected and China making its initial steps toward engagement with Latin America. A generation later, Latin

American–US relations are transformed. Those changes were not nearly as radical as Chávez wanted or confidently predicted, but they were important. By no means had the United States "lost" the region, which still cooperated extensively in countless areas, but Latin American policy makers had options that were not available before. In other words, the United States was still by far the most powerful country in the region and exerted tremendous influence, but there were more counterhegemonic projects than ever. Yet those were not just leftist governments. Increased autonomy was a near universal aspiration.

The extent of Latin American governments' push for autonomous policy making is historic and noteworthy. For decades, successfully pushing back against the United States meant a high economic price, and in some cases even armed force. Cuba is a famous long-term example, and more recently Venezuela also was hit by major sanctions, though they did not come for many years. Now, El Salvador and Nicaragua—both deeply damaged by the United States during the Cold War—are able to reject the United States in many ways without paying anywhere near the same price. Autonomy without retaliation is a recurrent theme in the Latin American literature, and it's been achieved more than ever before.

Further, over the past two hundred years, the United States vigorously rejected the presence of outside governments. It was, in fact, the basis for the 1823 Monroe Doctrine, and the Cold War was focused squarely on using force to counter any perceived Soviet presence. Yet after 2000, China's role ballooned in particular, and other countries also expanded their partnerships to varying degrees. The end of the Cold War changed that element of US policy significantly. Even when US policy makers vociferously opposed extra-hemispheric relationships, they were far less likely to use coercion.

Nonetheless, ideology and nationalism served as a brake on the development of regional autonomy movements. Brazil, for example, shifted its position markedly after changes of government. Plus, neither Hugo Chávez nor Venezuela's oil bonanza were permanent, and after Chávez's death, Venezuela ceased to be a regional leader. The organizations he helped found remained either limited in influence or lost legitimacy. Other examples abound where national-level political developments blocked regional efforts. Autonomy has rarely been a successful regional effort. Puig himself noted that integration per se didn't necessarily lead to autonomy unless there was a conscious collective effort to reduce dependency on the dominant power (Puig 1980, 154–55).

Given the US history of viewing Latin America as a "backyard" to be monitored and at times outright controlled, it is ironic that the embrace of autonomy stemmed in part from US policy itself. Insistence on export-led market economies prompted Latin American leaders to look for new trading partners. Later, Donald Trump's erratic and insult-laden policies accelerated that trend. It is now a reality of Latin American–US relations, and now more than ever it is a good time for US analysts to consider more Latin American views about the evolution of the relationship.

NOTES

CHAPTER 1

1. For a broad discussion and a bibliography of major works, see Tickner 2014.
2. For a political history of the Latin American–US relations, see Weeks 2015.
3. For a good summary of the concept's development, see Simonoff 2016.
4. He held this position under President Héctor Cámpora for three months in 1973. The entire purpose of Cámpora's brief presidency was to pave the way for the return of Juan Perón by removing the barriers to his candidacy the military dictatorship had erected before leaving power. Once that was achieved, Cámpora handed the presidential sash to Perón and Puig resigned.
5. For the former, see Gunder Frank 1986. For the latter, see the seminal work by Cardoso and Faletto (1979). Fernando Henrique Cardoso later became president of Brazil.
6. In his analysis of dependency theory, Robert Packenham (1992) asserts that the goal of all variants of dependency is actually a vague notion of Marxist socialism, and not autonomy per se. That is debatable, but it does highlight how the intellectual roots of dependency are leftist, whereas those of autonomy are much more centrist.
7. As Kenneth Waltz, whose *Theory of International Politics* is the most influential example of realism, puts it, the international system is "self-help" (Waltz 1979).
8. Realism spawned its own variants, often aimed at showing how cooperation between states can indeed take place based on shared norms or interests that go beyond just security. For example, Keohane (1984) argues that states have complementary interests and are interested in cooperating with each other, including through the creation of international organizations, to reduce conflict. It is worth noting, however, that his analysis centers exclusively on advanced market economy countries.
9. On this point, see Bernal-Meza 2013. He also favored going beyond just economic integration.
10. Puig 1980, 153. To illustrate, he uses the case of the United States disputing British power in the nineteenth century, which fundamentally changed their relationship to US benefit.
11. For a concise discussion in English, see Escudé 2014. The more detailed Spanish book is Escudé 1992.

12. Peripheral Realism developed in Argentina and was reflected in particular in the foreign policies of President Carlos Menem (Sahni 2001).
13. Jaguaribe 1979. He does not specify exactly how many of these resources are necessary. At a minimum, it is clear that by virtue of its size Brazil qualifies.
14. See his letters to the vice president of Colombia about carefully cultivating ("with dulcet and persuasive words") both the United States and England without entangling in their affairs (Lecuna and Bierck 1951, 479, 499).
15. For a well-articulated example, see Crandall 2011.
16. All of the data comes from the World Bank. https://wits.worldbank.org/CountrySnapshot/en/LCN/textview.
17. "Nuance" is an especially overused term. For a memorable dissection of the term, see Healy 2017.

CHAPTER 2

1. See the Castro Speech Database at the University of Texas at Austin. http://lanic.utexas.edu/project/castro/db/1979/19791012.html.
2. Trading partner information comes from the World Bank website. https://wits.worldbank.org/CountrySnapshot/en/CUB. Despite the US embargo on Cuba, there is latitude for US export of agricultural goods for "humanitarian" purposes, but they must be in cash. The law allows no credit or financing, which limits the scope of the trade.
3. Sánchez's description of Chávez is memorable: "From the time when he became president, in 1999, until his untimely death in 2013, Chávez, through a deft montage of monuments and dancing, presided over Venezuelan politics as the quintessential dancing Jacobin, for the most part keeping the restless Venezuelan population focused on his monumentalized-cum-dancing persona" (Sánchez 2016, 327).
4. Reasons included the death of Mao Zedong in 1976, which opened the door for change. Further, the Cultural Revolution (1966–1976) was unpopular, and the Chinese Community Party saw the need to take an entirely new direction based on the advice of their economic planners. See Chow 2004.
5. All data comes from the World Bank website. https://wits.worldbank.org/CountryProfile/en/Country/GTM/Year/2000/TradeFlow/EXPIMP.
6. Data from the US Energy Information Administration. See https://www.eia.gov.
7. The Pew Research Center has data for Brazil (80 percent with little or no confidence), Mexico (77 percent), and Argentina (86 percent). See Pew Research Center 2008.
8. The 1992 and 1994 attacks in Buenos Aires are important exceptions. In 1992,

a car bomb killed twenty-nine at the Israeli embassy, while in 1994 another bomb killed eighty-five at the Mutual Israeli-Argentine Association. These attacks have been attributed to the Iranian government, which has been a matter of intense speculation and controversy.

9. One of these was satellite-guided bombs, which eventually killed FARC leader Mono Jojoy and twenty of his soldiers in 2010.

10. For example, President Clinton expanded the scope of what should be considered a crime in immigration, constructing more border fencing, increasing the number of immigrants being detained, and developing memoranda of understanding with local law enforcement.

11. Unlike the United States, in Latin America "liberal" is not synonymous with "left." In fact, liberal generally means the opposite of the US usage, referring to liberal or neoliberal economics rather than progressive politics. "Neoliberal" is a commonly used term, often pejorative, that refers to market economics.

12. Though Lula was quite emphatic: "I believe that we can surprise the world in terms of the relationship of Brazil and the United States" (George W. Bush Archives 2003).

13. Created in 1999, the Group of 20, or G20, is a collection of governments (nineteen plus the European Union) that convene periodically to discuss global economic challenges. Participation entails recognition that the member government's economy is considered significant.

14. Trading partner information comes from the World Bank website. https://wits.worldbank.org/CountryProfile/en/Country/SLV/Year/2015/TradeFlow/EXPIMP.

CHAPTER 3

1. See the archived transcript of Zoellick participating in a press roundtable two years later when he was deputy secretary of state. https://2001-2009.state.gov/s/d/former/zoellick/rem/54974.htm.

2. It is notable that half of Amorim's memoir of his time as foreign minister is dedicated to discussing Brazil's relations with the Middle East.

3. All data in this section is from the World Bank website. https://wits.worldbank.org/CountryProfile/en/Country/BRA/StartYear/1989/EndYear/2016/TradeFlow/Export/Indicator/XPRT-TRD-VL/Partner/CHN/Product/all-groups.

4. Jiang also went to Chile, Argentina, Uruguay, Cuba, and Venezuela, all of which offered opportunities in commodities that China needed.

5. That relationship included a bizarre moment in 2006 when Uruguay and Argentina had a dispute over the construction of a pulp mill on the Uruguay River. Argentina protested, claiming it would pollute the river. Vázquez later said he

even thought of war and called President Bush for support in case it erupted (*El Observador* 2011). Eventually the crisis was resolved peacefully.

6. All data is from the World Bank website https://wits.worldbank.org/CountryProfile/en/Country/URY/Year/2000/TradeFlow/EXPIMP.

7. For a well-written account of the process, see Blustein 2005.

8. Duhalde was one of five presidents who served in a period of ten days after Fernando de la Rúa's resignation on December 20, 2001.

9. All data on Argentine trade is from the World Bank website: https://wits.worldbank.org/CountryProfile/en/Country/ARG/Year/2003/TradeFlow/EXPIMP.

10. The Bush administration paid particular attention to the Triborder Area, which comprises roughly a million people and which developed a reputation for lawlessness. In 2004, for example, it cited companies operating in concert with Hezbollah in the area. See https://www.treasury.gov/press-center/press-releases/Pages/js1720.aspx.

11. There were other initiatives as well: Petrosur, Petroandina, and Petroamérica, but they became mostly vehicles for cooperation and not for widespread distribution of oil.

12. More specifically, if the price of oil is more than $40 per barrel, 30–70 percent is financed and the rest paid at 1 percent over twenty-five years. If it's below $40, then 5–25 percent is financed over seventeen years at 2 percent interest (Petrocaribe Development Fund 2018).

13. Ecuadorian president Rafael Correa used a similar strategy. Between his 2006 election and 2010, he reduced the professional diplomatic staff to almost nothing, leaving only personnel with ties to the government and no experience (*El Comercio* 2010).

14. This occurred right around the time that conservative Christian Pat Robertson said on the air that the United States government should kill Hugo Chávez, which would be easier than starting a war (Goodstein 2005). The Venezuelan government, which viewed Robertson as close to the White House, was not amused.

15. According to the original General Agreement on Tariffs and Trade from 1947, a customs union is an agreement where "the duties and other regulations of commerce imposed at the institution of any such union or interim agreement in respect of trade with contracting parties not parties to such union or agreement shall not on the whole be higher or more restrictive than the general incidence of the duties and regulations of commerce applicable in the constituent territories prior to the formation of such union or the adoption of such interim agreement, as the case may be." This is a tongue-twisting way of saying the countries agree to a common tariff amongst themselves, which is sometimes zero, but also a common tariff for countries outside the agreement. See https://www.wto.org/english/tratop_e/region_e/region_art24_e.htm.

16. Decision 24 was revoked in 1991 as the neoliberal era dawned.

17. Two years later, the World Bank published an assessment of Bolivian water privatization, labeling Santa Cruz a "cooperative model" while Cochabamba was "unsuccessful privatization" (World Bank 2002, 2). It concluded drily that a "pragmatic approach tailored to local circumstances should be adopted for effective institutional development" (World Bank 2002, 3).
18. Certainly, he mentioned the United States all the time and sometimes reveled in insulting President Bush, whom he referred to as a terrorist after he won the election (*Al Jazeera* 2005). But his overall goals were broader than just rejecting Bush and US policy.
19. Trade data is from the World Bank website. https://wits.worldbank.org/CountryProfile/en/Country/BOL/StartYear/2005/EndYear/2010/TradeFlow/Export/Indicator/XPRT-TRD-VL/Partner/CHN/Product/all-groups.

CHAPTER 4

1. Those efforts angered some conservatives in the US Senate, who tried unsuccessfully to torpedo his nomination to be ambassador to Brazil because he had engaged in dialogue with Bolivia, Ecuador, Honduras, Nicaragua, and Venezuela. One of his sins was to "improve relations with President Correa" in Ecuador (Harper 2009).
2. And it should be noted that since Ecuador is dollarized, the SUCRE could only allow for limited autonomy. No matter what kind of trade Ecuador engages in, the dollar will be present in some manner.
3. It replaced and broadened the 1991 Andean Preference Act.
4. The United States was involved because the Venezuelan involved happened to be an FBI informant. He implicated others, who were arrested in Miami on charges of acting as agents of the Venezuelan government.
5. An English translation can be found at http://pdba.georgetown.edu/Constitutions/Ecuador/english08.html.
6. As noted later in the book, Ecuador left the agreement unilaterally in 2013. Peru was not renewed in 2010 because it was already entering a free trade agreement with the United States.
7. Normal diplomatic relations were not re-established for another three years.
8. Source: US Energy Information Administration website. https://www.eia.gov/dnav/pet/hist/LeafHandler.ashx?n=pet&s=mttimusve1&f=a.
9. All trade data is from https://wits.worldbank.org/.
10. The posture statement is the US Army's account to Congress about its roles, activities, and accomplishments. US Southern Command is the US Army's command center for Latin America.

CHAPTER 5

1. For example, "A 'pink tide' of progressive governments swept the Americas, promising to reverse decades of miserable poverty and entrenched privilege" (Livingstone 2009, 1).
2. At the same time, it is worth pointing out that the report highlighted how much Chinese foreign direct investment in the Western Hemisphere (upwards of $40 billion) was concentrated in tax havens in the Cayman Islands and the British Virgin Islands. Trade was therefore by far the most important engine of growth elsewhere.
3. The cable was publicized by Areddy (2010).
4. Similar offers, often with anonymous sources, popped up from time to time later as well.
5. Small planes sprayed glyphosate, commonly known in US households as Roundup. As the product instructions tell consumers, "Make sure the plants you're about to treat are the ones you don't want" (https://www.roundup.com/en-us/library/using-roundup-weed-grass-killer-products-properly/how-do-i-apply-roundup-weed-grass-killer). In Colombia, it was sprayed over everything.
6. Cuba was expelled from the OAS in 1962 but had originally been a member. It was invited back in 2009 and declined.
7. The email was publicized by Wikileaks (2009).
8. See Merke, Reynoso, and Schenoni (2020) for a good overview of that literature.
9. He also got along with Daniel Ortega, who allowed him to seek asylum when he faced corruption charges and in 2019 even gave him Nicaraguan citizenship, thus cementing his protection from Salvadoran courts.
10. For an English-language version of the constitution, see https://www.constituteproject.org/constitution/Bolivia_2009.pdf.
11. For trade data, see https://www.census.gov/foreign-trade/balance/c3350.html#2009.
12. See US Energy Information Administration 2018. The agency is part of the statistical arm of the US Department of Energy.
13. The announcement came not too long after his creation of a vice minister of the supreme social happiness of the people (Clarín.com 2013).
14. E.g. see Slipak 2014.
15. The Drug Enforcement Agency did feel compelled to respond to its expulsion, filing lawsuits against top Bolivian officials for drug trafficking, which in turn led to indictments (Grim and Wing 2015). The DEA even had a name for this effort: Operation Naked King.
16. For full text, see Public Law 104-114, 1996.

CHAPTER 6

1. Such a statement was not typical for a former president to say of a current president, to the point that the fact-checking website Snopes felt compelled to confirm that three different people heard it. https://www.snopes.com/news/2017/03/31/bush-trumps-inauguration-weird-sht/.
2. Chilean political scientist Robert Funk pointed this out in a conversation with the author on the Understanding Latin American Politics podcast, March 13, 2017. http://weeksnotice.blogspot.com/2017/03/podcast-episode-27-how-latin-america.html.
3. This has been the case from the time of Latin American independence, when the liberator Simón Bolívar called for unity and to his great frustration never achieved it.
4. The declaration also calls for PROSUR to have a structure that is "not costly," presumably a stab at the notion that Hugo Chávez used funds to advance his goals without attention to long-term structures, efficiency, or organization (not unlike the history of the San Diego Padres).
5. Even there, the leader of a failed coup led by US military contractors in 2020 said he had "encouragement" from the administration (in addition to Juan Guaidó himself) and plotted in Trump hotels in Washington, DC, and in Florida (Delgado et al. 2020).
6. Similarly, those voters were receptive to the assertion that Joe Biden would copy the Venezuelan economic model in the United States, a message Trump repeated many times leading up to the 2020 presidential election.
7. The United Nations started holding this vote annually in 1992 (with the exception of 2020 because of COVID-19). The resolution's title is "Necessity of ending the economic, commercial and financial embargo imposed by the United States of America against Cuba." See https://undocs.org/en/A/75/L.97. Typically, the only countries voting against it are the United States, Israel, and several very small countries in the Pacific.
8. In other words, Congress did not outline any crimes she allegedly committed, but instead focused on her management of the economy.
9. Lava Jato means "car wash" in Portuguese, and the investigation into money laundering and corruption got that name because the first example it uncovered took place at a car wash. The investigation began in 2014 and continued until 2021.
10. AMLO, a committed antimasker, shared that view.
11. The Sputnik vaccine did arrive in 2021, and Maduro received the first dose.
12. India, in fact, was increasing its exports of pharmaceuticals in general to Latin America, where demand (and therefore profit) was consistently high.
13. These are the larger countries, namely Argentina, Brazil, Chile, Ecuador, Mexico, Peru, and Venezuela.

14. Her analysis was based on polls conducted by Vanderbilt University in their AmericasBarometer surveys.
15. The Spanish-language version is T-MEC (Tratado *México*-Estados Unidos-Canadá), which rolls off the tongue more easily.
16. For example, Biden's US trade representative, Katherine Tai, was a central figure in negotiating the USMCA.

CHAPTER 7

1. US policy makers, most prominently Sen. Marco Rubio (R-FL) also accused them of espionage and suppression of free speech, which in turn led to a 2021 law barring defense funding from colleges and universities that hosted them.
2. One can reasonably assume Venezuela would have either voted against or abstained, but it lost voting rights from the United Nations for failure to pay dues.
3. The countries were Argentina, Bolivia, Brazil, El Salvador, Honduras, Mexico, Saint Kitts and Nevis, and Saint Vincent and the Grenadines.
4. This data comes from the US Customs and Border Protection website: https://www.cbp.gov/newsroom/stats/nationwide-encounters.

BIBLIOGRAPHY

Acua Popocatl, Raúl Gustavo, Rafael Alberto Durán Gómez, and Selene Jiménez Bautista. 2020. "El T-MEC, confrontado con el enfoque del Nuevo Regionalismo de la CEPAL." *VinculaTégica*, July 15. http://ri.uaemex.mx/handle/20.500.11799/109484.
Administration of Barack Obama. 2016. "Notice—Continuation of National Emergency With Respect to Venezuela." March 3. https://www.govinfo.gov/content/pkg/DCPD-201600122/pdf/DCPD-201600122.pdf.
AFP. 2009. "La Jornada: Chávez y Funes estrechan lazos en materia energética." May 21. https://www.jornada.com.mx/2009/05/21/mundo/027n3mun.
Agence France-Presse. 1998. "Castro Congratulates Chavez on His 'Overwhelming Victory.'" December 7.
Agence France-Presse. 2020. "'Prevent, Discourage, Confront': South American States Tackle Chinese Fishing Boats." *The Guardian*, November 4. http://www.theguardian.com/environment/2020/nov/05/prevent-discourage-confront-south-american-states-tackle-chinese-trawlers.
Agence France-Presse. 2021. "Bolivia rechaza 'sesgado' informe de Biden que critica su lucha antidrogas." September 16. https://www.france24.com/es/minuto-a-minuto/20210916-bolivia-rechaza-sesgado-informe-de-biden-que-critica-su-lucha-antidrogas.
Agencia EFE. 2022. "El Salvador pone bajo secreto información de remesas con billetera bitcón." March 11. https://www.efe.com/efe/america/economia/el-salvador-pone-bajo-secreto-informacion-de-remesas-con-billetera-bitcoin/20000011-4759005.
Agencia de Información Paraguaya. 2020. "Paraguay y Colombia coinciden en cooperar para fortalecer la integración regional." November 8. https://www.ip.gov.py/ip/paraguay-y-colombia-coinciden-en-cooperar-para-fortalecer-la-integracion-regional/.
Agencia Venezolana de Noticias. 2013. "Nicolás Maduro: ¡Qué Viva La Felicidad Suprema! ¡Qué Viva La Navidad!" November 1. http://www.avn.info.ve/

contenido/maduro-decretamos-llegada-navidad-porque-queremos-paz-del-pueblo.

Ahumada, Consuelo. 2020. "La implementación del Acuerdo de paz en Colombia: entre la 'paz territorial' y la disputa por el territorio." *Problemas del desarrollo* 51, no. 200 (March): 25–47.

Ajenjo Fresno, Natalia. 2007. "Honduras: Nuevo Gobierno Liberal Con La Misma Agenda Política." *Revista de Ciencia Política (Santiago)* 27: 165–81.

Alden, Chris, and Marco Antonio Vieira. 2005. "The New Diplomacy of the South: South Africa, Brazil, India and Trilateralism." *Third World Quarterly* 26, no. 7 (October 1): 1077–95.

Al Jazeera. 2005. "Morales Calls Bush a 'Terrorist.'" December 20. https://www.aljazeera.com/news/2005/12/20/morales-calls-bush-a-terrorist.

Al Jazeera. 2021. "Mexico to Host Summit of New Latin America 'Pink Tide' Leaders." September 17. https://www.aljazeera.com/news/2021/9/17/mexico-to-host-summit-of-new-latin-america-pink-tide-leaders.

Almeida, Paulo Roberto de. 2004. "Uma Política Externa Engajada: A Diplomacia Do Governo Lula." *Revista Brasileira de Política Internacional* 47, no. 1 (June): 162–84.

Alvarez, Fernando E., David Argente, and Diana Van Patten. 2022. "Are Cryptocurrencies Currencies? Bitcoin as Legal Tender in El Salvador." NBER Working Paper Series, April. https://www.nber.org/papers/w29968#:~:text=We%20use%20evidence%20from%20a,accept%20bitcoin%20for%20all%20payments.

Alvarez, María Victoria. 2021."A Theory of Hegemonic Stability in South American Regionalism? Evidence from the Case of Brazil in UNASUR and Venezuela in ALBA." *Contexto Internacional* 43, no. 1 (April): 55–76.

AMLO. 2019. "Firman modificaciones al T-MEC en Palacio Nacional; generará crecimiento y bienestar en las tres naciones, asegura presidente – AMLO." December 10. https://lopezobrador.org.mx/2019/12/10/firman-modificaciones-al-t-mec-en-palacio-nacional-generara-crecimiento-y-bienestar-en-las-tres-naciones-asegura-presidente/.

Amorim, Celso. 2010. "Brazilian Foreign Policy under President Lula (2003–2010): An Overview." *Revista Brasileira de Política Internacional* 53, no. SPE (December): 214–40.

Amorim, Celso. 2017. *Acting Globally: Memoirs of Brazil's Assertive Foreign Policy*. Lanham, MD: Hamilton Books.

Anderson, Jon Lee. 2001. "The Revolutionary." *New Yorker*, September 3. https://www.newyorker.com/magazine/2001/09/10/the-revolutionary.

Areddy, James. 2010. "Wikileaks: China Profits Off Cheap Venezuelan Oil." *Wall Street Journal*, December 15. https://www.wsj.com/articles/BL-CJB-12223.

Avritzer, Leonardo. 2009. *Participatory Institutions in Democratic Brazil*. Baltimore: Johns Hopkins University Press.

Azpuru, Dinorah. 2021. "Four Years Later, Biden Faces a Different Latin America." *Global Americans*, January 26. https://theglobalamericans.org/2021/01/four-years-later-biden-faces-a-different-latin-america/.

Bachelet, Pablo. 2017. "State Department Documents Reveal U.S. Dealings with Venezuela's Chavez." *McClatchy*, October 23. http://www.mcclatchydc.com/news/politics-government/article24473125.html.

Backer, Larry Catá, and Augusto Molina. 2010. "Cuba and the Construction of Alternative Global Trade Systems: ALBA and Free Trade in the Americas." *University of Pennsylvania Journal of International Law* 31, no. 3 (Spring): 679–752.

Baribeau, Simone. 2006. "Chavez: Venezuela to Withdraw from Andean Community of Nations." Venezuelanalysis.com, April 21. https://venezuelanalysis.com/news/1706.

Barros, Pedro Silva, and Julia Borba Gonçalves. 2019. "Fragmentação da Governança Regional, o Grupo de Lima e a política externa brasileira." *Mundo e Desenvolvimento: Revista do Instituto de Estudos Econômicos e Internacionais* 2, no. 3 (December 28): 6–39.

BBC (British Broadcasting Corporation). 2004. "Argentina Gets China Investment." November 17. http://news.bbc.co.uk/2/hi/americas/4018219.stm.

BBC (British Broadcasting Corporation). 2010. "Obama Says Venezuela Has Right to Russian Nuclear Aid." *BBC News*, October 19, US & Canada. https://www.bbc.com/news/world-us-canada-11580469.

BBC (British Broadcasting Corporation). 2012. "US Denies Mexico Drug War Failure." February 28, Latin America & Caribbean. https://www.bbc.com/news/world-latin-america-17187231.

BBC (British Broadcasting Corporation). 2014. "Venezuela's Maduro Breaks Diplomatic Links With Panama." March 6. https://www.bbc.com/news/world-latin-america-26461530.

Becerril, Andrea, Rosa Elvira Vargas, and Enrique Mendez. 2006. "Admite Presidencia influencia de EU en el veto a ley sobre drogas." *La Jornada*, May 5.

Bellos, Alex. 2000. "Opec Leader Wants the West over a Barrel." *The Guardian*, September 29, World news. https://www.theguardian.com/world/2000/sep/29/oil.business1.

Benzi, Daniele, and Ximena Zapata. 2013. "Geopolítica, economía y solidaridad internacional en la nueva cooperació sur-sur: El caso de la Venezuela bolivariana y Petrocaribe." *América Latina Hoy* 63: 65–89.

Bernal-Meza, Raúl. 2013. "Heterodox Autonomy Doctrine: Realism and Purposes, and Its Relevance." *Revista Brasileira de Política Internacional* 56, no. 2 (December): 45–62.

Berti, Lucas. 2020. "Argentina President Sends Dubious Message after Bolsonaro Diagnosis." *Brazilian Report*, July 8. https://brazilian.report/coronavirus-brazil-live-blog/2020/07/08/argentina-president-sends-dubious-message-after-bolsonaro-diagnosis/.

Biden, Joe. 2015. "A Plan for Central America." *New York Times*, January 30.

Blanco, Ramon. 2017. "The Brazilian Engagement with Peace Operations: A Critical Analysis." *Revista Brasileira de Política Internacional* 60, no. 2. https://doi.org/10.1590/0034-7329201700206.

Blustein, Paul. 2005. *And the Money Kept Rolling In (and Out)*. New York: PublicAffairs.
Boersner, Adriana, and Makram Haluani. 2011. "Moscú Mira Hacia America Latina." *Nuava Sociedad* 236 (noviembre-diciembre): 16–26.
Borger Alex, and Julian Bellos. 2002. "US 'gave the Nod' to Venezuelan Coup." *The Guardian*, April 17. http://www.theguardian.com/world/2002/apr/17/usa.venezuela.
Bolsonaro, Eduardo. 2021. *Twitter*, January. https://twitter.com/BolsonaroSP/status/1348411227672899587.
Bolton, John. 2020. *The Room Where It Happened: A White House Memoir*. New York: Simon & Schuster.
Borzutzky, Silvia. 2010. "Socioeconomic Policies: Taming the Market in a Globalized Economy." In *The Bachelet Government: Conflict and Consensus in Post-Pinochet Chile*, edited by Silvia Borzutzky and Gregory Weeks, 87–116. Gainesville: University Press of Florida.
Brazilian Report. 2020. "Pandemic Makes Brazil Even More Reliant on China." The Wilson Center, September 4. https://www.wilsoncenter.org/blog-post/pandemic-makes-brazil-even-more-reliant-china.
Briceño-Ruiz, José, Thomas Legler, and Juan Pablo Prado Lallande. 2021. "Growing Up as the New Kid on the Block: The Pacific Alliance Turns 10." *Latin American Policy* 12, no. 1 (May): 193–204.
Brooks, Brad, and Lisandra Paraguassu. 2019. "Brazil's Bolsonaro Says He Is Open to Hosting a U.S. Military Base." *Reuters*, January 3. https://www.reuters.com/article/us-brazil-politics-idUSKCN1OX1SR.
Bukele, Nayib. 2022. *Twitter*. February 16. https://twitter.com/nayibbukele/status/1494066643625988107.
Buquet, Daniel, and Daniel Chasquetti. 2005. "Elecciones Uruguay 2004: Descifrando El Cambio." *Revista de Ciencia Política (Santiago)* 25, no. 2: 143–52. https://doi.org/10.4067/S0718-090X2005000200006.
Bureau of International Narcotics and Law Enforcement Affairs. 2009. "2009 International Narcotics Control Strategy Report (INCSR)." February 27. https://2009-2017.state.gov/j/inl/rls/nrcrpt/2009/vol1/116520.htm.
Burges, Sean, and Fabricio Chagas Bustos. 2016. "It Will Get Worse Before It Gets Better: Impeachment and the Quagmire of Political Corruption in Brazil." April 21. http://www.coha.org/it-will-get-worse-before-it-gets-better-impeachment-and-the-quagmire-of-political-corruption-in-brazil/.
Cáceres, Luis René. 2017. "Consideraciones sobre la dolarización en El Salvador." *Realidad: Revista de Ciencias Sociales y Humanidades*, no. 128 (May 27): 209–41.
Calderón Chelius, Leticia. 2021. "Claves para entender la política migratoria Mexicana en tiempos de López Obrador." *Revista Cadernos de Campo* 30 (January/June): 99–122.
Canelas, Manuel, and Francisco J. Verdes-Montenegro. 2011. "La nueva política exterior boliviana (2005–2010): más autonomía y nuevos desafíos." In *"¡Ahora es*

cuándo, carajo!": Del as alto a la transformación del Estado en Bolivia, edited by Íñigo Errejón and Alfredo Serrano, 239–66. España: El Viejo Topo.

Cardoso, Fernando Henrique (with Brian Winter). 2006. *The Accidental President of Brazil: A Memoir*. New York: PublicAffairs.

Cardoso, Fernando Henrique, and Enzo Faletto. 1979. *Dependency and Development in Latin America (Dependencia Y Desarrollo En América Latina, Engl.)*. Berkeley: University of California Press.

Carney, Stephen A. 2011. *Allied Participation in Operation Iraqi Freedom*. Washington, DC: Center for Military History, US Army. https://history.army.mil/html/books/059/59-3-1/CMH_59-3-1.pdf.

Castañeda, Jorge G. 1993. *Utopia Unarmed: The Latin American Left After the Cold War*. New York: Alfred A. Knopf.

Castañeda, Jorge G. 2006. "Latin America's Left Turn." *Foreign Affairs* 85, no. 3: 28–43. https://doi.org/10.2307/20031965.

Castro, Fidel. 2014. "Mensaje del compañero Fidel sobre Eugenio George." *Granma*, June 2. http://www.granma.cu/cuba/2014-06-02/estimados-companeros-delinder.

CEPAL. 2015. "Latin American Economic Outlook 2016: Towards a New Partnership With China." Paris: OECD Publishing. http://repositorio.cepal.org/bitstream/handle/11362/39663/1/S1501060_en.pdf.

Ceppi, Natalia. 2014. "La Política Exterior de Bolivia En Tiempos de Evo Morales Ayma." *Si Somos Americanos* 14, no. 1 (June): 125–51.

Chabat, Jorge. 2013. "La seguridad en la política exterior de Calderón." *Foro Internacional* 53, no. 3/4: 729–49.

Chetwynd, Gareth. 2004. "Lula Seals Deal to Feed China's Booming Cities." *The Guardian*, May 28. http://www.theguardian.com/world/2004/may/28/china.brazil.

Chiba, Yasuyoshi. 2022. "Moscú: Ucrania está bombardeando una ciudad en Donbass para luego hacerlo pasar por un ataque de las tropas rusas." *RT*, April 28. https://actualidad.rt.com/actualidad/428335-ministerio-defensa-rusia-kiev-tropas.

China Daily. 2001. "Jiang Zemin to Start Latin America Tour." April 1. http://www.china.org.cn/english/2001/Apr/9917.htm.

Chow, Gregory C. 2004. "Economic Reform and Growth in China." *Annals of Economic and Finance* 5: 127–52.

Clarín.com. 2013. "Insólita medida de Maduro: crea el 'Viceministerio para la Suprema Felicidad Social.'" October 24. https://www.clarin.com/mundo/maduro-viceministerio-suprema-felicidad-social_0_HJ9xpCGjwXe.html.

Clem, Ralph S., and Anthony P. Maingot, eds. 2011. *Venezuela's Petro-Diplomacy: Hugo Chávez's Foreign Policy*. Gainesville: University Press of Florida.

CNN. 2016. "Inaugural Address: Trump's Full Speech." *CNN Digital*, January 1. https://www.cnn.com/2017/01/20/politics/trump-inaugural-address/index.html.

Congress.gov. 2021. "Text - S.1064 - 117th Congress (2021–2022): RENACER Act." November 10. http://www.congress.gov/.

Congressional Research Service. 2020. "China's Engagement with Latin America and the Caribbean." November. https://crsreports.congress.gov/product/pdf/IF/IF10982.

Congressional Research Service. 2021. "Latin America and the Caribbean: Impact of Covid-19." February 25. https://fas.org/sgp/crs/row/IF11581.pdf.

Constable, Pamela. 2006. "U.S. Officials Soften Stance Toward Bolivia's New Leftist President." February 21. http://www.washingtonpost.com/wp-dyn/content/article/2006/02/20/AR2006022001089.html.

Constable, Pamela. 2008. "Bolivian President Evo Morales Visits Washington, Talks of Fresh Start With U.S. Under Obama." November 20. http://www.washingtonpost.com/wp-dyn/content/article/2008/11/19/AR2008111903743.html.

Cooper, Andrew F., and Thomas F. Legler. 2006. *Intervention Without Intervening?: The OAS Defense and Promotion of Democracy in the Americas*. New York: Palgrave Macmillan. http://ebookcentral.proquest.com/lib/uncc-ebooks/detail.action?docID=307897.

Corporación Latinobarómetro. 2008. "Informe 2008." Corporación Latinobarómetro. http://www.latinobarometro.org/docs/INFORME_LATINOBAROMETRO_2008.pdf.

Corrales, Javier. 2009. "Using Social Power to Balance Soft Power: Venezuela's Foreign Policy." *Washington Quarterly* 32, no. 4: 87–114.

Correa-Cabrera, Guadalupe. 2022. "The End of the Mérida Initiative?" *Georgetown Journal of International Affairs* 23, no. 1 (Spring): 59–64.

Correo del Orinoco. 2016. "Ambas Naciones Han Suscrito Más de 300 Acuerdos Visita de Jiang Zemin En 2001 Impulsó Cooperación Entre China y Venezuela." April 14. http://www.correodelorinoco.gob.ve/visita-jiang-zemin-2001-impulso-cooperacion-entre-china-y-venezuela/.

Cote-Muñoz, Natalia. 2019. "China's Green Investments Won't Undo Its Environmental Damage to Latin America." Council on Foreign Relations blog, April 25. https://www.cfr.org/blog/chinas-green-investments-wont-undo-its-environmental-damage-latin-america.

Craham, Neville. 2019. "Sanctions on Venezuela Preventing PetroCaribe Debt Payments – Clarke." March 4. http://jamaica-gleaner.com/article/news/20190304/sanctions-venezuela-preventing-petrocaribe-debt-payments-clarke.

Crandall, Russell. 2006. *Gunboat Democracy: U.S. Interventions in the Dominican Republic, Grenada, and Panama*. Lanham, MD: Rowman & Littlefield.

Crandall, Russell. 2008. *The United States and Latin America After the Cold War*. New York: Cambridge University Press.

Crandall, Russell. 2011. "The Post-American Hemisphere." *Foreign Affairs*, June 1. https://www.foreignaffairs.com/articles/americas/2011-05-01/post-american-hemisphere.

Cunha Filho, Clayton M., André Luiz Coelho, and Fidel I. Pérez Flores. 2013. "A Right-to-Left Policy Switch? An Analysis of the Honduran Case under Manuel Zelaya." *International Political Science Review* 34, no. 5 (November 1): 519–42.

Davis, Bob. 2010. "Latin America: Lessons for Europe." *Wall Street Journal*, December 6, US. https://www.wsj.com/articles/SB10001424052748703350104575652723255241184.

Delgado, Antonio Maria, Kevin G. Hall, and Shirsho Dasgupta. 2020. "Venezuela Coup Plotters Met at Trump Doral. Central Figure Says U.S. Officials Knew of Plan." *Miami Herald*, October 31. https://www.miamiherald.com/news/nation-world/world/americas/article246819562.html.

DemocraciaSUR. 2007. "Ecuador: discurso de toma de posesión de Rafael Correa como president." January 22. http://democraciasur.com/2007/01/22/ecuador-discurso-de-toma-de-posesion-de-rafael-correa-como-presidente/.

Democracy Now! 2006. "Bolivian President Evo Morales on Latin America, U.S. Foreign Policy and the Role of the Indigenous People of Bolivia." September 22. http://www.democracynow.org/2006/9/22/bolivian_president_evo_morales_on_latin.

Democracy Now! 2010. "Bolivian President Evo Morales on President Obama: 'I Can't Believe a Black President Can Hold So Much Vengeance Against an Indian President.'" April 23. http://www.democracynow.org/2010/4/23/bolivian_president_evo_morales_to_president.

Deutsche Welle. 2018. "With UNASUR Floundering, Latin America Longs for Integration." DW.COM, August 14. https://www.dw.com/en/with-unasur-floundering-latin-america-longs-for-integration/a-45083122.

Díaz-Canel, Miguel. 2019. "Miguel Díaz-Canel Bermúdez on Twitter." Twitter, February 20. https://twitter.com/DiazCanelB/status/1098202265519902720.

Dinatale, Martín. 2020. "La Argentina permanecerá en el Grupo Lima pero rechazará una declaración contra Venezuela." Infobae, October 13. /politica/2020/10/13/la-argentina-permanecera-en-el-grupo-lima-pero-rechazara-una-declaracion-contra-venezuela/.

Doctor, Mahrukh. 2015. "Brazil's Role in Institutions of Global Economic Governance: The WTO and G20." *Global Society* 29, no. 3 (July 3): 286–300.

Domínguez, Pedro. 2021. "AMLO: relación con Donald Trump fue buena y en beneficio de México." *Milenio*, January 20. https://www.milenio.com/politica/amlo-relacion-donald-trump-beneficio-mexico.

Duarte Villa, Rafael. 2004. "Dos Etapas an La Política Venezolana Frente a Estados Unidos En El Período de Hugo Chávez." *Cuadernos Del Cendes* 21, no. 55: 21–45.

Durand, Jorge. 2013. "La 'desmigratización de la relación bilateral: Balance del sexenio de Felipe Calderón." *Foro Internacional* 53, no. 3/4 (July–December): 750–70.

ECLAC (Economic Commission for Latin America and the Caribbean). 2010. "Latin America and the Caribbean in the World Economy, 2009–2010." Economic Commission for Latin America and the Caribbean. https://repositorio.cepal.org/bitstream/handle/11362/1175/1/S1000784_en.pdf.

ECLAC (Economic Commission for Latin America and the Caribbean). 2014. "Preliminary Overview of the Economies of Latin America and the Caribbean, 2013." November 28. https://www.cepal.org/es/publicaciones/balance-preliminar-de-las-economias-de-america-latina-y-el-caribe-2013.

El Comercio. 2010. "La Cuota Política En La Cancillería Ha Desplazado a Diplomáticos de Carrera." April 19. https://www.elcomercio.com/actualidad/politica/cuota-politica-cancilleria-desplazado-diplomaticos.html.

El Nuevo Día. 2020. "¿Se acerca la hora de cambiar la política contra las drogas?" December 14. http://www.elnuevodia.com.co/nuevodia/actualidad/politica/458804-se-acerca-la-hora-de-cambiar-la-politica-contra-las-drogas.

El Nuevo Diario. "Guatemala Considera Retirarse de Petrocaribe." July 3. https://www.elnuevodiario.com.ni/politica/290596-guatemala-considera-retirarse-petrocaribe/.

El Observador. 2011. "Las declaraciones que provocaron el retiro de Vázquez." October 12. https://www.elobservador.com.uy/las-declaraciones-que-provocaron-el-retiro-vazquez-n211122.

El Universal. 2020. "'No soy autoritario', responde AMLO a intelectuales." September 18. https://elporvenir.mx/nacional/no-soy-autoritario-responde-amlo-a-intelectuales/140723.

Ellis, R. Evan. 2009. *China in Latin America: The Whats and Wherefores*. Boulder, CO: Lynne Rienner Publishers.

Ellis, R. Evan, Kelly Senters Piazza, Adam Greer, and Daniel Uribe. 2022. "China's Use of Soft Power in Support of its Strategic Engagement." *Journal of the Americas* 2: 159–82.

Embassy of the Russian Federation to the United Kingdom of Great Britain and Northern Ireland. 2016. "The Foreign Policy Concept of the Russian Federation." November 30. https://www.rusemb.org.uk/rp_insight/.

Emerson, R. Guy. 2010. "Radical Neglect? The 'War on Terror' and Latin America." *Latin American Politics and Society* 52, no. 1: 33–62.

Erikson, Daniel P. 2008. "Obama & Latin America: Magic or Realism?" *World Policy Journal* 25, no. 4: 101–7.

Escudé, Carlos. 1992. *Realismo periférico: fundamentos para la nueva política exterior argentina*. Buenos Aires: Planeta.

Escudé, Carlos. 2014. "Realism in the Periphery." In *Routledge Handbook of Latin America in the World*, edited by Jorge I. Domínguez and Ana Covarrubias, 45–57. New York: Routledge.

Espinal, Flavio Darío. 2022. "Cumbre de las Américas: un Puente hacia ningún lugar." *Diario Libre*, June 3. https://www.diariolibre.com/opinion/en-directo/2022/06/02/la-cumbre-es-un-encuentro-que-no-deja-nada-en-concreto/1866770.

Estado Plurinacional de Bolivia, Ministerio de la Presidencia. 2021. "President ratifica la lucha contra el narcotráfico tras la interceptación de 210 toneladas de sustancias controladas en el 2021." December 30. https://www.presidencia.gob.bo/index.php/prensa/noticias/1796-presidente-ratifica-la-lucha-contra-el-narcotrafico-tras-la-intercepcion-de-210-toneladas-de-sustancias-controladas-en-el-2021.

Estado Plurinacional de Bolivia, Viceministerio de Comunicación. 2020. "Conaltid presenta la estrategia nacional contra el narcotráfico 'Unidos, libres de drogas.'" February 28. https://comunicacion.gob.bo/?q=20200228/28857.

European Commission. 2017. "Uruguay: President Tabaré Vázquez Visits the European Commission." September 17. http://europa.eu/rapid/press-release_IP-07-1344_en.htm.

Executive Office of the President of the United States. 2019. "National Drug Control Strategy." January. https://www.state.gov/wp-content/uploads/2019/02/288960.pdf.

Executive Office of the President of the United States. 2022. "National Drug Control Strategy." April. https://www.whitehouse.gov/wp-content/uploads/2022/04/National-Drug-Control-2022Strategy.pdf.

Falomir Lockhart, Nicolás. 2013. "La identidad de UNASUR: ¿Regionalismo post-neoliberal o post-hegemónico?" *Revista de Ciencias Sociales*, no. 140. https://doi.org/10.15517/rcs.v0i140.12316.

Faria, Carlos Aurélio Pimenta de, and Clarisse Goulart Paradis. 2013. "Humanism and Solidarity in Brazilian Foreign Policy under Lula (2003–2010): Theory and Practice." *Brazilian Political Science Review* 7, no. 2: 8–36.

Felbab-Brown, Vanda. 2020. "The Upcoming Friction in US-Mexico Relations." *Brookings Institute Blog*. December 4. https://www.brookings.edu/blog/order-from-chaos/2020/12/04/the-upcoming-friction-in-us-mexico-relations/.

Ferro Clérico, Lilia. 2006. "Democracia y política exterior: Uruguay (1985–2006)." *América Latina Hoy* 44. http://www.redalyc.org/resumen.oa?id=30804406.

Fieser, Ezra. 2013. "Venezuela's Regional Energy Program Petrocaribe Wobbles." *Christian Science Monitor*, November 15. https://www.csmonitor.com/World/Americas/2013/1115/Venezuela-s-regional-energy-program-Petrocaribe-wobbles.

Flores, Francisco. 2013. "El Salvador Can Shine Again." *Harvard International Review*, February 11. http://hir.harvard.edu/article/?a=3036.

French, John. 2020. *Lula and His Politics of Cunning: From Metalworker to President of Brazil*. Chapel Hill: University of North Carolina Press, 2020.

Frenkel, Alejandro. 2019. "Prosur: el ultimo Frankenstein de la integración Sudamericana." *Nueva Sociedad* (June). https://nuso.org/articulo/prosur-integracion-america-latina-derecha-alianza/.

Foer, Franklin. 2006. "The Talented Mr. Chávez." *The Atlantic*, May. https://www.theatlantic.com/magazine/archive/2006/05/the-talented-mr-ch-vez/304809/.

Forero, Juan. 2001. "Venezuela's New Oil Law Is Seen as a Risk to Growth." *New York Times*, December 4, World. https://www.nytimes.com/2001/12/04/world/venezuela-s-new-oil-law-is-seen-as-a-risk-to-growth.html.

Forero, Juan. 2009. "Obama and Chávez Start Sparring Early." *Washington Post*, January 19, 2009. http://www.washingtonpost.com/wp-dyn/content/article/2009/01/18/AR2009011802325.html.

Fortin, Carlos, Jorge Heine, and Carlos Ominami. 2001. *El no alineamiento Activo y America Latina: Una doctrina para el nuevo siglo*. Santiago, Chile: Catalonia.

Fox, Vicente (and Rob Allyn). 2007. *Revolution of Hope: The Life, Faith, and Dreams of a Mexican President*. New York: Viking.

Frank, Dana. 2018. *The Long Honduran Night: Resistance, Terror, and the United States in the Aftermath of the Coup*. Chicago: Haymarket Books.

Franko, Patrice. 2007. *The Puzzle of Latin American Economic Development*. Lanham, MD: Rowman & Littlefield.

French, John. 2020. *Lula and His Politics of Cunning: From Metalworker to President of Brazil*. Chapel Hill: University of North Carolina Press.

Frenkel, Alejandro. 2019. "Prosur: el ultimo Frankenstein de la integración Sudamarica." *Nueva Sociedad Opinión*, June 29. https://nuso.org/articulo/prosur-integracion-america-latina-derecha-alianza/.

Fuentes, Claudio. 2006. "La Apuesta Por El 'Poder Blando': Política Exterior de La Concertación 2000–2006." In *El Gobierno de Ricardo Lagos: La Nueva Vía Chilena Hacia El Socialism*, edited by Robert L. Funk, 105–22. Santiago: Ediciones Universidad Diego Portales.

Garrison, Cassandra. 2020. "In Latin America, a Biden White House Faces a Rising China." *Reuters*, December 14. https://www.reuters.com/article/us-latam-usa-china-insight-idUSKBN28O18R.

Gedan, Benjamin N. 2021. "In Latin America, U.S. Popularity Is Already Bouncing Back." *Foreign Policy*, February 19. https://foreignpolicy.com/2021/02/19/latin-america-united-states-diplomacy-regional-cooperation/.

Gentile, Carmen. 2003. "Analysis: Powell Woos Latin America." *UPI*, June 11. https://www.upi.com/Analysis-Powell-woos-Latin-America/32821055378749/.

George W. Bush White House Archives. 2018. "President Bush Welcomes Brazilian President Lula to White House." June 11. https://georgewbush-whitehouse.archives.gov/news/releases/2003/06/20030620-3.html.

Giraudo, Maria Eugenia. 2020. "Dependent Development in South America: China and the Soybean Nexus." *Journal of Agrarian Change* 20, no. 1: 60–78.

Gleaner, The. 2022. "CARICOM Mulls Participation in Summit of the Americas." *The Gleaner*, May 8. https://jamaica-gleaner.com/article/news/20220508/caricom-mulls-participation-summit-americas.

Global Times. 2022. "'No Longer US Backyard,' Latin America Sends United Message." *Global Times*, June 7. https://www.globaltimes.cn/page/202206/1267442.shtml.

Gobierno Bolivariano de Venezuela. 2021. "Venezuela condena polarización política y espiral de violencia en EEUU." January 6. https://mppre.gob.ve/comunicado/venezuela-condena-polarizacion-politica-violencia-eeuu/.

Gobierno de México. 2016. "In the World Drug Problem, Let Us Shift from Prohibition

Alone to Effective Prevention and Regulation: Enrique Peña Nieto." April 19. https://www.gob.mx/epn/prensa/in-the-world-drug-problem-let-us-shift-from-prohibition-alone-to-effective-prevention-and-regulation-enrique-pena-nieto.
Gobierno de Mexico. 2020. "Videoconferencia Especial entre Cancilleres de China y de América Latina y el Caribe para atención de la pandemia por Covid-19." July 22. http://www.gob.mx/sre/prensa/videoconferencia-especial-entre-cancilleres-de-china-y-de-america-latina-y-el-caribe-para-atencion-de-la-pandemia-por-covid-19?idiom=es.
Golinger, Eva. 2018. *Confidante of "Tyrants": The Inside Story of the American Woman Trusted by the US's Biggest Enemies*. Oxford: New Internationalist.
Goodman, Joshua. 2021. "Chinese Loans to Latin America Plunge as Virus Strains Ties." *AP News*, February 22. https://apnews.com/article/business-global-trade-coronavirus-pandemic-asia-china-bc3c896d89842f8a50a601963899af57.
Goodstein, Laurie. 2005. "Robertson Suggests U.S. Kill Venezuela's Leader." *New York Times*, August 24, Politics. https://www.nytimes.com/2005/08/24/politics/robertson-suggests-us-kill-venezuelas-leader.html.
Government of Canada. 2020. "Lima Group Joint Statement." August 14. https://www.international.gc.ca/world-monde/international_relations-relations_internationales/latin_america-amerique_latine/2020-08-14-lima_group-groupe_lima.aspx?lang=eng.
Granma. 2005. "Acuerdo de Cooperación Energética Petrocaribe." July 1. http://www.granma.cu/granmad/2005/07/01/interna/articulo05.html.
Grim, Ryan, and Nick Wing. 2015. "Operation Naked King: U.S. Secretly Targeted Bolivia's Evo Morales in Drug Sting." *Huffington Post*, September 15. https://www.huffpost.com/entry/operation-naked-king-evo-morales_n_55f70da2e4b077ca094fdbe1.
Gruss, Bertrand. 2014. "After the Boom—Commodity Prices and Economic Growth in Latin America and the Caribbean." IMF Working Paper, August. https://www.imf.org/en/Publications/WP/Issues/2016/12/31/After-the-BoomCommodity-Prices-and-Economic-Growth-in-Latin-America-and-the-Caribbean-41846.
Guevara, Aleida. 2005. *Chávez: Venezuela and the New Latin America*. Melbourne: Ocean Press.
Gunder Frank, Andre. 1986. "The Development of Underdevelopment." In *Promise of Development: Theories of Change in Latin America*, edited by Peter F. Klarén and Thomas J. Bossert, 111–23. Boulder, CO: Westview Press.
Gutiérrez Castillo, Elba. 2006. "Trump, AMLO y los migrantes atrapados." *Nexos*, April 1. https://www.nexos.com.mx/?p=47463.
Hakim, Peter. 2006. "Is Washington Losing Latin America?" *Foreign Affairs* 85, no. 1: 39–53.
Harper, Liz. 2009. "At the DC Watering Hole: Senate Continues to Hold Tom Shannon's Nomination to Be the U.S. Ambassador to Brazil." *Americas Quarterly*, October 15. https://www.americasquarterly.org/node/1004/.

Harrison, Chase, Luisa Horwitz, and Carin Zissis. 2022. "Timeline: Tracking Latin America's Road to Vaccination." *AS/COA*, June 6. https://www.as-coa.org/articles/timeline-tracking-latin-americas-road-vaccination.
Healy, Kieran. 2017. "Fuck Nuance." *Sociological Theory* 35, no. 2 (June 1): 118–27.
Heine, Jorge. 2006. "China, Chile and Free Trade Agreements." *Estudios Internacionales* 38, no. 152: 143–47.
Hernández, David. 2022. "Conyuntura internacional y nacional del actual gobierno." *Revista CON-SECUENCIAS* 1, no. 1: 61–66.
Hernández Bermúdez, Orietta E. 2020. "La política exterior del Estado Plurinacional de Bolivia en el marco del proceso de cambio (2009–2019)." *Universidad de La Habana* 290 (July-December): 250–67. http://scielo.sld.cu/scielo.php?script=sci_arttext&pid=S0253-92762020000200250.
Herrera Chaves, Benjamín. 2006. "El 'nuevo orden mundial' entre la dispersión del poder y la hegemonía." *Polis. Revista Latinoamericana*, no. 13 (April 14). http://journals.openedition.org/polis/5329.
Hey, Jeanne A. K. 2003. "Ecuador: Foreign Policy on the Brink." In *Latin American and Caribbean Foreign Policy*, edited by Frank O. Mora and Jeanne A. K. Hey, 185–205. Lanham, MD: Rowman & Littlefield.
Hidalgo, Juan Carlos. 2009. "Obama Congratulates Correa." *Cato Institute Blog*, June 11.
Hidalgo, Juan Carlos. 2011. "Juan Manuel Santos Calls for a Discussion on the Legalization of Cocaine." *Cato Institute Blog*, November 14. https://www.cato.org/blog/juan-manuel-santos-calls-discussion-legalization-cocaine.
Human Rights Watch. 2020. "Q&A: Trump Administration's 'Remain in Mexico' Program." January 29. https://www.hrw.org/news/2020/01/29/qa-trump-administrations-remain-mexico-program.
Hunt, Edward. 2019. "Staying the Course in Mexico: The Role of the US in the Drug War, 2006–Present." *Third World Quarterly* 40, no. 6: 1184–1205.
Hunter, Wendy. 2003. "Brazil's New Direction." *Journal of Democracy* 14, no. 2 (2003): 151–62.
Iber, Patrick. 2015. *Neither Peace nor Freedom: The Cultural Cold War in Latin America*. Cambridge, MA: Harvard University Press.
IMFBlog. 2020. "Pandemic Persistence Clouds Latin America and Caribbean Recovery." October 22. https://blogs.imf.org/2020/10/22/pandemic-persistence-clouds-latin-america-and-caribbean-recovery/.
Infobae. 2020. "'El neoliberalismo fue un proyecto incoherente': Eréndira Sandoval propone a la CELAC armar un frente común contra la corrupción." *Infobae*, November 25. /america/mexico/2020/11/25/el-neoliberalismo-fue-un-proyecto-incoherente-irma-erendira-sandoval-propone-a-la-celac-armar-un-frente-comun-contra-la-corrupcion/.
Instituto de Iberoamérica. 2006. "Historia del FMLN." http://americo.usal.es/oir/opal/Documentos/ElSalvador/FMLN/Historia%20del%20FMLN.pdf. September 19.

Inter-American Commission on Human Rights. 2021. *Nicaragua: Concentration of Power and the Undermining of the Rule of Law*. OEA/Ser,L/V/II. October 25. https://www.oas.org/en/iachr/reports/pdfs/2021_Nicaragua-EN.pdf.
International Trade Administration website. n.d. "USMCA vs NAFTA: Major Differences Between USMCA and NAFTA in Key Chapters." https://www.trade.gov/usmca-vsnafta.
Inzunza, Gerardo. 2017. "Juan Manuel Santos Replies to Trump's Threat to Decertify Colombia." *Colombia Focus* (blog), September 21. https://colombiafocus.com/juan-manuel-santos-replies-to-trumps-threat-to-decertify-colombia.
IPS Correspondents. 2008. "Venezuela: Castro, Menem y EEUU felicitan a Hugo Chávez." February 28, 2018. https://ipsnoticias.net/1998/12/venezuela-castro-menem-y-eeuu-felicitan-a-hugo-chavez/.
Isacson, Adam. 2017. "Four Common Misconceptions About U.S.-Bound Drug Flows Through Mexico and Central America." *WOLA Blog*, June 20. https://www.wola.org/analysis/four-common-misconceptions-u-s-bound-drug-flows-mexico-central-america/.
Isacson, Adam, and Sarah Kinosian. 2017. "U.S. Military Assistance and Latin America." Washington Office on Latin America, April 27. https://www.wola.org/analysis/u-s-military-assistance-latin-america/.
Jaguaribe, Helio. 1979. "Autonomía Periférica y Hegemonía Céntrica." *Estudios Internacionales* 12, no. 46: 91–130.
Jegarajah, Sri. 2017. "Pacific Alliance Looks to Asia as NAFTA, TPP Face Uncertainty." *CNBC*, May 21. https://www.cnbc.com/2017/05/21/pacific-alliance-looks-to-asia-as-nafta-tpp-face-uncertainty.html.
Jenkins, Rhys, Enrique Dussel Peters, and Mauricio Mesquita Moreira. 2008. "The Impact of China on Latin America and the Caribbean." *World Development* 36, no. 2: 235–53.
Jenne, Nicole, and Sebastián Briones Razeto. 2018. "Integración Regional y La Política Exterior de Chile. ¿Paradoja o Acomodo?" *Estudios Internacionales* 50, no. 189 (April): 9–35.
Jones, Bart. 2007. *¡Hugo! The Hugo Chávez Story From Mud Hut to Perpetual Revolution*. Hanover, NH: Steerforth Press.
Jourdan, Adam, Marco Aquino, and Matt Spetalnick. 2022. "Exclusive: Under Biden, China Has Widened Trade Lead in Much of Latin America." *Reuters*, June 8. https://www.reuters.com/world/americas/exclusive-under-biden-china-has-widened-trade-lead-much-latin-america-2022-06-08/.
Kassab, Hanna S., and Jonathan D. Rosen. 2016. "Regional Differences in Obama's Foreign Policy: A Theoretical Approach." In *The Obama Doctrine in the Americas*, edited by Hanna S. Kassab and Jonathan D. Rosen, 307–27. Lanham, MD: Lexington Books.
Keohane, Robert O. 1984. *After Hegemony: Cooperation and Discord in the World Political Economy*. Princeton, NJ: Princeton University Press.

KhabarOnline. 2012. "US Does Not Favor Independent Latin America: Iran MP." December 30. https://english.khabaronline.ir/news/183806/US-does-not-favor-independent-Latin-America-Iran-MP.

King, John. 2007. "Obama Again Stirs Up Decades-Old Debate on Cuba." August 21. Cnn.com. http://www.cnn.com/2007/POLITICS/08/21/obama.cuba/.

Kirchner, Cristina. 2012. *Twitter*, October 7. https://twitter.com/CFKArgentina/status/255138728698331137.

Kosevich, Ekaterina. 2021. "Historia de la cooperación política y económica entre Rusia y México a principios del siglo XXI (2000–2019)." *América Latina en la historia económica* 28, no. 3 (Sept.-Dec.): 1–21.

Koven, Barnett S., and Cynthia McClintock. 2016. "The Obama Administration and Peru." In *The Obama Doctrine in the Americas*, edited by Hanna S. Kassab and Jonathan D. Rosen, 155–84. Lanham, MD: Lexington Books.

Kozloff, Nikolas. 2011. "Wikileaks Cables: The Great Equaliser in Peru." *Al Jazeera*, June 2. https://www.aljazeera.com/features/2011/6/2/wikileaks-cables-the-great-equaliser-in-peru/.

Kraul, Chris, and Patrick McDonnell. 2008. "Russia Seeking Inroads among Latin Nations." *Los Angeles Times*, November 27. https://www.latimes.com/archives/la-xpm-2008-nov-27-fg-medvedev27-story.html.

Kurtz-Phelan, Daniel. 2013. "What Is IBSA Anyway?" *Americas Quarterly*, Spring. http://www.americasquarterly.org/content/what-ibsa-anyway.

La Nación. 2013. "Ecuador renuncia a preferencias arancelarias de EE. UU." June 27. https://www.nacion.com/economia/ecuador-renuncia-a-preferencias-arancelarias-de-ee-uu/RL4NNJF5OBG4RNO536JRKHUNJE/story/.

La Nación. 2016. "El viaje de George Bush a la Argentina en 2005: la gira que hundió la relación bilateral." February 18. https://www.lanacion.com.ar/1872180-el-viaje-de-george-bush-a-la-argentina-en-2005-la-gira-que-hundio-la-relacion-bilateral.

La Vanguardia. 2009. "Hugo Chávez dice que China es el mayor motor para conducir al mundo más allá de crisis." April 8. https://www.lavanguardia.com/internacional/20090408/53678214573/hugo-chavez-dice-que-china-es-el-mayor-motor-para-conducir-al-mundo-mas-alla-de-crisis.html.

Latin American Commission on Drugs and Democracy. 2009. "Drugs and Democracy: Toward a Paradigm Shift." http://www.ungassondrugs.org/images/stories/towards.pdf.

Laufer, Rubén. 2020. "El proyecto Chino 'La Franja y La Ruta' y América Latina: ¿Otro norte para el sur?" *Revista Interdisciplinaria de Estudios Sociales*, no. 20: 9–52.

Lecuna, Vicente, and Harold A. Bierck Jr. 1951. *Selected Writings of Bolivar*. New York: Colonial Press, Inc.

Lee, Rensselaer, and Patrick Clawson. 1993. "Crop Substitution in the Andes." Office of National Drug Control Policy, December. https://www.ncjrs.gov/pdffiles1/Digitization/146794NCJRS.pdf.

Lehman, Kenneth. 2006. "A 'Medicine of Death? U.S. Policy and Political Disarray in Bolivia, 1985–2006." In *Addicted to Failure: U.S. Security Policy in Latin America and the Andean Region*, edited by Brian Loveman, 130–68. Lanham: MD: Rowman and Littlefield.

Leogrande, William M. 1990. "From Reagan to Bush: The Transition in US Policy Towards Central America." *Journal of Latin American Studies* 22, no. 3 (October): 595–621.

Leogrande, William M., and Peter Kornbluh. 2014. *Back Channel to Cuba: The Hidden History of Negotiations Between Washington and Havana*. Chapel Hill: University of North Carolina Press.

Levitsky, Steven, and Kenneth M. Roberts. 2011. "Latin America's 'Left Turn': A Framework for Analysis." In *The Resurgence of the Latin American Left*, edited by Steven Levitsky and Kenneth M. Roberts, 1–28. Baltimore: Johns Hopkins University Press.

Lima Group. 2021. "Statement from the Lima Group." Government of Canada, January 5. https://www.international.gc.ca/world-monde/international_relations-relations_internationales/latin_america-amerique_latine/2021-01-05-lima_group-groupe_lima.aspx?lang=eng.

Linthicum, Kate. 2022. "Mexico's President Vowed to End the Drug War. Instead He's Doubled the Number of Troops in the Streets." *Los Angeles Times*, August 19.

Livingstone, Grace. 2009. *America's Backyard: The United States and Latin America from the Monroe Doctrine to the War on Terror*. London: Zed Books.

Long, Tom. 2015. *Latin America Confronts the United States: Asymmetry and Influence*. Cambridge: Cambridge University Press.

López Maya, Margarita. 2003. "The Venezuelan 'Caracazo' of 1989: Popular Protest and Institutional Weakness." *Journal of Latin American Studies* 35, no. 1 (February): 117–37.

Los Angeles Times. 2002. "Uruguay Cuts Diplomatic Ties to Cuba." April 24. http://articles.latimes.com/2002/apr/24/news/mn-39626.

Lucero, Jose Antonio. 2001. "Crisis and Contention in Ecuador." *Journal of Democracy* 12, no. 2 (April): 59–73.

Luna, Juan Pablo, and Cristóbal Rovira Kaltwasser, eds. 2014. *The Resilience of the Latin American Right*. Baltimore: Johns Hopkins University Press.

MacFarquhar, Neil. 2008. "Upheaval on Wall St. Stirs Anger in the U.N." *New York Times*, September 23, World. https://www.nytimes.com/2008/09/24/world/24nations.html.

Malamud, Andrés. 2011. "Argentine Foreign Policy Under the Kirchners: Ideological, Pragmatic, or Simply Peronist?" In *Latin American Foreign Policies*, 87–102. New York: Palgrave Macmillan. https://doi.org/10.1057/9780230118270_6.

Malamud, Andrés. 2019. "Overlapping Regionalism, No Integration: Conceptual Issues and The Latin American Experiences." *Politica Internacional*, 46–59.

Malamud, Andrés, and Gian Luca Gardini. 2012. "Has Regionalism Peaked? The Latin

American Quagmire and Its Lessons." *International Spectator: Italian Journal of International Affairs* 47, no. 1 (March 1): 116–33.

Mapstone, Naomi. 2012. "Humala Moves Away From Peru's Left." *Financial Times*, June 8. https://www.ft.com/content/c8244050-a96e-11e1-9972-00144feabdc0.

Marcondes, Danilo, and Emma Mawdsley. 2017. "South–South in Retreat? The Transitions from Lula to Rousseff to Temer and Brazilian Development Cooperation." *International Affairs* 93, no. 3: 681–99.

Mariano, Marcelo Passini. 2015. *A Política Externa Brasileira e a Integração Regional*. Sao Paulo: Editora Unesp. http://editoraunesp.com.br/catalogo/9788568334638,a-politica-externa-brasileira-e-a-integracao-regional.

Marmouyet, Françoise. 2019. "PetroCaribe Challenge: The Campaign Mobilising Haitians against Corruption." *France 24*, February 15. https://www.france24.com/en/20190215-petrocaribe-challenge-social-media-campaign-mirambeau-haiti-corruption-moise.

Martinez, Elias David Morales, and Mariana P. O. de Lyra. 2018. "The Role of UNASUR in the South American Democratic Crises (2008–2015). *Revista Carta Internacional* 13, no. 1: 98–126.

Mather, Steven. 2010. "Venezuela Pays for First ALBA Trade with Ecuador in New Regional Currency." Venezuelanalysis.com, July 7. https://venezuelanalysis.com/news/5480.

Maxwell, Kenneth. 2002. "Brazil: Lula's Prospects." *New York Review of Books*, December 5. http://www.nybooks.com/articles/2002/12/05/brazil-lulas-prospects/.

McDermott, Jeremy. 2008. "Colombian President Accuses Hugo Chavez of Genocide." *Telegraph*, March 5, World. https://www.telegraph.co.uk/news/worldnews/southamerica/colombia/1580810/Colombian-president-accuses-Hugo-Chavez-of-genocide.html.

McPherson, Alan. 2014. *The Invaded: How Latin Americans and Their Allies Fought and Ended U.S. Occupations*. New York: Oxford University Press.

Mejía, Daniel. 2016. "Plan Colombia: An Analysis of Effectiveness and Costs." Foreign Policy at Brookings, July. https://www.brookings.edu/wp-content/uploads/2016/07/mejia-colombia-final-2.pdf.

MercoPress. 2005. "Mesa: 'No Venezuela Meddling in Bolivian Affairs.'" June 13. https://en.mercopress.com/2005/06/13/mesa-no-venezuela-meddling-in-bolivian-affairs.

MercoPress. 2020. "Chile, Colombia, Ecuador, and Peru Join Forces to Combat Illegal Fishing." November 6. https://en.mercopress.com/2020/11/06/chile-colombia-ecuador-and-peru-join-forces-to-combat-illegal-fishing.

Merke, Federico, and Diego Reynoso. 2016. "Dimensiones de Política Exterior En América Latina Según Juicio de Expertos: Experts' Perception of Foreign Policy Dimensions." *Estudios Internacionales (Santiago)* 48, no. 185: 107–30.

Merke, Federico, Diego Reynoso, and Luis Leandro Schenoni. 2020. "Foreign Policy Change in Latin America: Exploring a Middle-Range Concept." *Latin American Research Review* 55, no. 3: 413–29.

Meyer, Bill. 2009. "Honduras Coup Shows Hugo Chavez's Influence and Power in Latin America Is Limited: Analysis." cleveland.com, July 28. http://www.cleveland.com/world/index.ssf/2009/07/honduras_coup_shows_hugo_chave.html.

Michelutti, Lucia. 2017. "'We Are All Chávez': Charisma as an Embodied Experience." *Latin American Perspectives* 44, no. 1 (January 1): 232–50. https://doi.org/10.1177/0094582X16666023.

Ministerio de Relaciones Exteriores (Cuba). 2022. "Cuba: Llamas a preserver la paz y la seguridad internacional." *Granma*, February 22. https://www.granma.cu/mundo/2022-02-22/llamamos-a-preservar-la-paz-y-la-seguridad-internacionales-22-02-2022-23-02-41.

Ministry of Foreign Affairs of the People's Republic of China. 2018. "First Ministerial Meeting of China-CELAC Forum Grandly Opens in Beijing." August 1. https://www.fmprc.gov.cn/mfa_eng/zxxx_662805/t1227318.shtml.

Miro, Jordi. 2014. "Los Diplomáticos Venezolanos Carecen de Preparación." *El Nuevo Herald*, November 12. https://www.elnuevoherald.com/noticias/mundo/america-latina/venezuela-es/article3798781.html.

Moak, Ken. 2020. "Bolsonaro's Mixed China Policies Could Burn Brazil." *Asia Times*, December 17. https://asiatimes.com/2020/12/bolsonaros-mixed-china-policies-could-burn-brazil/.

Mora, Frank O., and Jeanne A. K. Hey, eds. 2003. *Latin American and Caribbean Foreign Policy*. Lanham, MD: Rowman & Littlefield.

Morales, Pablo Sebastian. 2021. "International Broadcasters and Country Image Management: Comparing Audience Perceptions of China, Russia and Iran in Latin America." *Global Media and China* 6, no. 1 (March): 100–115.

Morandé, José A. 2003. "Chile: The Invisible Hand and Contemporary Foreign Policy." In *Latin American and Caribbean Foreign Policy*, edited by Frank O. Mora and Jeanne A. K. Hey, 243–64. Lanham, MD: Rowman & Littlefield.

Morasso, Carla. 2016. "La orientación autonomista de la política exterior argentina (2003–2015)," June. http://rephip.unr.edu.ar/xmlui/handle/2133/6715.

Moreno, Carlos. 2007. "Integración Lationamericana: ALCA vs. ALBA." *Presente y Pasado. Revista de Historia* 12, no. 23 (June): 155–78.

Mufson, Steven. 1999. "In Panama, Ports in a Storm." *Washington Post*, December 8. http://www.washingtonpost.com/wp-srv/WPcap/1999-12/08/008r-120899-idx.html.

Muñoz, Heraldo. 2008. *A Solitary War: A Diplomat's Chronicle of the Iraq War and Its Lessons*. Golden, CO: Fulcrum.

Murphy, Annie. 2012. "'Who Rules In Honduras?' Coup's Legacy of Violence." NPR.org, February 12. https://www.npr.org/2012/02/12/146758628/who-rules-in-honduras-a-coups-lasting-impact.

Myers, Margaret, and Ricardo Barrios. 2021. "How China Ranks Its Partners in LAC." *The Dialogue*, February 3. https://www.thedialogue.org/blogs/2021/02/how-china-ranks-its-partners-in-lac/.

Obama, Barack. 2007. "Our Main Goal: Freedom in Cuba." *Miami Herald*, August 21.

Oddone, Carlos Nahuel, and Leonardo Granato. 2007. "Los nuevos proyectos de integración regional vigentes en América Latina: la alternativa bolivariana para nuestra América y la comunidad sudamericana de naciones." *OIKOS (Rio de Janeiro)* 6, no. 1. http://www.revistaoikos.org/seer/index.php/oikos/article/view/17.

O'Keefe, Thomas Andrew. 1996. "How the Andean Pact Transformed Itself into a Friend of Foreign Enterprise." *International Lawyer* 30, no. 4: 811–24.

Oliva, Carla V. 2010. "Argentina's Relations With China." In *Latin America Facing China: South-South Relations Beyond the Washington Consensus*, edited by Alex E. Fernández Jilberto and Barbara Hogenboom, 99–114. New York: Berghahn Books.

Oliveros, Luis. 2020. "Impacto de Las Sanciones Financieras y Petroleras Sobre La Economía Venezolana." Washington, DC: Washington Office on Latin America, October. https://www.wola.org/wp-content/uploads/2020/10/Oliveros-informe-completo-2.pdf.

OPEC. 2004. *Annual Report 2003*. Organization of the Petroleum Exporting Countries Public Relations & Information Department. https://www.opec.org/opec_web/static_files_project/media/downloads/publications/AR002003.pdf.

OPEC. 2008. *Annual Report 2007*. Organization of the Petroleum Exporting Countries Public Relations & Information Department. https://www.opec.org/opec_web/static_files_project/media/downloads/publications/AR2007.pdf.

OPEC. 2010. *Annual Report 2009*. Organization of the Petroleum Exporting Countries Public Relations & Information Department. https://www.opec.org/opec_web/static_files_project/media/downloads/publications/AR2009.pdf.

Organization of American States. 2001. "Statement From the OAS General Assembly." September 11. http://www.oas.org/charter/docs/comuni_eng/E_005.htm.

Osborn, Catherine. 2022. "Washington Learns to Live With Regional Differences on Ukraine." *Foreign Policy Latin America Brief*, April 29. https://foreignpolicy.com/2022/04/29/united-states-brazil-argentina-mexico-russia-ukraine-war/

Packenham, Robert. 1992. *The Dependency Movement: Scholarship and Politics in Development Studies*. Cambridge, MA: Harvard University Press.

Padgett, Tim. 2013. "The Obama Administration Looks to Latin America After Years of Neglect." *Time*, May 13. https://world.time.com/2013/05/13/has-washington-finally-discovered-latin-america/.

Pan American Health Organization. 2022. "Latin American Manufacturers Complete First Training in mRNA Technology in Bid to Improve Regional Vaccine Production." March 24. https://www.paho.org/en/news/24-3-2022-latin-american-manufacturers-complete-first-training-mrna-technology-bid-improve.

Paraguassu, Lisandra. 2018. "Six South American Nations Suspend Membership of Anti-U.S. Bloc." April 21. *Reuters*. https://www.reuters.com/article/us-unasur-membership/six-south-american-nations-suspend-membership-of-anti-u-s-bloc-idUSKBN1HR2P6.

Pearce, Stephanie. 2018. "The First Five Years of the Sucre: Successes and Limitations of ALBA's Regional Virtual Currency." In *Understanding ALBA: Progress, Problems, and Prospects of Alternative Regionalism in Latin America and the Caribbean*, edited by Ana Cusack, 73–90. London: Institute of Latin American Studies.

Pecequilo, Cristina Soreanu, and Corival Alves do Carmo. 2013. "Regional Integration and Brazilian Foreign Policy: Strategies in the South American Space." *Revista de Sociologia e Política; Curitiba* 21, no. 48 (December): 51–65.

People's Daily Online. 2006. "Chinese President Calls for Stronger China-Bolivia Links." January 10. http://en.people.cn/200601/09/eng20060109_233989.html.

Pérez-Hernáiz, Hugo Antonio. 2008. "The Uses of Conspiracy Theories for the Construction of a Political Religion in Venezuela." *International Journal of Humanities and Social Sciences* 2, no. 8: 970–81.

Perelló, Lucas. 2020. "Honduras Is Losing the Fight against Corruption." *Global Americans* (blog), January 16. https://theglobalamericans.org/2020/01/honduras-is-losing-the-fight-against-corruption/.

Pethokoukis, James. 2008. "Susan Schwab on the Colombian Trade Deal." *US News & World Report*, March 26. https://www.usnews.com/news/world/articles/2008/03/26/susan-schwab-on-the-colombian-trade-deal.

Petrocaribe Development Fund. 2018. "Overview of the PetroCaribe Development Fund." May 16. http://www.petrocaribejm.org/overview.

Pew Research Center. 2002. "What the World Thinks in 2002." *Pew Research Center's Global Attitudes Project* (blog), December 4. http://www.pewglobal.org/2002/12/04/what-the-world-thinks-in-2002/.

Pew Research Center. 2008. "Global Public Opinion in the Bush Years (2001–2008)." *Pew Research Center's Global Attitudes Project*, December 18. http://www.pewglobal.org/2008/12/18/global-public-opinion-in-the-bush-years-2001-2008/.

Pew Research Center. 2018. "U.S. Unauthorized Immigration Total Lowest in a Decade." *Pew Research Center's Hispanic Trends Project*, November 27. https://www.pewresearch.org/hispanic/2018/11/27/u-s-unauthorized-immigrant-total-dips-to-lowest-level-in-a-decade/.

Prebisch, Raúl. 1962. "The Economic Development of Latin America and Its Principal Problems." *Economic Bulletin for Latin America* VII, no. I (February): 1–22.

Public Law 104-114, 104th Congress. 1996. *Cuban Liberty and Democratic Solidarity (LIBERTAD) Act of 1996*. March 12. https://www.govinfo.gov/content/pkg/PLAW-104publ114/html/PLAW-104publ114.htm.

Public Papers of the Presidents of the United States, 2001: Book, 2, George W. Bush, July 1 to December 31, 2001. 2004. Washington, DC: Government Printing Office.

Puig, Juan Carlos. 1980. *Doctrinas Internacionales y Autonomía Latinoamericana*. Buenos Aires: Fundación Bicentenario de Simón Bolívar.

Pulecio, Jorge Reinel. 2005. "La estrategia Uribe de negociación del TLC." *Colombia Internacional*, no. 61: 12–32. https://doi.org/10.7440/colombiaint61.2005.01.

Quinn, Andrew. 2009. "Clinton: U.S. Worried by Venezuelan Arms Purchases."

Reuters, September 15. https://www.reuters.com/article/us-usa-venezuela-idUSTRE58E60S20090915.

Quirós, Ludmila. 2017. "Reconfiguración política y Gobernanza Regional en América Latina ¿Hacia dónde va el regionalismo post-liberal?" *Revista Andina de Estudios Políticos* 7, no. 2 (December 15): 111–31.

Ramírez, Carlos. 2002. "México recupera autonomía geopolítica ante EU-Biden." *24-Horas*, May 6. https://www.24-horas.mx/2022/05/06/mexico-recupera-autonomia-geopolitica-ante-eu-biden/.

Ramírez, Mariana Aparicio, Gustavo Adolfo Islas Cadena, and Ivan López Martínez. 2021. "Un diálogo entre discursos y hechos: el acercamiento del Mercado Común del Sur (Mercosur) y la Alianza del Pacífico (AP)." *Foro Internacional*, 45–79.

Ramonet, Ignacio. 2010. *Fidel Castro: Biografía a dos voces*. New York: Penguin Random House Grupo Editorial España.

Rauhala, Emily, and Yasmeen Abutaleb. 2020. "U.S. Says It Won't Join WHO-Linked Effort to Develop, Distribute Coronavirus Vaccine." *Washington Post*, October 29. https://www.washingtonpost.com/world/coronavirus-vaccine-trump/2020/09/01/b44b42be-e965-11ea-bf44-0d31c85838a5_story.html.

Ray, Rebecca, and Kevin Gallagher. 2015. "China-Latin America Economic Bulletin, 2015 Edition." Global Economic Governance Initiative, Discussion Paper 2015-9. September. https://www.bu.edu/pardeeschool/files/2015/02/Economic-Bulletin-2015.pdf.

Relea, Fracesc. 2004. "Guerra de declaraciones entre Argentina y Washington." *El País*. January 9, Internacional. https://elpais.com/diario/2004/01/09/internacional/1073602807_850215.html.

Reuters. 2009. "ANALYSIS-Honduras Coup Leaders Hunker Down for Isolation." August 3. https://www.reuters.com/article/idUSN03525204.

Reuters. 2014. "Brazil's Rousseff Lets Obama off the Hook for NSA Spying." July 10. https://www.reuters.com/article/us-brazil-usa-espionage-idUSKBN0FF2H820140710.

Reuters. 2021. "Taiwán dice que está ayudando a su aliado Paraguay a comprar vacunas COVID-19." Infobae, March 17. https://www.infobae.com/america/agencias/2021/03/17/taiwan-dice-que-esta-ayudando-a-su-aliado-paraguay-a-comprar-vacunas-covid-19-2/.

Rico, Maite. 2006. "Perú denuncia la injerencia de Chávez y retira a su embajador." *El País*, May 1, Internacional. https://elpais.com/diario/2006/05/01/internacional/1146434410_850215.html.

Riggirozzi, Pía, and Jean Grugel. 2015. "Regional Governance and Legitimacy in South America: The Meaning of UNASUR." *International Affairs* 91, no. 4 (July 1): 781–97. https://doi.org/10.1111/1468-2346.12340.

Robertson, Ewan. 2014. "UNASUR Moves toward Continental Freedom of Movement, Venezuela Makes 'Equality' Call." Venezuelanalysis.com, December 5. https://venezuelanalysis.com/news/11057.

Rohter, Larry. 1992. "The 1992 Campaign: Florida; Clinton Sees Opportunity to Break G.O.P. Grip on Cuban-Americans." *New York Times*, October 31, https://www.nytimes.com/1992/10/31/us/1992-campaign-florida-clinton-sees-opportunity-break-gop-grip-cuban-americans.html.

Rohter, Larry. 2000. "Dollar May Buy a Reprieve in Ecuador." *New York Times*, January 16, World. https://www.nytimes.com/2000/01/16/world/dollar-may-buy-a-reprieve-in-ecuador.html.

Rohter, Larry, and Elisabeth Bumiller. 2005. "Hemisphere Summit Marred by Violent Anti-Bush Protests." *New York Times*, November 5. https://www.nytimes.com/2005/11/05/world/americas/hemisphere-summit-marred-by-violent-antibush-protests.html.

Romero, Carlos. 2010. "Las Secuelas Regionales de La Crisis de Honduras." *Nueva Sociedad* 226 (March): 85–99.

Romero, Simon. 2008. "Regional Bloc Criticizes Colombia Raid in Ecuador." *New York Times*, March 6, World. https://www.nytimes.com/2008/03/06/world/americas/06venez.html.

Rosales, Antulio. 2016. "Deepening Extractivism and Rentierism: China's Role in Venezuela's Bolivarian Developmental Model." *Canadian Journal of Development Studies / Revue Canadienne d'études Du Développement* 37, no. 4: 560–77.

Rossone do Paula, Francine. 2018. *The Emergence of Brazil to the Global Stage: Ascending and Falling in the International Order of Competition*. London: Routledge.

Rueda, Carlos Roberto. 2018. "La nueva política exterior de Moreno." www.expreso.ec, November 7. https://www.expreso.ec/actualidad/politica-nacional-lenin-moreno-rafaelcorrea-unasur-BD2261407.

Russell, Roberto, and Juan Gabriel Tokatlian. 2003. "From Antagonistic Autonomy to Relational Autonomy: A Theoretical Reflection from the Southern Cone." *Latin American Politics & Society* 45, no. 1 (Spring): 1–24.

Russell, Roberto, and Juan Gabriel Tokatlian. 2016. "Contemporary Argentina and the Rise of Brazil." *Bulletin of Latin American Research* 35, no. 1: 20–33.

Rutenberg, Jim. 2007. "In Uruguay, Bush Finds Friendly Ear and Taste of Home." *New York Times*, March 11. https://www.nytimes.com/2007/03/11/world/americas/11prexy.html.

Sahni, Varun. 2001. "Peripheric Realism versus Complex Interdependence: Analyzing Argentine and Mexican Foreign Policies since 1988." *International Studies* 38, no. 1 (January 1): 17–27.

Salon. 2012. "Guatemalan President Calls Hunger a Security Issue." February 15. https://www.salon.com/2012/02/15/guatemala_president_calls_hunger_a_security_issue/.

San Martin, Nancy. 2007. "El Salvador Sticks by Iraq Coalition." *Seattle Times*, October 26. http://old.seattletimes.com/html/iraq/2003975544_iraq26.html.

Sanahuja, José Antonio, Pablo Stefanoni, and Francisco J. Verdes-Montenegro. 2022. "América Latina frente al 24-F ucraniano: entre la tradición diplomática y las tensiones políticas." *Fundación Carolina, Documentos de Trabajo* 62. https://www.fundacioncarolina.es/america-latina-frente-al-24-f-ucraniano-entre-la-tradicion-diplomatica-y-las-tensiones-politicas/.

Sánchez, Ilka Treminio, Fábio Kerche, and Esteban De Gori. 2021. "Latin America: Impact of the January 6 Insurrection at the U.S. Capitol." *AulaBlog*, February 2. https://aulablog.net/2021/02/11/latin-america-impact-of-the-january-6-insurrection-at-the-u-s-capitol/.

Sanchez, Omar. 2005."Argentina's Landmark 2003 Presidential Election: Renewal and Continuity." *Bulletin of Latin American Research* 24, no. 4 (October 1): 454–75.

Sánchez, Rafael. 2016. *Dancing Jacobins: A Venezuelan Genealogy of Latin American Populism.* New York: Fordham University Press.

Sanders, Richard M. 2022. "Why Brazil and Argentina Chose Russia Over Ukraine." *National Interest*. March 20. https://nationalinterest.org/feature/why-brazil-and-argentina-chose-russia-over-ukraine-201244.

Santos, Juan Manuel, Ernesto Zedillo, and Ruth Dreifuss. 2019. "Legalization Is the Only Viable Drug Policy." Project Syndicate, March 19. https://www.project-syndicate.org/commentary/drug-legalization-regulation-only-viable-policy-by-juan-manuel-santos-et-al-2019-03.

Santos Vieira de Jesus, Diego. 2010. "The Brazilian Way." *Nonproliferation Review* 17, no. 3 (November 1): 551–67. https://doi.org/10.1080/10736700.2010.517003.

Saraiva, José Flávio Sombra. 2014. "Autonomia Na Inserção Internacional Do Brasil: Um Caminho Histórico Próprio." *Contexto Internacional* 36, no. 1: 9–41.

Saraiva, Miriam Gomes. 2014. "Balanço Da Política Externa de Dilma Rousseff: Perspectivas Futuras?" *Relações Internacionais*, no. 44: 25–35.

Sarney, José. 1986. "Brazil: A President's Story." *Foreign Affairs*, September 1. https://www.foreignaffairs.com/articles/brazil/1986-09-01/brazil-presidents-story.

Schenoni, Luis, and Carlos Escudé. 2016. "Peripheral Realism Revisited." *Revista Brasileira de Política Internacional* 59, no. 1: 1–18.

Schor, Elana. 2008. "US Elections 2008: Obama Urges Thaw in US-Cuba Relations." *The Guardian*, May 23. https://www.theguardian.com/world/2008/may/23/barackobama.uselections20081.

Schoultz, Lars. 1998. *Beneath the United States: A History of U.S. Policy Toward Latin America.* Cambridge, MA: Harvard University Press.

Seelke, Clare Ribando, and Kristin Finklea. 2015. "U.S.-Mexican Security Cooperation: The Mérida Initiative and Beyond." *Congressional Research Service*, May 7. https://www.everycrsreport.com/files/20150507_R41349_1bac654f49733b184f1859ed02cbddf52230dbaa.pdf.

Seguimiento.co. 2020. "Colombia y Chile proponen que Prosur se eleve a rango de tratado en los países miembros." November 10. https://www.seguimiento.co/colombia/colombia-y-chile-proponen-que-prosur-se-eleve-rango-de-tratado-en-los-paises-miembros-41139.

Serbin, Andrés, and Andrei Serbin Pont. 2017. "The Foreign Policy of the Bolivarian

Republic of Venezuela: The Role and Legacy of Hugo Chávez." *Latin American Policy* 8, no. 2: 232–48. https://doi.org/10.1111/lamp.12122.

Seshasayee, Hari. 2021. "India and Latin America: Moving from Transactional to Permanent Healthcare Partners." *Georgetown Journal of International Affairs*, March 18. https://gjia.georgetown.edu/2021/03/18/india-and-latin-america-moving-from-transactional-to-permanent-healthcare-partners/.

Seshasayee, Hari. 2022. "Latin America: The Last Frontier for India's Foreign Policy." *Observer Research Foundation*, June 6. https://www.orfonline.org/expert-speak/the-last-frontier-for-indias-foreign-policy/.

Sevastopulo, Demetri, and Gideon Long. 2021. "US Development Bank Strikes Deal to Help Ecuador Pay China Loans." January 14. https://www.ft.com/content/affcc432-03c4-459d-a6b8-922ca8346c14.

Shannon, Thomas A. 2008. "U.S. Asst. Secretary of State for Western Hemisphere Affairs Thomas A. Shannon." Americas Society/Council of the Americas website, April 2. https://www.as-coa.org/articles/us-asst-secretary-state-western-hemisphere-affairs-thomas-shannon.

Sheridan, Mary Beth. 2022. "Mexico's President Meets Biden Amid Tension over Migration, Fentanyl." *Washington Post*, July 12.

Sheridan, Mary Beth, and Nick Miroff. 2002. "They Call Him the Eagle: How the U.S. Lost a Key Ally in Mexico as Fentanyl Took Off." *Washington Post*, December 12. https://www.washingtonpost.com/investigations/interactive/2022/the-eagle-mexico-drug-cartels/?itid=hp-top-table-main_p001_f001.

Simonoff, Alejandro. 2009. "Regularidades de La Política Exterior de Néstor Kirchner." *CONfines de Relaciones Internacionales y Ciencia Política* 5, no. 10 (December): 71–86.

Simonoff, Alejandro. 2016. "La vigencia del pensamiento autonómico de Juan Carlos Puig." *Ciclos en la Historia, la Economía y la Sociedad* 22, no. 44. http://digicodi.com.ar/index.php/ciclos/article/view/2.

Slipak, Ariel Martín. 2014. "Un análisis del ascenso de China y sus vínculos con América Latina a la luz de la Teoría de la Dependencia." *Realidad Económica* 282: 99–124.

Soares de Lima, Maria Regina, and Monica Hirst. 2006. "Brazil as an Intermediate State and Regional Power: Action, Choice and Responsibilities." *International Affairs* 82, no. 1: 21–40.

Spagat, Elliott, Joshua Goodman, and Chris Megerian. 2012. "Biden Scrambles to Avoid Americas Summit Flop in Los Angeles." *AP News*, June 5.

Spanish Newswire Services. 1998a. "President Felicitó Hufo Chávez Por Su Triunfo Electoral." December 8.

Spanish Newswire Services. 1998b. "Presidente Parlacen: Triunfo Chávez Es 'Tragedia Para America,'" December 9.

Sullivan, Marc P., and Rebecca M. Nelson. 2017. "Argentina: Background and U.S. Relations." Congressional Research Service Report, June 16. https://fas.org/sgp/crs/row/R43816.pdf.

Tan, Rebecca. 2018. "Trump Referred to Mexico's Incoming Leader as 'Juan Trump,' Former White House Official Says." *Washington Post*, July 9. https://www.washingtonpost.com/news/worldviews/wp/2018/07/09/trump-referred-to-mexicos-incoming-leader-as-juan-trump-former-white-house-official-says/.

TASS Russian News Agency. 2022. "Argentina Keeps in Contact with Russia Despite Situation Around Ukraine, Says Envoy." March 7. https://tass.com/politics/1418467?utm_source=google.com&utm_medium=organic&utm_campaign=google.com&utm_referrer=google.com.

Tedesqui Vargas, Luis Marcelo. 2020. "Luis Fernando López: 'El Chapare es un micro-Estado narcoterrorista independiente.'" *El Deber*, January 19. https://eldeber.com.bo/pais/luis-fernando-lopez-el-chapare-es-un-micro-estado-narcoterrorista-independiente_163203.

Telegraph, The. 2009. "Hugo Chavez Threatens Military Action in Honduras." June 29, World. https://www.telegraph.co.uk/news/worldnews/centralamericaandthecaribbean/honduras/5681368/Hugo-Chavez-threatens-military-action-in-Honduras.html.

Telegraph, The. 2012. "Hugo Chavez Announces Venezuela Making Drones and Kalashnikov Rifles." June 14, World. https://www.telegraph.co.uk/news/worldnews/southamerica/venezuela/9330968/Hugo-Chavez-announces-Venezuela-making-drones-and-Kalashnikov-rifles.html.

TeleSur. 2016. "CFK: Hugo Chávez ayudó a Argentina en los momentos difíciles." July 28. https://www.telesurtv.net/news/CFK-Hugo-Chavez-ayudo-a-la-Argentina-cuando-el-mundo-nos-dio-la-espalda-20160728-0070.html.

TeleSur. 2018. "Evo Morales Criticizes Ecuador's Withdrawal From ALBA." August 26. https://www.telesurenglish.net/news/Evo-Morales-Critisizes-Ecuadors-Withdrawl-From-ALBA-20180826-0001.html.

Tickner, Arlene B. 2014. "Autonomy and Latin American International Relations Thinking." In *Routledge Handbook of Latin America in the World*, edited by Jorge I. Domínguez and Ana Covarrubias, 74–84. New York: Routledge.

Tokatlian, Juan Gabriel. 2022. "1994–2022: La cumbre de las Américas y el 'síndrome de la superpotencia frustrada.'" *Nueva Sociedad*. https://nuso.org/articulo/cumbredelasamericas-estadosunidos/?fbclid=IwAR1PmrOcK4Txi7Wpl8JyHaigcBdxFQoRzvl3KwwBglq-1fx8z3-pOvaSTes.

Toro, Alfredo. 2011. "El ALBA Como Instrumento de 'Soft Balancing.'" *Pensamiento Propio* 33 (Enero-Junio): 159–84.

Towers, Marcia, and Silvia Borzutzky. 2004. "The Socioeconomic Implications of Dollarization in El Salvador." *Latin American Politics and Society* 46, no. 3 (September 1): 29–54.

Trotta, Daniel. 2009. "Honduran Catholic Hierarchy Opposes Zelaya, Chavez." *Reuters*, July 15.

Tussie, Diana. 2021. "No Alineamiento Activo (NAA) y Rregionalismo Post Hegemónico: Traslapes e Intersecciones." In *El No Alineamiento Activo y Américas*

Latina: Una Doctrina Para el Nuevo Siglo, edited by Carlos Fortin, Jorge Heine, and Carlos Ominami, 283–301. Santiago, Chile: Catalonia.

United Nations Development Programme. 2016. "Reflections on Drug Policy and its Impact on Human Development: Innovative Approaches." April. https://www.undp.org/publications/reflections-drug-policy-and-its-impact-human-development-innovative-approaches-member.

United Press International. 2001. "Putin, Venezuela's Chavez Blast U.S." May 14. https://www.upi.com/Archives/2001/05/14/Putin-Venezuelas-Chavez-blast-US/5974989812800/.

United States Census Bureau. 2022. "Foreign Trade." https://www.census.gov/foreign-trade/balance/c2190.html.

United States Department of Homeland Security. 2019. "Fact Sheet: DHS Agreements With Guatemala, Honduras, and El Salvador." October 28. https://www.dhs.gov/sites/default/files/publications/19_1028_opa_factsheet-northern-central-america-agreements_v2.pdf.

United States Department of State. 2005. "Country Reports on Terrorism." US Department of State, April 27, 2005. https://2009-2017.state.gov/j/ct/rls/crt/45392.htm.

United States Department of State. 2007. "The Merida Initiative: United States - Mexico - Central America Security Cooperation." October 22. https://2001-2009.state.gov/r/pa/prs/ps/2007/oct/93800.htm.

United States Department of State. 2008. "Joint Press Conference on the Merida Initiative High-Level Consultative Group." December 19. https://2001–2009.state.gov/secretary/rm/2008/12/113401.htm.

United States Department of State. 2013. "Daily Press Briefing." January 3. https://2009-2017.state.gov/r/pa/prs/dpb/2013/01/202480.htm.

United States Department of State, Office of Electronic Information, Bureau of Public Affairs. 2002. "The OAS and the Democratic Charter." May 3. https://2001-2009.state.gov/p/wha/rls/rm/9992.htm.

United States Energy Information Administration. 2018. "Country Analysis Brief: Venezuela." June 21. https://www.eia.gov/beta/international/analysis_includes/countries_long/Venezuela/venezuela.pdf.

United States House of Representatives. 1988. "State Department and Intelligence Community Involvement in Domestic Activities Related to the Iran/Contra Affair." September 7. https://nsarchive2.gwu.edu/NSAEBB/NSAEBB40/04302.pdf.

United States House of Representatives, Committee on Foreign Affairs. 2008. "The New Challenge: China in the Western Hemisphere." Washington, DC: US Government Printing Office, June 11.

United States Senate, Committee on Foreign Relations. 2002. "Aid to 'Plan Colombia': The Time for U.S. Assistance Is Now, a Report to the Committee on Foreign Relations, United States Senate, by Joseph R. Biden, Jr., 106th Congress, May

2000." Washington, DC: US Government Printing Office. https://www.govinfo.gov/content/pkg/CPRT-106SPRT64135/html/CPRT-106SPRT64135.htm.

United States Senate, Committee on Foreign Relations. 2022. "Risch, Menendez, Cassidy Introduce Legislation to Mitigate Risks of El Salvador's Adoption of Bitcoin." February 16. https://www.foreign.senate.gov/press/ranking/release/risch-menendez-cassidy-introduce-legislation-to-mitigate-risks-of-el-salvadors-adoption-of-bitcoin.

United States Southern Command. 2008. "U.S. Southern Command 2008 Posture Statement." https://securityassistance.org/sites/default/files/0UI0I1204838891.pdf.

United States Southern Command. 2009. "U.S. Southern Command 2009 Posture Statement." https://securityassistance.org/sites/default/files/0UI0I123742009.pdf.

United States Southern Command. 2022. "Statement of General Laura J. Richardson, Commander, United States Southern Command, Before the 117th Congress, Senate Committee on Armed Services." March 24. https://www.armed-services.senate.gov/imo/media/doc/SOUTHCOM%20SASC%20Posture%20Final%202022.pdf.

United States Trade Representative. 2008. "U.S. Trade Representative Schwab Announces Proposed Suspension of Bolivia's Tariff Benefits." September 26. https://web.archive.org/web/20090105194149/http://www.ustr.gov/assets/Document_Library/Press_Releases/2008/September/asset_upload_file663_15152.pdf.

Valença, Marcelo M., and Gustavo Carvalho. 2014. "Soft Power, Hard Aspirations: The Shifting Role of Power in Brazilian Foreign Policy." *Brazilian Political Science Review* 8, no. 3: 66–94.

Velázquez Flores, Rafael. 2008. "La relación entre el Ejecutivo y el Congreso en materia de política exterior durante el sexenio de Vicente Fox: ¿Cooperación o conflicto?" *Política y gobierno* 15, no. 1: 113–58.

Vigevani, Tullo, and Gabriel Cepaluni. 2012. *Brazilian Foreign Policy in Changing Times: The Quest for Autonomy from Sarney to Lula*. Lanham, MD: Lexington Books.

Visentini, Paulo G. Fagundes, and André Luiz Reis da Silva. 2010. "Brazil and the Economic, Political, and Environmental Multilateralism: The Lula Years (2003–2010)." *Revista Brasileira de Política Internacional* 53, no. SPE (December): 54–72.

Walker, Robert T. 2019. "In Brazil's Rainforests, the Worst Fires Are Likely Still to Come." *The Conversation*, September 9. http://theconversation.com/in-brazils-rainforests-the-worst-fires-are-likely-still-to-come-122840.

Waltz, Kenneth Neal. 1979. *Theory of International Politics*. New York: McGraw-Hill.

Watson, Penny L. 2017. "Iran's Latin America Strategy: 2005 to Present." *Democracy and Security* 13, no. 2: 127–43.

Weekly Compilation of Presidential Documents. 2006. US Government Printing Office, March 13.

Weeks, Gregory. 2006. "Fighting Terrorism While Promoting Democracy: Competing Priorities in U.S. Defense Policy Toward Latin America." *Journal of Third World Studies* XXIII, no. 2: 59–77.

Weeks, Gregory. 2008. *U.S. and Latin American Relations*. London: Pearson Longman, 2008.

Weeks, Gregory. 2009. "Crisis in Honduras." *Two Weeks Notice: A Latin American Politics Blog*. June 27. http://weeksnotice.blogspot.com/2009/06/crisis-in-honduras.html.

Weeks, Gregory. 2012. "Uruguay and China." *Two Weeks Notice*, April 29. http://weeksnotice.blogspot.com/2012/04/uruguay-and-china.html.

Weeks, Gregory. 2015. *U.S. and Latin American Relations*. Malden, MA: John Wiley & Sons.

Weeks, Gregory. 2018. "Global Responses to Rex Tillerson's Trip to Latin America." *Global Americans*. https://theglobalamericans.org/2018/02/global-responses-rex-tillersons-trip-latin-america/.

Wehner, Leslie. 2011. "Chile's Rush to Free Trade Agreements." *Revista de Ciencia Política* 31, no. 2. http://www.redalyc.org/resumen.oa?id=32422457003.

Western Hemisphere Drug Policy Commission. 2020. "Report of the Western Hemisphere Drug Policy Commission." December 1. https://foreignaffairs.house.gov/_cache/files/a/5/a51ee680-e339-4a1b-933f-b15e535fa103/AA2A3440265D-DE42367A79D4BCBC9AA1.whdpc-final-report-2020-11.30.pdf.

Weyland, Kurt. 2009. "The Rise of Latin America's Two Lefts: Insights from Rentier State Theory." *Comparative Politics* 41, no. 2 (January 1): 145–64.

White House. 2013. "President Obama Meets with President Humala of Peru." June 11. https://obamawhitehouse.archives.gov/blog/2013/06/11/president-obama-meets-president-humala-peru.

White House. 2014. "Statement by the President on Cuba Policy Changes." December 17. https://obamawhitehouse.archives.gov/the-press-office/2014/12/17/statement-president-cuba-policy-changes.

White House. 2017. "Remarks by President Trump on the Policy of the United States Towards Cuba." The White House, June 16. https://www.whitehouse.gov/briefings-statements/remarks-president-trump-policy-united-states-towards-cuba/.

White House. 2020. "President Obama Meets with Salvadoran President Funes." September 22. https://obamawhitehouse.archives.gov/node/9713.

White House. 2021a. "Remarks by President Trump at the 45th Mile of New Border Wall | Reynosa-McAllen, TX." January 12. https://www.whitehouse.gov/briefings-statements/remarks-president-trump-45th-mile-new-border-wall-reynosa-mcallen-tx/.

White House. 2021b. "UPDATED: ONDCP Releases Data on Coca Cultivation and Potential Cocaine Production in the Andean Region." July 16.

White House. 2022a. "Readout of President Biden's Call with Venezuela Interim

President Juan Guaidó." June 8. https://www.whitehouse.gov/briefing-room/statements-releases/2022/06/08/readout-of-president-bidens-call-with-venezuelan-interim-president-juan-guaido/.

White House. 2022b. "Fact Sheet: The Los Angeles Declaration on Migration and Protection U.S. Government and Foreign Partner Deliverables." June 10. https://www.whitehouse.gov/briefing-room/statements-releases/2022/06/10/fact-sheet-the-los-angeles-declaration-on-migration-and-protection-u-s-government-and-foreign-partner-deliverables/.

White House. 2022c. "Fact Sheet: Second Meeting of the U.S.-Mexico High-Level Security Dialogue." October 13. https://www.whitehouse.gov/briefing-room/statements-releases/2022/10/13/fact-sheet-second-meeting-of-the-u-s-mexico-high-level-security-dialogue/.

Wikileaks. 2006a. "Seared Bleu: The Socialist Convictions of Michelle Bachelet." Wikileaks Public Library of US Diplomacy. December 29. https://wikileaks.org/plusd/cables/06SANTIAGO2661_a.html.

Wikileaks. 2006b. "Initial Meeting with Evo Morales: Brass Tacks." Wikileaks Public Library of US Diplomacy, January 3. https://wikileaks.org/plusd/cables/06LAPAZ6_a.html.

Wikileaks. 2008. "Bahia Summits, Part 2: Bringing Latin America and the Caribbean Together . . . Around Cuba." Public Library of US Diplomacy. December 20. https://wikileaks.org/plusd/cables/08BRASILIA1637_a.html.

Wikileaks. 2010. "Ambassador Shannon's Meeting with Mod Jobim." Public Library of US Diplomacy, February 18. https://wikileaks.org/plusd/cables/10BRASILIA51_a.html.

Winter, Brian. 2015. "The Incredible Unknown Bond between Joe Biden and Brazil's Dilma Rouseff." *Americas Quarterly*, June 29. https://www.americasquarterly.org/article/the-incredible-unknown-bond-between-joe-biden-and-brazils-dilma-rousseff/.

Wise, Carol. 2020. *Dragonomics: How Latin America Is Maximizing (or Missing Out On) China's International Development Strategy*. New Haven, CT: Yale University Press.

World Bank. 2002. "Bolivia Water Management: A Tale of Three Cities." Précis. World Bank, Spring.

Xinhua News Agency. 1998. "Chavez Recognized as Venezuela's President-Elect by States." December 7.

Zapata, Sandra. 2017. "Regionalismo y cooperación sur-sur en la primera década del siglo XXI en América Latina: reconfiguraciones y repaso a la idea de autonomía." *Revista Andina de Estudios Políticos* 7, no. 2 (December 31): 67–91.

Zelicovich, Julieta. 2011. "El lugar del MERCOSUR en la política exterior argentina durante los gobiernos de Néstor Kirchner y Cristina Fernández de Kirchner." *Relaciones Internacionales* 20, no. 41. https://revistas.unlp.edu.ar/RRII-IRI/article/view/1192.

Zhu, Zhiqun. 2010. *China's New Diplomacy: Rationale, Strategies and Significance*. London: Ashgate.
Zibechi, Raúl. 2015. "Interconnection Without Integration in South America: 15 Years of IIRSA." *Upside Down World*, October 8. http://upsidedownworld.org/archives/international/interconnection-without-integration-in-south-america-15-years-of-iirsa/.

INDEX

Abrams, Elliott, 125
Accountability for Cryptocurrency in El Salvador (ACES) Act (2022), 146
active non-alignment, 6
Admadinejad, Mahmoud, 47
ALBA (Alianza Bolivariana para los Pueblos de Nuestra América). See Bolivarian Alliance for the Peoples of our America (ALBA)
ALBA-CARIBE fund, 59, 138
ALCA (Área de Libre Comercio de las Américas), 56
Allende, Salvador, 73
Alliance for Progress, 44
Alliance for the Peoples of our America (ALBA). See Bolivarian Alliance for the Peoples of our America (ALBA)
Al Qaeda, 27, 29
Alvarez, María Victoría, 138
AMLO. See López Obrador, Andrés Manuel
Amorim, Celso, 45, 46–47, 48
Andean Community, Andean Pact (Comunidad Andina), 61–62, 76
Andean Free Trade Area, 76
Andean Trade Preference Act (1991), 86
Andean Trade Promotion and Drug Eradication Act (2002), 77, 86, 106–7

Añez, Jeanine, 157
Angra Nuclear Power Plant (Rio de Janeiro), 46
antagonistic autonomy, 21
antinarcotics policies/operations, 63, 70, 140
Arce, Luis, 142, 157
Área de Libre Comercio de las Américas (ALCA), 56
ARENA party (El Salvador), 41
Argentina: autonomy of, 142; and China, 24, 53–54, 84; emergency loans to, 52; experience with terrorism, 56; foreign policy of, 55, 83; Peronist Party (formerly Partido Justicialista), 52, 53; policy of currency "convertibility," 52; Radical Party, 53; as second largest export destination for US, 72; in South American Common Market (Mercosur), 37. See also Duhalde, Eduardo; Fernández, Alberto; Kirchner, Cristina Fernández de; Kirchner, Néstor
Arias, Oscar, 101–2
Arteaga, Rosalía, 84
Assange, Julian, 107
asylum cooperative agreements, 132
Australia: in Latin America, 120–21; and Peru, 121

autonomy: according to Chávez, 18; according to Escudé, 6; according to Puig, 2–4; antagonistic autonomy, 21; Chávez's death as marking beginning of end of region-wide autonomy initiatives, 110; as connected to geography, 142; debates about in Latin America, 4–5; by diversification, 38; etymology of, 2; heterodox autonomy, 5, 16, 34, 137; loss of in Latin America, 2; pursuit of in Latin America, 7–9; radical autonomy, 16, 118, 124, 148; as rarely being a successful regional effort, 159–60; relational autonomy, 5, 21; secessionist autonomy, 4, 57; trade as vehicle for, 139; without retaliation as recurrent theme in Latin American literature, 159
Azpuru, Dinorah, 136

Bachelet, Michelle, 14, 73–76, 81, 102, 108, 118
Bahia Summit (2008), 45
Balladres, Ernesto Pérez, 18
bandwagoning, 4
Barros, Pedro Silva, 126
Batista, Fulgencio, 16, 109
Batlle, Jorge, 50
Belt and Road Initiative (China), 93, 135
Benitez, Adbo, 123
Benzi, Daniele, 59
Bicentennial Framework for Security, Public Health, and Safe Communities, 158
Biden, Joe, 14, 31, 96, 103, 109, 112, 132, 135, 136, 139, 141, 144–45, 146, 148, 149, 150, 151, 153, 154, 155, 156, 158
bin Laden, Osama, 27
bitcoin, 146–47
Blinken, Antony, 149

Bolivar, Simón, 8, 19, 20, 43
Bolivarian Alliance for the Peoples of our America (ALBA), 56–58, 61–62, 65–66, 70, 72
Bolivia: as case study of successful balance between needs of subsistence farmers and need to prevent export of coca for cocaine production, 116; and China, 64, 70, 105; and Comunidad Andina, 61; foreign policy of, 64, 72; gas exportation in, 28; and Iran, 70; Movement Toward Socialism (MAS) party, 63, 70, 105; as third largest export destination for US, 72; as trying to break away from free market model, 10; "United, Free of Drugs" strategy, 157; US decertification of, 115–16; US in anticoca business in, 71; US suspension of designation as beneficiary country, 86. See also Añez, Jeanine; Arce, Luis; Morales, Evo; Sánchez de Lozada, Gonzalo (Goni)
Bolsonaro, Eduardo, 132
Bolsonaro, Jair, 121, 130, 134, 136, 138, 152, 155
Bolton, John, 124–25
Borzutzky, Silvia, 74
Brazil: autonomy reversal in, 129–33; and China, 47–48; corruption in, 129–30; devaluation of dollar by, 52; as diversifying trading partners, 39; foreign policy of, 46, 48, 102–3, 129–30; invitation to participate in G20, 39; as largest export destination for US, 72; oil exportation in, 28; push for autonomy in, 38; renewed interest in South American economic development, 37; role in

international peacekeeping, 48; in South American Common Market (Mercosur), 37; view of as natural global player, 43–49; Worker's Party (PT), 74. See also Cardoso, Fernando Henrique; Rousseff, Dilma; Silva, Luiz Inácio Lula da (Lula); Temer, Michel
Briceño-Ruiz, José, 109
Brigada Hispanoamericana, 30
Bucaram, Abdalí ("El Loco"), 84–85
Bukele, Nayib, 146, 147, 150–51
Buquet, Daniel, 50
Burton, Dan, 89
Bush, George H. W., 15, 44
Bush, George W., 25–26, 27, 29, 30–31, 33, 34, 37–38, 42, 45, 47, 51, 54–55, 56, 63–64, 67, 69, 77, 78, 80, 86, 87, 90, 91, 92, 95, 115, 117, 119, 120, 133, 145

Cáceres, Luis René, 41
Caldera, Rafael, 21
Calderón, Felipe, 86, 87–89, 97, 116
Calderón Chelius, Leticia, 155
Calvalho, Gilberto, 45
Canelas, Manuel, 64
Capriles, Henrique, 110
Cardoso, Fernando Henrique, 36–37, 39, 44, 47, 80, 141
Caribbean Community (CARICOM), 153
Caribbean Summit (2001), 56
Cartagena Agreement (1969), 76
Castañeda, Jorge, 35
Castro, Fidel, 16–17, 18, 26, 33, 50, 53, 56, 57, 59, 62, 64, 91, 109, 118
Castro, Raúl, 45, 91, 118, 128
CELAC (Community of Latin American and Caribbean States), 17, 102, 114, 134, 138, 155
Central American Free Trade Agreement, 65, 148

CEPAL (Economic Commission for Latin America and the Caribbean, ECLAC) (UN), 3, 92, 139
Cepaluni, Gabriel, 6, 38, 45
Chasquetti, Daniel, 50
Chaves, Rodrigo, 156
Chávez, Hugo, 12, 13, 17–22, 24, 25, 26–27, 28, 33–34, 42, 43, 44, 49, 51, 53, 54, 55, 56, 57, 58, 59, 60–62, 64, 67, 70, 71, 72, 73, 74, 75, 76, 77, 83, 89, 91, 92, 93, 94, 95, 98, 99, 101, 105, 106, 108, 110, 120, 126, 127, 154
"Chicago Boys," 49
Chile: capitalism in, 74; and China, 75; and Comunidad Andina, 61; as diversifying trading partners, 39; as exemplifying complicated nature of Latin American left, 73; as featuring both left and right, 108; foreign policy of, 36, 74; international agreements of, 49–51; Party for Democracy (PPD), 36; Socialist Party, 73, 74; trade agreements of, 74, 75, 108. See also Bachelet, Michelle; Lagos, Ricardo; Piñera, Sebastián
Chile-China Free Trade Agreement, 75
China: and Argentina, 24, 53–54, 84; and Bolivia, 64, 70, 105; and Brazil, 47–48; and Chile, 75; as consumer of Latin America raw materials, 149; continued role of in Latin America, 149–50; continuing influence of, 113–14; Dominican Republic's recognition of, 135; and Ecuador, 107, 136; and El Salvador, 135, 147; exports from Latin America to, 92–93; foreign policy of, 138; and Guatemala, 24–25; in Latin America, 80, 88–89, 93, 119, 120, 121, 134, 142–43. See also specific countries; Latin America as

China (*continued*)
showing concern about increased economic dependence on, 137; Latin America percentage of exports to, 11; loans from, 10, 82, 84, 92, 137; new focus of on Latin America, 23, 34; Panama's recognition of, 135; percentage of Latin American imports from, 11; and Peru, 121; rise of, 22–25; share of Latin American trade, 11; trust in by Latin American countries, 136; and Uruguay, 51, 113; vaccines from, 149; and Venezuela, 24, 61, 88–89, 111; view of Latin American policy makers of, 23–24
Chivo Wallet, 147
Chomsky, Noam, 26
CICIG (International Commission against Impunity in Guatemala) (UN), 133, 140
citizen power (poder ciudadano), 65
citizen revolution (revolución ciudadana), 85
civil wars, 15
climate change/climate policy, 70, 121–22, 130, 156
Clinton, Bill, 15, 18, 31, 32, 45, 96
Clinton, Hillary, 94, 103
coca cultivation, 31, 62, 63, 70–71, 77, 88, 97, 106, 114, 115, 116, 157, 158
cocaine, 31, 63, 70, 71, 116, 157
Cochabamba Water War (2000), 62
Cold War, 5, 7–8, 12, 15, 17, 33, 42, 51, 69, 95, 102, 107, 128, 159
Colombia: and Comunidad Andina, 61; oil exportation in, 28; relations with US, 31; trade agreements of, 77–79; war on drugs in, 97. See also Duque, Iván; Petro, Gustavo; Santos, Juan Manuel; Uribe, Alvaro

Community of Latin American and Caribbean States (CELAC), 17, 102, 114, 134, 138, 155
Comunidad Andina (Andrean Community, Andean Pact), 61–62, 76
Confucius Institutes, 149
Congressional Research Service Report: on China's status as trading partner, 136; on Kirchner governments, 83; on Mérida Initiative, 87
conservative, use of term, 36
convertibility (of currency), purpose of, 52
Cooper, Andrew, 100
Corrales, Javier, 34
Correa, Rafael, 19, 41, 68, 84–85, 92, 106, 107, 110, 138
corruption: anticorruption initiative in Honduras, 133; attempt at solution to, 138, 141; in Brazil, 129–30; effect of drug war on, 114; in El Salvador, 147; in Guatemala, 140; in Haiti, 60; within PDVSA, 110–11; US influence in Central America regarding, 132–33; in Venezuela, 111–12, 127
COSIPLAN (South American Council of Infrastructure and Planning), 82
Costa Rica: Arias, Oscar, 101; Chaves, Rodrigo, 156; and Escazú Agreement, 121, 156
Countering Iran in the Western Hemisphere Act (2012), 94
counternarcotics policies/operations, 77, 88, 115
COVID-19: effects of, 152–53; impact of, 133–38, 145; vaccine creation and distribution, 134–35, 143, 152, 153
Crandall, Russell, 7
Cruz, Ted, 117
Cuba: alignment with Soviet Union, 17;

economic embargo of, 16, 95–96, 109, 117, 128–29; as main example of Latin America autonomy, 109; 1959 revolution, 16; radical autonomy of, 124; and Russia, 90, 128; shift in export partners, 17; shift of to China and European countries, 16; US approach to, 128–29; US as thawing relations with, 117–18; on US State Sponsor of Terrorism list, 127; and Venezuela, 118. See also Batista, Fulgencio; Castro, Fidel; Castro, Raúl

Declaration of Brasilia (2003), 46
Deferred Action for Childhood Arrivals (DACA) (2014), 96–97
Democratic Unity Roundtable (MUD) coalition (Venezuela), 112
dependency theory, 2, 3, 10, 19, 26, 36, 72, 104, 109, 113, 137
deregulation, as structural adjustment, 9
Development Bank of Latin America, 134
Development Programme (UN), 116
Díaz-Canel, Miguel, 128
dollarization: defined, 40; as exception, 39–42; purpose of, 52
Dominican Republic: and Brigada Hispanoamericana, 30; recognition of China, 135
Dominican Republic-Central America Free Trade Agreement (DR-CAFTA), 148
Drago, Luis, 100
Drago Doctrine (1902), 100
drug cartels, 31, 86, 116, 142
drugs/drug policy, 63, 66, 97, 105, 115, 116, 140–43, 157–58. See also coca cultivation; cocaine; fentanyl; marijuana; narcotics; war on drugs

drug trafficking, 31, 67, 78, 115, 116, 141, 157–58
Duhalde, Eduardo, 52
Duque, Iván, 123

Economic Commission for Latin America and the Caribbean (ECLAC, CEPAL) (UN), 3, 92, 139
Ecuador: and China, 107, 136; and Comunidad Andina, 61; dollarization in, 40–41, 42; and European Free Trade Association, 121; oil exportation in, 28. See also Correa, Rafael; Mahuad, Jamil; Moreno, Lenín
Eisenhower, Dwight, 44
Ejército de Liberación Nacional (ELN), 127–28
El Chapo, 116
El Salvador: ARENA party, 41; and Brigada Hispanoamericana, 30; and China, 135, 147; corruption in, 147; dependence on export of primary products, 12; dollarization in, 41–42; and emigration to US, 32–33; Farabundo Marti National Liberation Front (FMLN), 99; as model case for dependency theory, 104; and Russia, 147; and Turkey, 147; US sanctions on, 147. See also Bukele, Nayib; Funes, Mauricio
Enterprise for the Americas initiative, 44
environmental action/protection, 51, 82, 121–22, 156–57
Escazú Agreement (Regional Agreement on Access to Information, Public Participation and Justice in Environmental Matters in Latin America and the Caribbean) (2018), 121, 156–57

Escudé, Carlos, 5, 6, 12–13
Espinal, Flavio Darío, 154
Espinosa, Patricia, 87
European Free Trade Association, 121
Evrofinance Mosnarbank, 127
export-led development, new focus on, 10

Farabundo Marti National Liberation Front (FMLN), 99, 104
FARC (Fuerzas Armadas Revolucionarias de Colombia), 78, 85, 88, 97, 127, 140
Faria, Carlos Aurélio Pimenta de, 48
FDI (foreign direct investment), 114
Feierstein, Mark, 130–31
fentanyl, 116, 142
Fernández, Alberto, 126, 134, 151
financial crisis (2008): echoes of, 145–46; implications of, 79–80, 92, 93
Financial Times, on Humala's election, 108
flexibility, impact of increasing in, 15–16
Flores, Francisco, 41
FMLN (Farabundo Marti National Liberation Front), 99, 104
Foreign Affairs: Hakim article, 68; Sarney article, 38
Foreign Assistance Act (1985), 63
foreign direct investment (FDI), 114
"Foreign Policy Concept of the Russian Federation," 128
Forum for South American Progress (PROSUR), 123
Fox, Vicente, 27, 30–31, 66–67, 141
Frank, Dana, 65–66
free market model: breaking away from, 10; as norm, 18
free trade agreements (FTAs), 49–50, 57, 77, 78, 107, 108, 119, 121, 139. See also specific agreements
Free Trade Area of the Americas (FTAA), 34, 37, 45, 46, 51, 54, 56, 80, 82, 120

French, John, 38
Frenkel, Alejandro, 123
Frente Amplio, 50, 51
Fuentes, Claudio, 36
Fuerzas Armadas Revolucionarias de Colombia (FARC), 78, 85, 88, 97, 127, 140
Fujimori, Alberto, 20, 108
Fujimori, Keiko, 108
Funes, Mauricio, 104–5

G3. See India-Brazil-South Africa Dialogue Forum (IBSA, G-3)
G8, 46
G20, Brazil's invitation to participate in, 39
García, Alán, 77, 108–9
Gaviria, Cesar, 141
Geisel, Ernesto, 45
General Agreement on Tariffs and Trade (1947), 164n15
Giammettei, Alejandro, 132
Giraudo, Maria Eugenia, 137
Global Partnership Dialogue (2012), 103
globalization: asymmetric globalization, 37; and Latin America's market reforms, 24; neoliberal globalization, 53
global politics, as defined by anarchy, 4
Golinger, Eva, 58
Gonçalves, Julia Borba, 126
Goni. See Sánchez de Lozada, Gonzalo (Goni)
Granato, Leonardo, 57
Guaidó, Juan, 124, 125, 126, 153, 155
Guatemala: and China, 24–25; corruption in, 140; and emigration to US, 32–33; and Petrocaribe, 60; and US, 24–25. See also Giammettei, Alejandro; Morales, Jimmy; Pérez Molina, Otto
Guevara, Aleida, 56

Haddad, Fernando, 130
Haiti, corruption in, 60
Hakim, Pater, 68
Heavy Investment Fund, 88–89
hegemony, of US, 8–9, 10, 12, 16, 34, 42, 53, 66, 68, 74
Hegemony or Survival (Chomsky), 26
Heine, Jorge, 75
Helms-Burton law (1996), 89, 96, 117
heterodox autonomy, 4, 16, 34, 137
Hirst, Monica, 44
Honduras: and ALBA, 65–66; and Brigada Hispanoamericana, 30; coup in, 98–102; crisis brewing in, 65–66; and emigration to US, 32–33; Liberal Party, 65; and Petrocaribe, 65; Support Mission Against Corruption and Impunity in Honduras (MACCIH), 133. See also Lobo, Porfirio; Micheletti, Roberto; Zelaya, José Manuel
Huawei, 136
Hu Jintao, 54, 64
Humala, Ollanta, 76, 108–9
Hussein, Saddam, 27
Hyde, Henry, 44

ICE (Immigration and Custom Enforcement), 32
IIRSA (Initiative for the Integration of Regional Infrastructure in South America), 37, 81–82
IMF. See International Monetary Fund (IMF)
immigration: Calderón de-emphasis of, 87–88; "caravans" of Central American migrants, 132; from Cuba, 156; Deferred Action for Childhood Arrivals (DACA) (2014), 96–97; effects of 9/11 on, 31–32; Migration Protection Protocols (MPP) ("Remain in Mexico" policy), 131; Obama as enlisting help on, 116; Regional Conference on Migration, 155; and Summit of the Americas (2022), 156; during Trump administration, 119, 132; "wet foot, dry foot" Cuba immigration policy, 118, 156
Immigration and Custom Enforcement (ICE), 32
Immigration and Naturalization Service (INS), 32
Immigration Reform and Control Act (1986), 31
India: COVID-19 vaccines to Argentina, Brazil, and Mexico, 135; private sector trade in Latin America, 152–53
India-Brazil-South Africa Dialogue Forum (IBSA, G-3), 46
Initiative for the Integration of Regional Infrastructure in South America (IIRSA), 37, 81–82
INS (Immigration and Naturalization Service), 32
Institutional Revolution Party (PRI) (Mexico), 30
Insulza, José Miguel, 99, 100, 101
Inter-American Development Bank, 38, 134
international anarchy, 2
International Commission against Impunity in Guatemala (CICIG) (UN), 133, 140
International Monetary Fund (IMF), 37, 39, 40, 44, 52, 53, 54, 134, 147
Iran: and ALBA, 58; and Bolivia, 70; in Latin America, 94; Lula on, 46–47; and Venezuela, 127
Iraq, as oil exporter, 28

Jaguaribe, Helio, 5–6

Jamaica, and Petrocaribe, 60
January 6, 2021, Latin America reaction to, 145
Jiang Zemin, 23, 24, 47
Jobim, Nelson, 49
Johnson & Johnson, 152

Kaltwasser, Cristóbal Rovira, 35
Kennedy, John F., 44
Kirchner, Cristina Fernández de, 19–20, 82–84, 108
Kirchner, Néstor, 19, 52–56, 64, 70, 82–83
Kubitschek, Juscelino, 44

Lagos, Ricardo, 27, 36, 39, 73, 75, 154
Latin America: and China (see China); effect of financial crisis (2008) on, 79; electoral revolution in, 15–42; impact of COVID-19 on, 133–38; and India, 135, 152–53; perspective of 9/11 by, 29–30; as returning to heterogeneity and skepticism of unity, 120; and Russia (see Russia); as showing concern about increased economic dependence on China, 137; and the United States (see United States)
Latinobarómetro poll, on George W. Bush, 69
Laufer, Rubén, 137
Lava Jato, 129
leftist leadership: Bachelet, Michelle, 75, 118; categories of, 35–36; Chávez, Hugo, 42, 44; Correa, Rafael, 41; Cuba's Cold War autonomy as inspiration for, 17; diversity of, 102–10; Farabundo Marti National Liberation Front (FMLN), 99; growth of, 1, 10, 12, 20, 67; Humala, Ollanta, 108;

Kirchner, Néstor, 70; leftist populists, 20; Lula, 37, 70; moderate left, 35, 56; Morales, Evo, 64; Ortega, Daniel, 89; populist left, 20, 35, 36; radical left, 35; reformist left, 36; as riding high, 92; US attacks on, 16. See also pink tide/pink wave
Legler, Thomas, 100, 109
Lehman Brothers, 79, 80
Levitsky, Steven, 20
Liberal Party (Honduras), 65
Lima Group, 125–26
Lobo, Porfirio, 99, 105
López Obrador, Andrés Manuel (AMLO), 121, 126, 130, 131, 134, 139, 141–42, 153, 154, 155–56, 158
Lugo, Fernando, 112
Lula. See Silva, Luiz Inácio Lula da (Lula)
Luna, Juan Pablo, 35

Maduro, Nicolás, 61, 72, 93, 110, 111, 112–13, 118, 124, 125, 126, 134, 150
Mahuad, Jamil, 40, 85
Maisto, John, 21, 27
marijuana, 52, 114, 116, 141
MAS (Movement Toward Socialism) party (Bolivia), 63, 70, 105
McKinley, Michael, 108
Medvedev, Dimitry, 89–90
Menem, Carlos, 18, 24, 53
Menendez, Bob, 146
Mercosur. See South American Common Market (Mercosur)
Mérida Initiative (2007), 86–87, 116, 158
Merke, Federico, 75
meth, 116
Mexico: drug cartels in, 116, 142; and emigration to US, 32–33; foreign policy of, 86; Institutional Revolution Party (PRI), 30. See also

Calderón, Felipe; Fox, Vicente; López Obrador, Andrés Manuel (AMLO); Peña Nieto, Enrique; Zedillo, Ernesto
Micheletti, Roberto, 98, 99, 100
Michelutti, Lucia, 111
Migration Protection Protocols (MPP), 131
MINUSTAH (Stabilizing Mission in Haiti) (UN), 48, 49
moderate left, 35, 56
Moderna, 152
Moïse, Jovenel, 60
Monroe Doctrine (1823), 159
Morales, Evo, 19, 62–65, 69–72, 81, 86, 92, 105–6, 110, 157
Morales, Jimmy, 140
Morandé, José, 36
Morasso, Carla, 53, 83
Moreno, Lenín, 58, 137–38
Mourão, Hamilton, 152
Movement Toward Socialism (MAS) party (Bolivia), 63, 70, 105
MPP (Migration Protection Protocols), 131
MUD (Democratic Unity Roundtable) coalition (Venezuela), 112
Mujica, José, 107
Muñoz, Heraldo, 27

NAFTA (North American Free Trade Agreement), 119, 122, 131, 139
Napolitano, Janet, 114
narcotics, 21, 25, 63, 67, 86, 97, 106, 114, 115, 141, 157. See also drugs/drug policy
National Drug Control Strategy (2022 report), 157–58
New York Times, on Venezuela's increased spending, 27
Nicaragua: and Brigada Hispanoamericana, 30; and Russia, 90, 128; Sandinistas, 104; and Taiwan, 148; trade in, 148; US sanctions on, 147, 148–49. See also Ortega, Daniel
Noboa, Gustavo, 40–41
Non-Aligned Movement, 5, 16
nonintervention, principle of as central to most Latin American governments, 100
Noriega, Roger, 30, 33–34, 55, 63
North American Free Trade Agreement (NAFTA), 119, 122, 131, 139

OAS. See Organization of American States (OAS)
Obama, Barack, 14, 47, 69, 70, 80, 90–91, 94–97, 98–99, 101, 103, 104–5, 106–7, 108, 111–12, 114, 115, 116, 117–18, 121, 127, 128–29, 140, 145, 151, 156, 158
Oddone, Carlos Nahuel, 57
oil diplomacy, 28
oil strike (2002), 28, 33
Oliveros, Luis, 127
opioids, 140
Organization of American States (OAS): according to Cooper and Legler, 100; actions of post-9/11, 29; anticorruption initiative in Honduras, 133; on Colombia attack on FARC camp, 85; COVID-19 information portal, 134; Cuba's expulsion from, 17; Inter-American Commission on Human Rights, 147–48; as most visible regional entity, 101; Obama administration's use of, 112–13; suspension of Russia's observer status, 150; use of, 21
Organization of the Petroleum Exporting Countries (OPEC), 22, 28
Ortega, Daniel, 26, 33, 128

Oye Trump (Listen Up Trump) (AMLO), 130

Pacific Alliance (2011), 108–9, 122
Panama: dollarization in, 40; recognition of China, 135; US invasion of (1989), 15
Panama Canal, 23
Pan American Health Organization, 153
Pan Americanism, 44
Paradis, Clarisse Goulart, 48
Paraguay: COVID-19 vaccines from Taiwan, 135; in South American Common Market (Mercosur), 37. See also Benitez, Adbo; Lugo, Fernando
Paris Agreement, 121, 130
Partido Colorado, 50
Partido Nacional, 50
Party for Democracy (PPD) (Chile), 36
Pastrana, Andrés, 31
Patriota, Antonio, 103
Paula, Rossone do, 43
PDVSA (Petróleos de Venezuela), 58, 110–11, 126–27
Peña Nieto, Enrique, 116–17
Pentagon, attack on (9/11/2001), 27
Pérez, Carlos Andrés, 18, 110
Pérez Hernáiz, Hugo, 113
Pérez Jimenez, Marcos, 124
Pérez Molina, Otto, 114, 141
peripheral realism, 5, 6, 16
Peronist Party (formerly Partido Justicialista) (Argentina), 52, 53
personalism, 20
Peru: and Australia, 121; and China, 121; and Comunidad Andina, 61. See also Fujimori, Alberto; García, Alán; Humala, Ollanta; Toledo, Alejandro
Petro, Gustavo, 158
Petrocaribe, 58–62, 65, 111

petro-diplomacy, 28
Petróleos de Venezuela (PDVSA), 58, 110–11, 126–27
Pew Research Center, on US image, 29
Pfizer, 135, 152
Piñera, Sebastián, 108, 123
pink tide/pink wave, 20–21, 74, 92, 105, 107
Pinochet, Augusto, 49
Plan Colombia, 21, 31, 96, 141, 144
populism, use of term, 20
populist left, 20, 35, 36
post-hegemonic regionalism, 154
PPD (Party for Democracy) (Chile), 36
Prado Lallande, Juan Pablo, 109
Prebish, Raúl, 3
PRI (Institutional Revolution Party) (Mexico), 30
privatization of state industry, as structural adjustment, 9
PROSUR (Forum for South American Progress), 123
PSUV (Socialist Party) (Venezuela), 112
PT (Worker's Party) (Brazil), 37, 38
Puig, Juan Carlos, 2, 16, 34, 57, 137, 160
Putin, Vladimir, 21, 58, 61, 89, 90, 93, 128, 150

Quirós, Ludmila, 138

radical autonomy, 16, 18, 118, 124
radical left, 35
Radical Party (Argentina), 53
Reagan, Ronald, 15
realism, 4, 6
realist theory, 2, 4
reformist left, 36
Regional Agreement on Access to Information, Public Participation and Justice in Environmental Matters in Latin America and the Caribbean (Escazú Agreement) (2018), 121, 156–57

Regional Conference on Migration, 155
regionalism, 154, 155, 156
regional unity, 53, 62, 123, 138
Reich, Otto, 26, 30
Reina, Carlos Roberto, 18
relational autonomy, 5, 21
"Remain in Mexico" policy, 131
RENACER Act (2021), 148
"Responsible Pragmatism," 45
retribution, for pursuing policies that US deemed as threatening, 4
Revolutionary Armed Forces of Colombia (FARC). See Fuerzas Armadas Revolucionarias de Colombia (FARC)
Reynoso, Diego, 75
Rice, Condoleezza, 70
right leadership, 35–36
Rio Group, 102
Risch, Jim, 146
Roberts, Kenneth M., 20
Rodriguez Maradiaga, Oscar, 98
Rohrabacher, Dana, 23
Romero, Carlos, 100
Rousseff, Dilma, 102–3, 107–8, 129, 138
Rubio, Marco, 117
Rumsfeld, Donald, 69
Russell, Roberto, 5
Russia: arms deal with Venezuela, 61; and Cuba, 90, 128; and El Salvador, 147; "Foreign Policy Concept of the Russian Federation," 128; invasion of Ukraine, 145, 150–52, 155; in Latin America, 89–90, 93, 151–52; Latin American reaction to invasion of Ukraine, 150–52; loans to Venezuela, 94; and Nicaragua, 90, 128; and Venezuela, 90, 94, 111, 127. See also Putin, Vladimir

Samper, Ernesto, 31

San José Accords (1980), 58–59
Sánchez, Rafael, 20
Sánchez de Lozada, Gonzalo (Goni), 62
Sandinistas, 104
Santiago Declaration, 123
Santos, Juan Manuel, 108, 114, 116, 141
Saraiva, José, 44
Sarney, José, 38, 44
Schwab, Susan, 78
secessionist autonomy, 4, 57
seigniorage, 40
September 11, 2001: effects of, 25–33; impact of on Mexico-US relations, 66–67
Shannon, Thomas, 49, 69, 95
Shining Path guerrillas, 77
Silva, André Luiz Reis da, 46
Silva, Luiz Inácio Lula da (Lula), 14, 37–39, 42, 43–44, 45–49, 54, 64, 67, 70, 84, 95, 99, 103, 130, 152, 155
Simonoff, Alejandro, 55
Sinovac, 152
Snowden, Edward, 107
Soares de Lima, Maria Regina, 44
Sobel, Clifford, 45
Socialist Party (Chile), 73, 74
Socialist Party (PSUV) (Venezuela), 112
soft power, 36, 59, 96, 111
South American Common Market (Mercosur), 37, 45, 49, 50, 51, 62, 80, 83, 122
South American Council of Infrastructure and Planning (COSIPLAN), 82
Soviet Union, impact on Latin America of fall of, 12
Spanish Alianza Bolivariana para los Pueblos de Nuestra América (ALBA), 56–58
Stabilizing Mission in Haiti (MINUSTAH) (UN), 48, 49
"State Sponsor of Terrorism" list, 117

structural adjustments, in Latin America, 9–10
subsidies, end of government subsidies as structural adjustment, 9
SUCRE (Unified System of Regional Compensation), 72–73
Summit for Democracy (2021), 146
Summit of the Americas (2005), 51, 54, 56
Summit of the Americas (2022), 153–54, 155, 156
supranationalism, 82

Taiwan: and COVID-19 vaccines, 135; and Nicaragua, 148
Temer, Michel, 47, 121, 129–30
tension without rupture, 21
terrorism, war on. See war on terror/war on terrorism
Tiananmen Square repression, 22
Tokatlian, Juan Gabriel, 5, 154
Toledo, Alejandro, 76, 77
trade barriers, lowering of as structural adjustment, 9–10
Transalba, 59
Trilateral Commission, 46
Trump, Donald, 14, 91, 112, 118, 119, 120, 121, 122, 124–29, 130–32, 133, 134, 135, 136, 137, 138, 139, 140, 141, 143, 144, 145, 146, 151, 156, 158, 160
Turkey, and El Salvador, 147
Tussie, Diana, 154
Twitter, 60, 110, 120, 128, 132, 146, 147

Ukraine, Russia's invasion of, 145, 150–52, 155
Unified System of Regional Compensation (SUCRE), 72–73
Union of South American Nations (UNASUR), 14, 37, 75, 80–82, 83, 84, 99, 112, 122–23
United Nations: condemnation of Russia's invasion of Ukraine, 150; Development Programme, 116; Economic Commission for Latin America and the Caribbean (ECLAC, CEPAL), 3, 92, 139; International Commission against Impunity in Guatemala (CICIG), 133, 140; Stabilizing Mission in Haiti (MINUSTAH), 48, 49
United States: attack of leftist governments/movements, 16; as contributing to Latin American governments looking elsewhere for trading partners, 106–7; economic embargo of Cuba, 16, 95–96, 109, 117, 128–29; exports from Latin America to, 92; foreign policy of, 120, 149; hegemony of, 8–9, 10, 12, 16, 34, 42, 53, 66, 68, 74; influence in Central America regarding corruption, 132–33; influence of, 9; invasion of Afghanistan, 27–28; percentage of Latin America exports to, 10–11, 11; percentage of Latin American imports from, 11; presidents of. See specific presidents; resistance to drug policies of, 86; sanctions from, 16, 46, 60, 72, 73, 94, 109, 111, 112, 124, 125, 126, 127, 147, 148–49, 150, 155, 159; security assistance to Latin America, 30; September 11, 2001 (see September 11, 2001); struggling to keep its own democracy alive, 146; on terrorist activity in Latin America, 55; trust in by Latin American countries, 136; war on terrorism (see war on terror/war on terrorism). See also specific agencies/departments

United States-Mexico-Canada Agreement (USMCA), 121–22, 139
Uribe, Alvaro, 31, 76, 77, 78, 79, 88, 99, 108
Uruguay: center-left leadership in, 50; and China, 51, 113; foreign policy of, 50–52; in South American Common Market (Mercosur), 37. See also Mujica, José
US Agency for International Development (USAID), 82, 134
US-Colombia Trade Promotion Agreement (2006), 78
US Customs and Border Protection, 156
US Department of Homeland Security, 31–32, 114, 132
US Drug Enforcement Agency, 67, 70, 71–72, 81, 115, 142
US Energy Information Administration, on Venezuela's oil production, 110
US Federal Reserve, 40
US International Development Finance Corporation, 137
USMCA (United States-Mexico-Canada Agreement), 121–22, 139
US Office of National Drug Control Policy, 71
US Senate Foreign Relations Committee, 108
US Southern Command, 90, 151
US State Department, International Narcotics Control Strategy Report (2009), 70–71

Valenzuela, Arturo, 95
Vázquez, Tabaré, 50–52
Venezuela: and China, 24, 61, 88–89, 111; and Comunidad Andina, 61–62; corruption in, 111–12, 127; coup in, 33–39; and Cuba, 118; dependence on export of primary products, 12; foreign policy of, 60; impacts of structural changes in, 18; and Iran, 127; and Mercosur, 62; as often exceptional case, 73; oil production in, 28; radical autonomy of, 124; as rebel state, 126; and Russia, 61, 90, 94, 111, 127; Socialist Party (PSUV), 112; as trying to break away from free market model, 10; and Unified System of Regional Compensation (SUCRE), 72; US sanctions on, 60, 72, 73, 94, 111, 112, 124, 127, 150, 155, 159. See also Chávez, Hugo; Guaidó, Juan; Maduro, Nicolás
Verdes-Montenegro, Francisco J., 64
Vigevani, Tullo, 6, 38, 45
Visentini, Paulo G. Fagundes, 46

Wang Yi, 134
war on drugs, 18, 30, 31, 69, 86, 96, 97, 114–17, 141, 158
war on terror/war on terrorism, 29, 30, 56, 66, 68
Washington Consensus, 37, 55
Watson, Penny L., 58
Western Hemisphere Drug Policy Commission, 140
"wet foot, dry foot" Cuba immigration policy, 118, 156
Wikileaks, 107
Wise, Carol, 143
Worker's Party (PT) (Brazil), 37, 38
World Bank, 62, 85, 134
World Health Organization (WHO), 134
World Trade Center, destruction of (9/11/01), 27
World Trade Organization (WTO), 22–23, 38, 46

Xi Jinping, 93, 114

Yang Shyangkun, 22
Yeltsin, Boris, 21

Zapata, Sandra, 59
Zedillo, Ernesto, 141
Zelaya, José Manuel, 65–66, 98–99, 100, 101, 104, 105
Zoellick, Robert, 46

www.ingramcontent.com/pod-product-compliance
Lightning Source LLC
Chambersburg PA
CBHW020822230426
43666CB00007B/1059